The Claim of Humanity in Christ

Princeton Theological Monograph Series

K. C. Hanson, Charles M. Collier, D. Christopher Spinks,
and Robin A. Parry, Series Editors

Recent volumes in the series:

Koo Dong Yun
*The Holy Spirit and Ch'i (Qi):
A Chiological Approach to Pneumatology*

Stanley S. MacLean
*Resurrection, Apocalypse, and the Kingdom of Christ:
The Eschatology of Thomas F. Torrance*

Brian Neil Peterson
*Ezekiel in Context: Ezekiel's Message Understood in Its Historical
Setting of Covenant Curses and Ancient Near
Eastern Mythological Motifs*

Amy E. Richter
Enoch and the Gospel of Matthew

Maeve Louise Heaney
Music as Theology: What Music Says about the Word

Eric M. Vail
Creation and Chaos Talk: Charting a Way Forward

David L. Reinhart
*Prayer as Memory: Toward the Comparative Study of Prayer
as Apocalyptic Language and Thought*

Peter D. Neumann
Pentecostal Experience: An Ecumenical Encounter

Ashish J. Naidu
*Transformed in Christ:
Christology and the Christian Life in John Chrysostom*

The Claim of Humanity in Christ
*Salvation and Sanctification in the Theology
of T. F. and J. B. Torrance*

ALEXANDRA S. RADCLIFF

Foreword by Andrew Purves

◆PICKWICK *Publications* · Eugene, Oregon

THE CLAIM OF HUMANITY IN CHRIST
Salvation and Sanctification in the Theology of T. F. and J. B. Torrance

Princeton Theological Monograph Series 222

Copyright © 2016 Alexandra S. Radcliff. All rights reserved. Except for brief quotations in critical publications or reviews, no part of this book may be reproduced in any manner without prior written permission from the publisher. Write: Permissions, Wipf and Stock Publishers, 199 W. 8th Ave., Suite 3, Eugene, OR 97401.

Pickwick Publications
An Imprint of Wipf and Stock Publishers
199 W. 8th Ave., Suite 3
Eugene, OR 97401

www.wipfandstock.com

PAPERBACK ISBN 13: 978-1-4982-3019-3
HARDCOVER ISBN 13: 978-1-4982-3021-6

Cataloguing-in-Publication data:

Radcliff, Alexandra S.

The claim of humanity in Christ : salvation and sanctification in the theology of T. F. and J. B. Torrance / Alexandra S. Radcliff.

xvi + 196 pp. ; 23 cm. Includes bibliographical references.

ISBN: 978-1-4982-3019-3 (paperback) | ISBN: 978-1-4982-3021-6 (hardback)

1. Torrance, Thomas F. (Thomas Forsyth), 1913–2007. 2. Torrance, James B., 1923–2003. 3. Theology. 4. Salvation—Christianity. 5. Sanctification. I. Title.

BT751 R31 2016

Manufactured in the U.S.A.   02/25/2016

New Revised Standard Version Bible: Anglicized Edition, copyright 1989, 1995, Division of Christian Education of the National Council of the Churches of Christ in the United States of America. Used by permission. All rights reserved.

To
Two Nicholases

Contents

Foreword by Andrew Purves | ix

Acknowledgments | xiii

Introduction | 1

Part 1: The Triune God of Grace and Salvation

1. The Father as Covenant not Contract God:
   Filial over Federal | 15

2. The Vicarious Humanity of the Son:
   Ontological over External | 48

3. Drawn to Participate by the Holy Spirit:
   Objective over Subjective | 84

Part 2: Sanctification and Human Participation

4. Christ Is Our Holiness:
   Objective over Subjective | 123

5. Growing Up into Christ:
   Ontological over External | 142

6. Fixing Our Eyes on Jesus:
   Filial over Federal | 167

Conclusion | 188

Bibliography | 195

Foreword

THERE IS GROWING WORLD-WIDE INTEREST IN THE THEOLOGY OF THOMAS F. Torrance, the Scottish theologian who died in 2007. Many new studies are published annually. An international online journal, *Participatio*, is now devoted to Torrance theology, as it is also the subject-matter for conferences and symposia. Alexandra Radcliff is a fresh, new voice who brings gracious and impressive care to her Torrance scholarship. This book is a well-conceived constructive project and a worthy addition to the growing secondary literature.

A foreword, of course, is not a scholarly review. It is an invitation to read the book because there is thoughtful and insightful writing between its pages that breaks ground and plants thoughts for further growth. Dr. Radcliff has written an important book that pushes Torrance theology into something of a neglected area, namely, sanctification in Christ. She has identified a clear subject for discussion and in my view has moved Torrance scholarship to a deeper understanding of the way in which the doctrine of sanctification can be developed in a helpful direction on the ground of Christology and soteriology. Her work is original, provocative and helpful for a number of reasons.

The analysis of and reflection on Torrance theology is not exclusively focused on Thomas F. Torrance, but includes also the work of his younger brother James B. Torrance. Giving both brothers their place gives this book a distinct character. Although each brother has his own rightful place, the sheer volume and intensity of published work by Thomas has, perhaps, overwhelmed or dominated Torrance scholarship and led to the neglect of important contributions on the part of James. Dr. Radcliff has done a fine job in placing the Torrance brothers not just side by side, but also by showing their common base in the doctrines of the person and work of Christ.

The book is beautifully and gently written and Dr. Radcliff helpfully summarizes her expositions along the way. The book especially exemplifies mastery of the thesis statement to make clear the direction of the ensuing discussion. This is important given the difficult and sometimes dense writing of Thomas F. Torrance. There is nothing here that is unclear.

Dr. Radcliff writes from within the Pentecostal-Charismatic tradition, and as such offers a gentle criticism of Torrance theology for the absence of exploration of the subjective nature of sanctification. This criticism is then turned around, as it were, to address the opposite perspective where subjective sanctification is worked out in external, logico-causal responses by the Christian. The positive contribution is that subjective sanctification can be built on Torrance theology when it is grounded in our participation in the vicarious humanity of Christ by the grace of the Holy Spirit. This is a point of profound theological, and, I believe, pastoral importance.

The heart of the book is the assessment that the soteriological categories most suitable to bring to expression the salvation wrought by the Triune God of grace are filial, ontological, and objective. The development of this foundation in Torrance theology is the major exposition in the book. Dr. Radcliff is aware that this is a direct challenge to soteriological categories that are developed in terms of federal theology, with an imposed penal instrumentality with regard to the cross of Christ. For T. F. Torrance especially, but also in J. B. Torrance, it is clear that an ontological relation with Christ on account of his incarnation and vicarious humanity calls for the human response of faith by the Spirit. This means that our response through the gift of the Spirit is a participation in Christ's response for us, which avoids a logico-causal semi-Pelagianism. Dr. Radcliff negotiates her way through this material in a masterful way. Set free from the burden of attempting to achieve sanctification, sanctification is no longer seen as a subsequent stage in the *ordo salutis*, as a second work of sanctification.

Dr. Radcliff correctly roots Torrance theology at this point in the vicarious humanity of Christ whereby justification and sanctification are held together in Christ as Christ's work for us. Now there is an easy flow to the doctrine of our participation by the Spirit in union with Christ. It would be hard to overemphasize the centrality of this for Torrance theology, and Dr. Radcliff narrates this with exceptional clarity. She rightly notes that the believer does not apply what Christ accomplished; the believer participates in what Christ has accomplished.

Dr. Radcliff argues that Torrance theology would be complimented by a greater appreciation of what humankind has received and is called to in Christ. The Torrance brothers did not much venture into what this might look like; we have in this book a worthy pressing of the issue. It is worth noting, too, that this pressing of Torrance scholarship to a deeper understanding of sanctification in Christ, especially in its subjective aspect, has impressive consequences for pastoral care. Pastoral care from a Christian perspective must always be concerned for more than therapeutic application. And there is now a growing body of pastoral theology, much of it from within the framework of Torrance theology, developing the theological apparatus for ministry grounded in Christ. The concern, surely, whatever the life situation, must be for a person's deeper life in Christ. Dr. Radcliff has given us theological tools for our further reflections on this ministry on the basis of her reflections on the theology of Thomas F. and James B. Torrance. At the end of the day this is pastoral theology for the future.

Andrew Purves
Jean and Nancy Davis Professor of Historical Theology
Pittsburgh Theological Seminary
July 2015

Acknowledgments

THIS WORK IS THE OUTCOME OF A DOCTORAL DISSERTATION EARNED AT the University of St. Andrews. I am thankful for the generous financial aid of the Donald M. Baillie Scholarship in Theology provided by St. Mary's College. I am exceedingly grateful to my supervisor, Alan Torrance, whose graciousness opened my eyes to the truth of the Gospel, and whose support surpassed my studies to pastoral care and plumbing advice too! I am also grateful for the kindness and encouragement of my examiners, Tom Noble, Paul Molnar, and Andrew Purves. The preparation for publication was not possible without the help of my faithful husband and fellow Torrance scholar, Jason Radcliff, who poured many hours into the painstaking details of formatting while I attended to our newborn son. Finally, I am thankful to the triune God of grace that this work has not been a burdensome endeavor but an enjoyable one, as is fitting to its content!

Introduction

THOMAS F. TORRANCE (1913–2007) AND JAMES B. TORRANCE (1923–2003) assert the radical claim that all of humanity has its true being in Christ. The whole of humanity is chosen by God the Father for salvation in Christ and the whole of humanity is redeemed by Christ's vicarious person and work. Humanity is wholly claimed in Christ prior to anything that we can contribute. This also places an unconditional and all-embracing claim upon humanity; God's grace demands our all. Yet sanctification is not a daunting, arduous endeavor. We are liberated to grow into the ontological reality of who we are in Christ as we freely share by the Holy Spirit in the incarnate Son's communion with the Father.

Whereas the Torrances' soteriology is deemed by its advocates to be liberating for the church, it is also being strongly criticized by contemporary Federal theologians who believe that it: (1) is internally incoherent; (2) leads to a license to sin; (3) fails to offer assurance of salvation; (4) undermines our human freedom and response; (5) implies universalism; (6) depends upon privileged knowledge; (7) conflates the atonement into the incarnation; (8) fails to take seriously Christ's death and human sin; and (9) undermines the Creator and creature distinction.[1] The current relevance of this book pertains to: (1) its engagement with the fervent criticism that the Torrances are presently attracting from Federal Calvinist theologians;[2] and (2) the further

---

1. There are also the criticisms that the Torrances' soteriology: denies a judicial understanding of the atonement; presents an atonement that is not efficacious for all; reduces salvation to a noetic concept; dismisses rational thought; and implies the sinfulness of God on account of his assumption of sinful humanity. All of these criticisms will be engaged within the course of the book.

2. This book also engages with points of contention raised by: the New Perspective on Paul, namely, that Christ's obedience to the law is legalistic and that our works by the Spirit are a necessary condition for final justification; and proponents of the Torrances' theology, such as the regret that "how" questions are not fully answered and that they do not give more of an account of the prospective nature of the Christian life. This book also presents its own criticism of the Torrances' theology, which can be

implications for sanctification which are constructively drawn out from the Torrances' soteriology, particularly in light of the current movement within Federal and conservative evangelical theology to recover Puritan theology for today. Extending the implications of the Torrances' soteriology for the doctrine of sanctification, this book argues for a liberating understanding that challenges what is argued to be a profoundly distorted and distortive perspective on humanity and the outworking of our sanctification. Determined by the eschatological orientation of the risen humanity of Christ, we have confidence to grow up into Christ as we freely share by the Spirit in his intimate relationship with the Father. This challenges anthropocentric schemes of sanctification which are introspective and entail a long, grueling battle with sin. Turned out of ourselves by the Spirit to Christ, the outworking of sanctification is argued to be the free and joyful gift of our being given to share in God's triune life of love.

Yet the relevance of this book is wider in scope than these academic debates. As Andrew Purves considers, "Puritanism and Federal Calvinism have metamorphosed into the psychologically orientated Christianity of the modern era."[3]

> Federal Calvinism is largely unknown by name in mainline Protestantism today, but its legacy remains clearly felt. It involves a fatal blunting of the evangelical dimension of the gospel of the love of God and a loss of confidence in assurance of salvation. Federal Calvinism undercut the heart of the gospel, in which the love of God is revealed in Jesus Christ, to whose life we are joined, by substituting a legal for a filial standing between God and ourselves, and by redirecting us to look to ourselves and our best efforts rather than to Christ.[4]

Although not everyone is seeking to recover Puritan theology, there is a sense in which its effects are still very much alive in modern Christianity:

> Calvin and Luther stressed that we look to Christ for the assurance of our salvation and not to our own, even our best, efforts. As Calvinists have insisted, the Christian must even repent of his or her virtues. Federal Calvinism, in contrast, imposed an anxious, introspective self-examination in search of the fruits of one's sanctification. Federal Calvinism comes to grief on the same issue that undoes Puritanism: the search for assurance turns inward. The doctrine of limited atonement and the

---

found restated in the Conclusion.

3. Purves, *Reconstructing Pastoral Theology*, 66.
4. Ibid.

consequent introspective piety left the residue of an intractable pastoral problem that directed attention away from confidence in what Christ has done.[5]

On account of this problem in the wider church today, this book seeks to assess the significance of the Torrances' claim for the interface between systematic and pastoral theology.

The Torrances' theology offers a valuable corrective to the tremendous burden placed on people today by preaching and teaching that, whether blatantly or subtly, "throws people back upon themselves" to earn their relationship with God and to try to achieve by their own efforts the kind of person that they ought to be.[6] Gary Deddo observes, "Despite the pattern of biblical teaching which begins with God and his faithfulness, we feel the pressure to preach and teach and motivate folks to obedience by addressing the naked will with raw commandments."[7] David W. Torrance considers, "Probably the great majority of sermons preached are telling people what to do."[8] Christian identity tends to be defined in terms of "Yes, I made a decision for Christ" or "I follow the teachings of Jesus" or "I attend church regularly."[9] This emphasis upon our own, independent religious activity leads to "frustration, failure and a lack of the real joy of the Lord."[10] "Because of this focus on ourselves," David W. Torrance regrets, "there is frequently in the Christian life a lack of assurance of salvation so that we are not really set free to serve!"[11] This problem is perpetuated by Federal theology and forms of conservative evangelicalism, particularly those committed to recovering

---

5. Ibid., 65–66.

6. The language of "throwing people back upon themselves" is a phrase that the Torrances often use to express the problem that people are made dependent upon their own contribution to truly be saved or sanctified, which is ultimately a hopeless task. As Paul Molnar explains, "For if we are thrown back on ourselves in any sense, then we are truly lost because then salvation in the end depends on our adding our last "weak link" to the chain of salvation. And that is exactly what we are unable to do just because of the nature of sin. That is hardly good news'" Molnar, *Incarnation and Resurrection*, 101–2. See Torrance (T. F. T. from here), *God and Rationality*, 58; Torrance (J. B. T. from here), *Worship, Community and the Triune God of Grace*, 34.

7. Gary Deddo, "The Christian Life and Our Participation in Christ's Continuing Ministry," 152.

8. Torrance (D. W. T. from here), "Introduction," 17.

9. Deddo, "The Christian Life," 138.

10. D. W. T., "Introduction," 19. Deddo argues that the weakness and burnout experienced in the church today occurs when Christian activity is not rooted in the unconditional grace of God. Deddo, "The Christian Life," 154.

11. Ibid.

a Puritan account of soteriology and sanctification. Yet the Torrances' claim that our being and action is irreducibly bound up with Christ is argued by its advocates to constitute a vitalizing remedy for the church today. Gerrit Scott Dawson asserts, "Such theology is a tonic for weariness to those who are labouring in the Church."[12]

A Contentious Claim

The claim that the whole of humanity has its true being objectively realized in Christ is a contentious one. Referring to the uproar and resistance caused by Martin Luther's proclamation of justification by faith, T. F. considers, "I find this kind of disturbance again and again in the reaction not only of people outside the Church, but even of would-be evangelical people within the membership of Church, for their refusal to accept unconditional grace seems to be due to the fact that it cuts so deeply into the quick of their souls."[13] T. F. recounts the story of a parishioner who refused to accept his preaching of unconditional grace. The parishioner protested, "Do you mean to say that although I have been an elder for forty years, that does not count at all for my salvation?" T. F. replied, "It is not what we are or do, but what Christ alone has done and continues to do for us as our Lord and Saviour, that counts. It is by his grace alone that we are put in the right with God, and by his grace alone that we are saved, and live day by day as Christians." Yet the parishioner still could not accept that his religious activity did not contribute to his salvation.[14] God's radical unconditional grace can be challenging to receive because, first, it constitutes the denial of our own contribution to salvation and yet, second, it also lays an immense claim upon our lives. T. F. asserts,

> Without any doubt the gospel of unconditional grace is very difficult for us, for it is so costly. It takes away from under our feet the very ground on which we want to stand, and the free will which we as human beings cherish so dearly becomes exposed

---

12. Dawson, "Introduction," 1.

13. T. F. T., "Preaching Jesus Christ," 30. See also T. F. T., "Thomas Torrance Responds," 323.

14. T. F. T., "My Parish Ministry: Alyth, 1940–43," 40. D. W. recalls T. F.'s ministry in Alyth: "His stress was upon the unconditional grace of the Lord Jesus Christ. They were called by God freely to accept as a gift his loving offer of salvation without which we are lost. Undoubtedly, this disturbed many of the congregation, as it disturbed many in his next congregation of Beechgrove in Aberdeen and many of his future students. It is often hard for good hardworking Kirk folk to accept that what *they* do does not avail for salvation." D. W. T., "Thomas Forsyth Torrance," 14.

as a subtle form of self-will—no one is free to escape from his self-will. It is the costliness of unconditional grace that people resent.[15]

A Liberating Claim

The unconditional nature of God's grace as articulated by the Torrances is found, by its proponents, however, to be profoundly liberating. God's prior claim of us in Christ sets us free to repose in and enjoy our salvation, rather than endeavoring to obtain it. T. F. explains, "Because he came as man to take our place, in and through his humanity our humanity is radically transformed, and we become truly human and really free to believe, love and serve him. That is the wonderful message of the Cross and resurrection."[16] T. F. writes, "It is in this message of the unconditional grace and vicarious humanity of the Lord Jesus Christ that people have often told me that they have found the healing and liberation that they never thought possible."[17]

An example of this healing and liberation is offered by David W. Torrance, the younger brother of T. F. and J. B. He was ministering to a man who was trying and failing to work up enough faith and repentance in order to receive salvation. D. W. said to him, "What you have to learn is to do nothing at all! . . . When Christ said on the cross 'It is finished,' he was saying 'I have done everything for your salvation. There is nothing left for you to do. Your salvation is complete and assured. The only thing left for you to do is simply to say Thank You! And then go on saying Thank You!'"[18] D. W. reflects how the good news of God's claiming of humanity in Christ liberated this man from his own efforts so that he could freely and joyfully offer himself back to God: "As the man listened, a spirit of relief came over him. His face relaxed. The struggle was over. I think he laughed. The worry and stress was over in the joyful recognition that Christ had done everything. He knew his salvation was assured. He was now for the first time set free to serve God."[19]

J. B. was convinced that the growing problems with "burn out" and pathological "weariness" among ministers, not least in his own Presbyterian tradition, reflected a failure to understand the unconditional grace of God

---

15. T. F. T., "Preaching Christ Today," 254.
16. Ibid.
17. Ibid., 255. See also T. F. T., "Thomas Torrance Responds," 323.
18. D. W. T., "Introduction," 19.
19. Ibid., 19–20.

and the liberation that results from reposing on the continuing priesthood of Christ.[20] Alasdair Heron reflects,

> James Torrance has the rare gift of enabling the simplest parishioners, the most perplexed theological students to sense that they are fledglings destined and called to fly in the atmosphere of the eternal grace of God. The warm humanity of his personality is not only a natural gift; it is the radiation of conviction, the conviction of one who knows himself to be constrained by the love of Christ and can therefore do none other than express and convey this witness to others as both claim and liberation.[21]

The Influence of the Torrances

The Torrances' theology exercises considerable influence.[22] Alister McGrath writes, "Thomas Forsyth Torrance is widely regarded, particularly outside Great Britain, as the most significant British academic theologian of the twentieth century . . . "[23] T. F. published prolifically and various theologians

---

20. See J. B. T., *Worship, Community and the Triune God of Grace*, 22–23.

21. Heron, "James Torrance," 3. J. B.'s son writes, "His life and theology were characterized by a joy borne of knowing the welcoming hospitality of God in Christ and the overwhelming and liberating sense of belonging which that generated. His overwhelming desire in life was that all might know that it applied to them too." Torrance (hereafter A. J. T.), "The Bible as Testimony to Our Belonging," 119.

22. This book is concerned with the Torrances' essential soteriological message of claim and liberation and their influence in this regard. However, their extensive ecumenical endeavors must also be noted, as well as T. F.'s work in theology and science. J. B. was Chairman of the international conversations between the World Alliance of Reformed Churches and the Lutheran World Federation, Chairman of the British Council of Churches' Commission on the Trinity, and Chairman of the Joint Commission on Doctrine of the Church of Scotland and the Scottish Roman Catholic Church. T. F. most notably initiated dialogue between the Reformed and the Orthodox Church. See T. F. T., ed. *Theological Dialogue Between Orthodox and Reformed Churches: Volume 1*; T. F. T., ed. *Theological Dialogue Between Orthodox and Reformed Churches: Volume 2*. For T. F.'s engagement with science, see T. F. T., *Theological Science*; T. F. T., *Reality and Evangelical Theology*. Robert T. Walker suggests that, although T. F. is well-known for his contribution to science, his greatest legacy is his dogmatic theology. See Walker, "Recollections and Reflections," 48.

23. McGrath, *T. F. Torrance*, xi. Molnar writes, "There is little doubt that Thomas Forsyth Torrance (1913–2007) is one of the most significant English-speaking theologians of the twentieth century." Molnar, *Thomas F. Torrance*, 1. Colyer writes, "Thomas F. Torrance is considered by many to be the most outstanding living Reformed theologian in the Anglo-Saxon world." Colyer, *How to Read T. F. Torrance*, 15. Colyer argues that T. F. might have had even more impact if it were not for his dense writing style,

have commented on the impact his writing had on them personally and not merely intellectually. Elmer Colyer comments, "Often in my study of Torrance's work I have found myself on my knees *coram deo* lost in wonder, praise and thanksgiving to the glorious Triune God, overwhelmed by the power and grandeur of the Gospel. I find myself personally and theologically transformed . . ."[24] Dawson writes of the impact upon him of both of the Torrances' work:

> From the moment I was re-introduced to the work of the Torrance brothers several years ago, something ignited in my soul. As I read, I felt like I held gold in my hands. Simultaneously, a hunger awoke and was satisfied. Ever was I directed to see a God higher and more wonderful than I had dared to imagine. Jesus Christ appeared to me through their words in the splendour of his glory and his all-embracing love.[25]

Although J. B.'s publications are fewer, he had a profound impact upon his students and others.[26] "There was more light in his lectures than I imagined possible," reflects C. Baxter Kruger.[27]

---

unmethodical publications, use of scientific concepts and the interrelated nature of his theology which necessitates comprehending it as a whole (See also Molnar, *Thomas F. Torrance*, 338). However, Robert T. Walker's editing of T. F.'s lecture materials now offers a helpful systematic organization of his theology. See T. F. T., *Incarnation*; T. F. T., *Atonement*.

24. Elmer Colyer, "Recollections and Reflections," 18. McGrath hails T. F. as "one of the most prolific of theological writers": "by the time of his retirement in 1979, Torrance had authored, edited or translated more than 360 pieces; since his retirement, he has added more than 250 further items to this already impressive list." McGrath, *T. F. Torrance*, xi.

25. Dawson, "Introduction," 1. D. W. writes, "On this issue of 'unconditional grace,' where both have been so criticised by evangelicals in the U.K. and the U.S.A., they have frequently seen conversions to Christ, both through their lecturing and their writing." D. W. T., "Thomas Forsyth Torrance," 27.

26. Although J. B. only published one book, *Worship, Community and the Triune God of Grace*, it continues to be reprinted and a considerable number of copies continue to be sold. It is unfortunate that J. B.'s theology has at times been confused with T. F.'s or even marginalized. For example, T. F. is mistakenly named as the author of J. B.'s book in the bibliography of Robert Webber, *Ancient-Future Faith*. Another example can be seen in the title of the 2013 Conference of the New Evangelical Theological Symposium: "Worship, Spirit and the Triune of God of Grace: The Trinitarian Relational Theology of T. F. Torrance." This plays upon the title of J. B.'s book whilst engaging with T. F. rather than J. B.

27. Kruger, *The Great Dance*, 21. See also Redding, "Calvin and the Cafe Church," 121. Douglas Campbell acknowledges that J. B.'s distinction between God as a covenant God and a contract God has had a revolutionary impact on his study of Paul.

The Torrances' influence continues through their students. Kruger's popular books have made J. B.'s theology accessible to a wide audience.[28] Colyer writes of lives transformed by teaching T. F.'s theology:

> Over many years of teaching T. F. Torrance's theology, and not least his understanding of the incarnational atoning reconciliation, I have repeatedly witnessed seminary students,' pastors' and lay persons' Christian lives transformed as a result of encountering Torrance's vision of the incarnate saviour.[29]

The Torrances' theology has even played a significant role in the transformation of a denomination, Grace Communion International, formerly The Worldwide Church of God.[30]

The Influences upon the Torrances

The Torrances seek to ground their theology in the revelation of God in Christ, the Scriptures, and the Christian tradition. Dawson writes, "They speak a daring, vital word that springs first from Scripture, then rises through the great Patristic writers, the creeds, the Reformers, and the evangelical theologians who have followed."[31] The Torrances draw upon patristic theology, especially, in the case of T. F., Athanasius and Cyril of Alexandria.

Campbell, *The Deliverance of God*, xxiv. Stein writes, "In his preaching, as in his dealings with people he has endeavoured to reflect the unconditional love of God. In that he has exercised considerable influence, not only here in Scotland, but wherever he has lectured abroad. It is frustrating that he has not written more." Stein, "The Legacy of the Gospel," 149.

28. See, for example, Kruger, *The Great Dance*; Kruger, *God is For Us*. Kruger's books have made the Torrances' theology more accessible not least most recently within the Pentecostal-Charismatic movement, which is especially notable because the Pentecostal-Charismatic movement has typically not been so concerned with intellectual theology (see Kennedy "Anti-intellectualism," 35). See, e.g., John Crowder, Sons of Thunder; David Vaughan and Joanne Gravell, The New Ecstatics; Godfrey Birtill, "It's a Wonderful Dance," https://www.youtube.com/watch?v=oLIasj5fUo4 for examples of Pentecostal-Charismatic appropriation of Torrance theology.

29. Colyer, "The Incarnate Saviour," 33. See also Colyer, *How To Read T. F. Torrance*, 18.

30. See Feazell, *The Liberation of the Worldwide Church of God*. See also Grace Communion International's "You're Included" online interview series: http://www.gci.org/yi.

31. Dawson, "Introduction," 4. Heron reflects, "James Torrance made no claim to be 'original' or to break fresh ground in academic theology. He was concerned far more to bear witness to the abiding foundation of all Christian faith as the promise leading us forward to the Kingdom of God." See Heron, "James Torrance," 5.

They stand within the Reformed tradition and are both deeply influenced by John Calvin. Both T. F. and J. B. are immense admirers and advocates of the theology of John McLeod Campbell, whom they regard as one of Scotland's greatest theologians despite the fact that his teaching on universal atonement and assurance led to his deposition from ministry in the Church of Scotland.[32] They are both greatly influenced by Karl Barth, with whom they studied in Basel, but T. F. also records the impact of his teachers, Daniel Lamont, William Manson and, most of all, Hugh Ross Mackintosh.[33] J. B.'s other influences include John MacMurray and Norman Kemp Smith, who were arguably the greatest Scottish philosophers of the twentieth century and both of whom had religious commitments.[34]

Shaped by their upbringing within a missionary family, the Torrances have a strongly practical orientation to their theology. Their brother, D. W., reflects,

> We were all three greatly influenced by our missionary parents, their dependence on the Word of God and prayer. They imparted to us their missionary concerns. Theology is the servant of ministry. If it does not lead us to personal faith in Jesus Christ in the unity of his person and work, then, as Tom often said, "our theology is only a paper theology."[35]

Both T. F. and J. B. chose to enter the ordained ministry as well as to have academic careers.[36] Their theology is intimately related to pastoral concerns. D. W. writes of T. F.:

> Tom was never primarily an academic theologian. He was primarily a churchman and pastor with a pastor's concern for the spiritual renewal of the church. It was out of his pastoral concern for the renewal of the church that he felt led—or compelled—into the academic world in order to try and forward that concern. His theology as a biblical theologian was centered on the saving, Triune grace of God centered in the person and

---

32. See T. F. T., *Scottish Theology*; J. B. T., "Introduction."

33. T. F. T., "*Itinerarium Mentis In Deum*," 7–18. See also H. R. Mackintosh, *The Divine Initiative*. Purves argues that, although T. F. is frequently labelled a Barthian, he is also his own person. Andrew Purves, "The Christology of Thomas F. Torrance," 71.

34. According to personal conversation with his son, Alan J. Torrance.

35. Speidell, "David W. Torrance Interview," 25–26.

36. See T. F. T., "My Parish Ministry: Alyth, 1940–43," for a personal account of some of T. F.'s parish ministry.

work of Christ, that grace which in Christ changes and transforms lives.[37]

Heron writes of J. B.:

> James Torrance is not and never was a cloistered academic, but a pastor, a guide for the perplexed, a man of faith whose goal and interest was above all the nurturing and guiding of others in the way of that same faith. Theological reflection, theological writing and theological teaching are for him firmly anchored in (and related to) the community of faith, a community far wider and broader than the purely academic. Theology as he understands and practices it is both existential and ecclesiastical. It is not merely a matter of dusty books or rarified ideas or brilliant theories; it is a personal quest and responsibility in the service of the Church, and as such involves not only the mind but also the heart of the theological teacher.[38]

The Torrances' pastoral and practical concerns mean that their theology truly engages with people's needs and has a transformative impact upon lives.

The Influence upon this Book

It is not my intention to evaluate the theological vision of the Torrances from some (mythical) detached, Archimedean point. It should be acknowledged that this book is shaped by questions that arise from standing within the Pentecostal-Charismatic movement. These questions will be distinct from ones which arise from the Torrances' own Reformed tradition. This book concurs with T. F. in some of his criticism of the Pentecostal-Charismatic movement, but also suggests how particular Pentecostal-Charismatic concerns might complement the Torrances' theology. This will be seen in the suggestion that Pentecostal-Charismatic experience might be considered to be a direct consequence of being drawn by the Spirit to participate in Christ's communion with the Father. A distinctively Pentecostal-Charismatic influence can also be seen in the argument for a greater confidence

---

37. Speidell, "David W. Torrance Interview." D. W. suggests that T. F.'s experience as a padre during the War was also formative in this regard: "His personal conversations with men facing danger and death, crystallized with greater intensity in his mind the necessity for a Christian faith that related to real life, a faith that could stand all the stresses and strains of life, and bring comfort and deliverance in Christ to the living and the dying." D. W. T., "Thomas Forsyth Torrance," 17.

38. Heron, "James Torrance," 2.

in the eschatological orientation of our humanity in Christ. However, the Pentecostal-Charismatic movement has its own shortcomings in that it can tend towards contractual relations with God.[39] Therefore, the tradition stands to benefit profoundly from the Torrancean insistence that the nature of Christ's claim on humanity involves liberation from an introverted concern with our own religious efforts.

The Scope of the Book

Part 1 of this book presents the significance of the Torrances' filial, ontological, and objective understanding of salvation, particularly given current criticism of this approach by contemporary Federal theologians. The Torrances' understanding challenges soteriologies that have an overarching federal or external framework, which lead to people being thrown back upon their own subjective endeavors to gain salvation. Chapter 1 explores how, according to the Torrances (particularly J. B.), God reveals himself in Christ as a covenantal God, not a contractual God, with primarily filial rather than judicial purposes for humanity. Prior to any contribution that we could make, God chooses the whole of humanity for salvation in Christ. This challenges the Federal Calvinist doctrines of double predestination and limited atonement. This chapter engages with the charges of incoherence and special knowledge. It also engages with the questions as to whether universal atonement leads to universalism, a license to sin, a lack of assurance of salvation, or the negation of our human freedom. Chapter 2 explores the Torrances' claim that the whole of humanity is saved by the person and work of Christ. This challenges the Federal Calvinist doctrines of penal substitution and forensic imputation that, according to the Torrances, do not reflect God's primarily filial purposes nor offer a true transformation of humanity. This chapter also engages with questions concerning the centrality of Christ's death and the seriousness of human sin, as also what it means to share in Christ's righteousness and to be justified by faith. Chapter 3 explores what place the Holy Spirit and humanity have in this objective, Christocentric scheme of salvation. It assesses the Torrances' conception of the Holy Spirit as drawing humanity to participate in Christ's intimate communion with the Father. In so doing, it seeks to challenge accounts of the Spirit wherein humanity is given an autonomous, logico-causal role in redemption, whether in our response of faith or through works in anticipation of final judgment. It also addresses the charge that salvation risks being reduced to a noetic concept, that it confuses the Creator and the creature,

---

39. See Ian Stackhouse's critique in Stackhouse, *The Gospel-Driven Church*.

and, furthermore, it considers whether the effect of this theology is to diminish the role of the Holy Spirit and devalue the place of the human response.

Part 2 seeks to explore constructively the implications of the Torrances' soteriology for the outworking of our sanctification, particularly in light of the current movement to recover the contemporary significance of Puritan theology. Chapter 4 roots sanctification objectively in Christ with justification and presents the outworking of sanctification as our participation by the Spirit in Christ's holiness. This challenges the belief that, having been justified by God, it is now our responsibility to work out our own sanctification. In particular it challenges the notion of a Federal second work or Pentecostal second blessing whereby sanctification is made subsequent to justification in the *ordo salutis* and people are thrown back upon their own resources to attempt to achieve it themselves. It also engages with the questions of whether our participation in Christ entails a loss of creaturely being and of our own human response. Chapter 5 argues for confidence in the outworking of our sanctification on account of our new eschatological orientation in the risen humanity of Christ. It challenges poor perspectives on the nature of humanity and the outworking of sanctification, whilst also addressing the charge of triumphalism and arrogance. Chapter 6 examines the nature of sin, repentance, and holiness. It challenges static, moralistic ethics and anthropocentric introspection and argues for a liberating understanding of the outworking of sanctification in dynamic, relational terms whereby we are turned "out of" ourselves by the Spirit to share in the Son's intimate communion with the Father. The conclusion revisits key issues and arguments and offers possible avenues for further exploration.

Part 1

The Triune God of Grace and Salvation

I

The Father as Covenant not Contract God
Filial over Federal

THE PURPOSE OF PART 1 OF THIS BOOK IS TO PRESENT THE SIGNIFICANCE OF the Torrances' filial, ontological, and objective soteriology, particularly in the face of current criticism by contemporary Federal theologians. The Torrances boldly challenged the Federal theology of their day when they believed that the preaching and teaching made salvation dependent upon our own efforts. This first chapter will explore the Torrances' belief that God the Father is revealed in his Son as a covenantal God, not a contractual God, with primarily filial rather than judicial purposes for humanity. Prior to any contribution that we could make, God chooses the whole of humanity for salvation in Christ. This liberates us to offer ourselves back to God wholeheartedly in freedom.

In order to understand where the Torrances stand within their Reformed tradition and the conflict that arises, it is helpful to consider Charles Partee's distinction between three kinds of Calvinism:

> (I) Conservative Calvinists, represented by Charles Hodge and his sympathizers, advance Scripture alone emphasizing its divinity before its humanity; (II) Liberal Calvinists, represented by Friedrich Schleiermacher and his sympathizers, advance faith alone emphasizing its subjectivity before its object; and (III) Evangelical Calvinists, represented by Karl Barth and his sympathizers, advance Christ alone emphasizing his person before his work.[1]

Conservative Calvinism, represented by Charles Hodge, Louis Berkhof, Richard Muller, the Canons of Dort (1618–1619), and the Westminster

---

1. Partee, "The Phylogeny of Calvin's Progeny," 26.

Confession (1648), seeks to be a faithful follower of Calvin.[2] Liberal Calvinism, driven by the challenge of contemporary issues, does not wish to be so restricted.[3] Evangelical Calvinism wishes to follow Calvin but is not so concerned with getting "back to" Calvin, on the grounds of *ecclesia reformata, semper reformanda*.[4] The Torrances have been grouped into this third way, along with figures such as Thomas Erskine, Edward Irving, John McLeod Campbell, and Karl Barth. "Evangelical Calvinism" has the vicarious humanity of Christ, and union with Christ, at its center. It claims to be in continuity with John Knox and the Scots Confession of 1560, and in contention with the Synod of Dort, the Westminster Assembly, and the Federal theology of Conservative Calvinism.[5]

Federal theology was the prevailing preaching and teaching of the Torrances' Scottish Reformed tradition in their time. Federal theology has had a history of dominance in the perspective of those wishing to adhere to Calvinism and it continues to have an abiding authority today.[6] It currently governs the North American Reformed perspective and "is considered, by many, to be the only orthodox Reformed theology acceptable."[7] According to Federal Calvinism, God made a covenant with Adam as the "federal" head of the human race. God created Adam to discern the laws of nature by reason and, if Adam was obedient, God would give him eternal life. If he was disobedient, it would lead to death. Adam disobeyed the law and, as federal head of the human race, his curse affected all of humanity. Out of his love, God made a new covenant, electing some to be saved by Christ. In order to forgive humanity, God had to satisfy his righteousness and justice and Christ therefore became a penal substitutionary sacrifice to atone for the sins of the elect.[8] This Federal scheme is expressed confessionally in the Irish Articles and in the Westminster Confession of Faith.[9]

---

2. Ibid., 28.

3. Ibid., 40 It is outwith the scope of this book to engage with the debate with liberalism.

4. Habets and Grow, "Introduction," 6–7.

5. Heron, "Foreword," xiv–xv. T. F. also uses the term "Evangelical Calvinism" himself. See T. F. T., *Scottish Theology*, 59–60.

6. McGowan, "Federal Theology as a Theology of Grace," 44.

7. Habets and Grow, "Introduction," 3.

8. McGowan, "Federal theology," 43. For a recent introduction to Federal theology, see Horton, *Pilgrim Theology*.

9. Ibid., 44. Purves writes of the Westminster Confession of Faith, "This confession has, since 1647, been the doctrinal standard of the Church of Scotland, shaping the Presbyterian mind ever since." Purves, *Reconstructing Pastoral Theology*, 64.

The Torrances believe that Federal theology is a distortion of Calvin's theology.[10] J. B. contends that the Federal doctrine of election presents God's relationship with humanity in contractual terms, which is foreign to Calvin's teaching of one eternal covenant of grace. J. B. argues that "old" and "new" do not denote two different covenants; they are two forms of the one eternal covenant.[11] Federal Calvinism presents a covenant of works for all and a covenant of grace only for the elect.[12] J. B. argues that this means that God is related to all of humanity in terms of law, but only to some in terms of grace.[13] Primacy is given to law over grace.[14] J. B. considers, "In the federal scheme, the focus of attention moves away from *what Christ has done for us* and for all humanity to *what we have to do* IF we would be (or know that we are) in covenant with God."[15] He observes that this leads to a lack of assurance regarding salvation and people turning inward upon themselves to examine whether they are bearing enough "fruit" as evidence of their salvation.[16]

There is much debate as to whether Federal Calvinism is faithful to Calvin.[17] More importantly, however, A. T. B. McGowan, who disagrees

10. J. B. T., "Introduction," 5.

11. Ibid.

12. J. B. T., "The Concept of Federal Theology," 24.

13. J. B. T., "The Incarnation and 'Limited Atonement,'" 92.

14. J. B. T., "The Concept of Federal Theology," 23. McGowan has sought to defend Federal theology from J. B.'s criticism, arguing that Federal theology is a theology of grace. McGowan, "Federal Theology as a Theology of Grace," 41–50. The same argument can be found in McGowan, *The Federal Theology of Thomas Boston*. Yet McGowan's highlighting of elements of grace within Federal theology does not adequately defend Federal theology from J. B.'s criticism that there is "an impoverishment and restriction of the concept of grace." J. B. T., "Introduction," 8. Whilst elements of grace can be found in Federal theology, grace is subordinated to an overarching legal framework which does not adequately reflect God's primarily filial purposes for humanity.

15. J. B. T., "Introduction," 7.

16. Ibid., 4.

17. Among those who argue that later Calvinists distorted Calvin's teaching are: Hall, "Calvin against the Calvinists," 19–37; Armstrong, *Calvinism and the Amyraut Heresy*; Rolston, "Responsible Man in Reformed Theology"; Kendall, *Calvin and English Calvinism to 1649*; Bell (a student of J. B.), *Calvin and Scottish Theology*. Among those who dispute this are: Paul Helm, *Calvin and the Calvinists*; McWilliams, "The Covenant Theology of the Westminster Confession of Faith and Recent Criticism," 109–24; Muller, *Calvin and the Reformed Tradition*; Muller, *After Calvin*. McGowan considers, "How can scholars come to such diametrically opposite positions and yet express them with such absolute assurance? The answer must surely be that the evidence is not compulsive in either direction." McGowan, *The Federal Theology of Thomas Boston*, 52.

with J. B.'s criticism of Federal theology, considers that the "crux" of J. B.'s argument does not concern a perceived lack of faithfulness to Calvin but rather "a misunderstanding of the nature of a Biblical covenant."[18] For the Torrances, the essential difficulty with Federal Calvinism is that it distorts the nature of *how* God relates to humanity in salvation because it does not subordinate human logical constructs to God's revelation of *who* he is in Christ. Lack of assurance in salvation and weariness from trying to obtain it can be remedied by a true understanding of God.

Who over How

"Who" over "how"

In order to understand *how* God acts in salvation, it is necessary to first ask *who* God is. This is the priority of the "who" question over the "how" question, which Dietrich Bonhoeffer wrote of in *Christology*.[19] He argues that Christology cannot be equated with soteriology. Christ cannot be known from his works. Rather, we understand God's works from knowing the person of Christ, who is the revelation of God the Father. We must therefore look to *who* God is in order to understand *how* he acts.[20]

This is the starting point for the Torrances.[21] J. B. perceives that if we do not begin with the "who" question, and allow our understanding to be shaped by God's self-revelation through his Son, we project anthropological notions onto God which have damaging consequences for how we understand salvation.[22] J. B. asserts, "Our dogmatic starting point in theology should be: Who is God?"[23] Correspondingly, T. F. argues that we cannot seek to understand God according to prior anthropological systems of logic. The method of knowing in theology must be appropriate to the subject of enquiry. God determines our knowledge of him and we are dependent upon his self-giving revelation.[24]

> Knowledge of this God cannot be moulded according to our plastic ideas or controlling archetypes; that would be idolatry.

---

18. McGowan, "Federal Theology as a Theology of Grace," 41.
19. Bonhoeffer, *Christology*, 37–39.
20. Ibid.
21. J. B. T., *Worship*, 58.
22. J. B. T., "Introduction," 1.
23. J. B. T., *Worship*, 58.
24. T. F. T., *Theological Science*, 26–27.

Rather must our knowing of God be brought into conformity with what He reveals of Himself, and under the control of what He gives us of Himself.[25]

Revelation through the Son

For the Torrances, we know *who* God the Father is according to his self-giving revelation through the incarnation of his Son. T. F. describes this revelation as God "objectifying" himself in Christ.[26] Jesus is able to show us who God is because he is *homoousios tō Patri* (of one being with the Father).[27] As Jesus said, "The Father and I are one" (John 10:30); "Whoever has seen me has seen the Father" (John 14:9); "No one knows the Father except the Son and anyone to whom the Son chooses to reveal him" (Matt 11:27). Of one being with the Father, Jesus is the very expression of the Father's heart. There is no difference in their mercy or love; Jesus is not the kinder side of a God who is also a wrathful Father.[28] As T. F. would often assert, "There is no God behind the back of Jesus."[29]

> God and Christ, the Father and the Son, are one in their being and nature—there is no God behind the back of Jesus Christ. As the one Mediator between God and Man who is himself both God and Man, Christ cannot be thought of in some intermediate way, as coming in between us and the wrath of God, or as changing God or making him merciful. Jesus Christ is God incarnate; what God is in Christ he ever was and is in himself. Christ's coming among us in the likeness of sinful flesh, in the likeness of flesh as it is in us sinners, in order to condemn sin in the flesh and reconcile us to God, is the very movement and expression of the Love of God.[30]

---

25. Ibid., 37.
26. Ibid., 29, 37, 43, 45; See also T. F. T., *The Ground and Grammar of Theology*, 165.
27. T. F. T., "Introduction," *The Incarnation*, xviii.
28. This misunderstanding is exemplified in such infamous preaching as Jonathan Edwards's. See Edwards, "Sinners in the Hands of an Angry God."
29. T. F. T., "Introduction," *The Incarnation*, xvii; T. F. T., *Scottish Theology*, 294.
30. T. F. T., *Scottish Theology*, 294.

Part 1: The Triune God of Grace and Salvation

"Filial" over "judicial"

Seeking to be faithful to God's self-revelation in Christ, the nineteenth-century minister, John McLeod Campbell, sought to promote a filial understanding of the atonement over a judicial understanding. He perceived that the judicial categories of the Federal Calvinism of his time had led to a lack of joy, peace, and assurance in salvation among his congregation.[31] Looking to God's self-revelation in Christ, McLeod Campbell saw grounds for their assurance, joy, and peace: Jesus's activity in salvation is one with the Father; the Son was not placating the wrath of the Father in order to receive forgiveness for humanity. The reconciliation that Jesus brings about is the very expression of the love of the Father. For McLeod Campbell, this does not deny a judicial element to atonement, but it means that it must be subsumed and only understood within God's overarching filial purposes for humanity.[32]

The Torrances admire and advance McLeod Campbell's concern to promote the "filial" over the "judicial."[33] They believe that, when we look to who God is through Christ, we see that the Father's dealings with humanity in salvation are primarily filial rather than judicial. The Torrances were therefore critical of their own tradition's Westminster Confession of Faith for having an overarching judicial framework. In contention with the Torrances, R. Michael Allen seeks to defend Federal theology by arguing that it does not distort the filial emphasis found in Scripture and Calvin.[34] He points to the significant place of adoption in the Westminster Confession, asserting, "Justification is for adoption. Thus, the kind of Calvin-against-the-Calvinists thesis propounded by Torrance . . . cannot be maintained, as if the relational focus of Calvin was lost amid the contractual and legal apparatus of his scholastic successors."[35] Allen contends, " . . . the Westminster Assembly manifests a serious commitment to putting the legal in its place—that is, as a parameter for relational union with the triune God."[36] However, the Torrances' contention with Federal theology is not that Federal theology

---

31. J. B. T., "Introduction," 3.

32. McLeod Campbell, *The Nature of the Atonement*. Commenting on McLeod Campbell's perspective, Purves writes, "The issue atonement must deal with is not broken law as much as a broken relationship with God, which leads to sin." Purves, *Reconstructing Pastoral Theology*, 63.

33. T. F. T., *Scottish Theology*, 293–312. T. F. commends McLeod Campbell as "one of the profoundest theologians in the history of Scottish theology since the Reformation of the Church of Scotland." T. F. T., *Scottish Theology*, 287.

34. Allen, *Justification and the Gospel*, 40.

35. Ibid., 44.

36. Ibid., 45.

denies God's filial purposes, but that they are restricted within an overarching legal "parameter."[37] Allen only reinforces the Torrances' concern.

T. F. believes that an overarching legal framework distorts the nature of the Father, presenting him primarily as a Judge and Lawgiver and only a Father to those who satisfy the requirements of the Law.[38] If you begin with a concept of God as Lawgiver, J. B. considers, there is the tendency to understand salvation in terms of God being conditioned into being gracious by human works or by Christ satisfying the conditions of the law. However, if you begin with the God revealed by Jesus as the triune God of grace, you will see his unconditional filial purposes whereby he draws us as his sons into communion with him.[39] Scripture speaks of God's intention "to bring many sons to glory" (Heb 2:10; cf. Eph 1:5). J. B. asserts, ". . . God's primary purpose for humanity is 'filial,' not just 'judicial,' where we have been created in the image of God to find our true being-in-communion, in 'sonship,' in the mutual personal relations of love."[40]

J. B. also perceives that a legal framework leads to a distortion of our understanding of humanity. He writes, "The federal scheme has substituted a *legal* understanding of man for a *filial*. That is, God's prime purpose for man is legal, not filial, but this yields an impersonal view of man as the object of justice, rather than as primarily the object of love."[41] J. B. considers that the Federal scheme can lead to the perception of humanity more as workers than as sons: "What our doctrine of God is, that is our anthropology. The counterpart of the contract God of the covenant of works is the individual with his / her legal rights—and a work ethic! The counterpart of the triune God of grace is the human person created for communion."[42] This resonates with the parable of the prodigal son, in which the father forgives his son before he has even had a chance to repent, and does not wish for his son to relate to him in terms of work and servanthood, but welcomes him back as family (Luke 15:11–31). The difficulty with an overarching legal framework is that it demands works from humanity for salvation. An overarching filial

---

37. Michael Horton argues that Federal theology holds together both the "legal and relational, judicial and familial." Horton, *Covenant and Salvation*, 130. However, for Horton, justification is "the forensic basis of union with Christ" (129). He writes, "Justification is exclusively juridical, yet it is the forensic origin of our union with Christ, from which all of our covenantal blessings flow" (139).

38. T. F. T., *Scottish Theology*, 128–33.

39. J. B. T., "Introduction," 1.

40. J. B. T., "The Doctrine of the Trinity in our Contemporary Situation," 15.

41. J. B. T., "Concept of Federal Theology," 35.

42. Ibid.

context declares that God has created humanity for communion.⁴³ The Torrances believe that the Father's dealings with us are not primarily in terms of law but rather in terms of Fatherhood and sonship.

Conclusion

The Torrances are convinced that, in considering *how* God acts in salvation, it is necessary to first ask *who* God is. We know *who* the Father is according to his self-giving revelation in the incarnation of his Son. Of one being with the Father, the Son is able to reveal the nature of the Father. The Torrances argue that this means that the Father and the Son are unified in their mission and that the Father's wrath is not pitted against the Son, conceived of as a kinder side of God. Rather, Jesus is the very expression of the Father's love for humanity. The Father's purposes are primarily filial rather than judicial. His love sought our salvation so that we might be adopted as sons and daughters in order to live in loving communion with him. This is of the utmost importance for people who lack joy, peace, and assurance in salvation.

Covenant versus Contract

Contract

Having considered *who* God is, it can be better understood *how* God acts in salvation. For the Torrances, the Father, who is one in his mission with the Son and has primarily filial purposes, does not relate to humanity in contractual terms. J. B. defines a contract as "a legal relationship in which two people or two parties bind themselves together on mutual conditions to effect some future result."⁴⁴ He suggests that contractual thinking arose in theology as a reflection of the structure of seventeenth century society in Britain, France, and New England.⁴⁵ The Torrances identify contractual thinking in Federal theology when salvation is made dependent upon our personal response.⁴⁶ Although God's grace may be upheld, contractual

---

43. Ibid., 35.
44. Ibid., 228.
45. Ibid., 227–28, 231.
46. T. F. T., *Scottish Theology*, 144.

thinking can unintentionally steal in when forgiveness is made conditional upon repentance, with devastating consequences for assurance of salvation.[47]

Contractual thinking is perpetuated today by forms of evangelical outreach such as the "Four Spiritual Laws" of Campus Crusade for Christ and "The 4 Points": "If you want to have that separation between you and God removed and have the punishment and guilt of all the wrong things you've ever done wiped away, then you can, right now! Just say this prayer and if you are sincere, God will see your heart and save you."[48] Michael Horton has observed that in evangelicalism "some Christians struggle to the point of despair over whether the quality and degree of their repentance is adequate for them to be forgiven, as if repentance were the ground of forgiveness and the former could be measured by the intensity of emotion, resolve, and victory over specific sins."[49] Martin Luther calls this "legal repentance."[50] J. B. perceives that the evangelical order of grace is reversed so that repentance is prior to forgiveness.[51] He observes, "It makes the imperatives of obedience prior to the indicatives of grace, and regards God's love and acceptance and forgiveness as conditional upon what we do—upon our meritorious acts of repentance."[52]

Covenant

The Torrances contend that God does not engage with humanity in contractual terms, but in covenantal terms. A covenant, in Biblical terms, is "a promise binding two people or two parties to love one another unconditionally."[53] Two kinds of covenant are seen in the Bible: *suntheke* (bilateral) and *diatheke* (unilateral). A bilateral covenant is made between two equals, for example, when a man and woman promise to take each other in marriage. A unilateral covenant, however, is made by one party for another. An example of this can be seen in Israel when a king made a covenant for his people, defining

---

47. J. B. T., "Covenant or Contract?," 58.

48. See the "Four Spiritual Laws" of Campus Crusade for Christ: http://www.campuscrusade.com/fourlawseng.htm; and "The 4 Points": http://www.the4points.com/INT/about_the4points.php?page=EVA; http://www.the4points.com/INT/about_the-4points.php?page=PT4&osCsid=e892fe3bcf239459b4e39fffa6bf7026. See also "Simply Share Jesus" and the "EvangeCube": http://www.simplysharejesus.com/.

49. Michael Horton, *Pilgrim Theology*, Kindle ed., Loc 5263.

50. John Calvin, *The Institutes of the Christian Religion*, III.2.iii.

51. J. B. T., "Covenant or Contract?," 57.

52. J. B. T., "Christ in our Place," 48.

53. J. B. T., "Covenant Concept," 228.

what kind of king he would be and what kind of people they would be.[54] As T. F. considers, God knew that Israel was incapable of fulfilling a bilateral covenant; therefore, he provided a way for Israel to respond to him. God made a unilateral covenant with Israel, asserting, "I will be your God and you shall be my people." Israel did not have to fulfill certain conditions to gain God's favor. This was a distinguishing factor from the activity of those who were not the people of Israel.[55] It is this kind of unilateral covenant which the Torrances argue that God has made with humanity.[56] God fulfills both sides of the covenant for our salvation in Christ. J. B. writes, "The God and Father of our Lord Jesus Christ is the God who has made a covenant *for us* in Christ, binding himself to man and man to himself in Christ."[57] T. F. declares the covenant in this way:

> God loves you so utterly and completely that he has given himself for you in Jesus Christ his beloved Son, and has thereby pledged his very Being as God for your salvation. In Jesus Christ God has actualised his unconditional love for you in your human nature in such a once for all way, that he cannot go back upon it without undoing the Incarnation and the Cross and thereby denying himself. Jesus Christ died for you precisely because you are sinful and utterly unworthy of him, and has thereby already made you his own before and apart from your ever believing in him. He has bound you to himself by his love in a way that he will never let you go, for even if you refuse him and damn yourself in hell his love will never cease. Therefore, repent and believe in Jesus Christ as your Lord and Saviour.[58]

We are not forgiven *if* we repent; we are forgiven, *therefore* we repent.[59] This is what Martin Luther calls "evangelical repentance."[60] J. B. draws upon McLeod Campbell's conviction that Christ vicariously confessed our sin for us.[61] He also points to the parable of the prodigal son who wanted to work his way into his father's favor, as in legal repentance, but the father accepted his son before he even had the opportunity (Luke 15:11–32).[62] J. B. argues

---

54. Ibid., 229.
55. T. F. T., *The Mediation of Christ*, 84.
56. J. B. T., "Covenant Concept," 229.
57. Ibid., 230.
58. T. F. T., *Mediation*, 94.
59. J. B. T., "Covenant or Contract?," 57.
60. Calvin, *Institutes*, III.2.iii.
61. J. B. T., "Christ in our Place," 49.
62. J. B. T., *Worship*, 57.

that, in the New Testament, forgiveness precedes repentance.[63] There are no conditions upon humanity to receive salvation. J. B. therefore repeatedly insists, "The God of the Bible, the God and Father of our Lord Jesus Christ is a covenant-God, and not a contract-God."[64]

Obligations of grace

The Torrances' claim that God places no conditions upon humanity for salvation has not been received without criticism. As J. B.'s son, Alan J. Torrance, considers, "JBT's exposition of this invariably gave rise to [the] concern, namely, that such a theology of grace risked weakening or diluting the force of the law thereby opening the door to a liberal if not licentious attitude towards our God-given obligations."[65] Yet this concern is a fundamental misunderstanding of grace. The desire to uphold godly behavior is certainly commendable; Paul is clear that we do not have a license to sin: "What then are we to say? Should we continue in sin so that grace may abound? By no means! How can we who died to sin go on living in it?" (Rom 6:1–2; cf. 6:15). However, Paul also emphasizes that grace leads to the end of sin. To introduce conditions for salvation is to keep us under the law. Paul asserts that sin abounds under the law (Rom 5:20). The very thing that people employ to seek to discourage disobedience perversely fuels it.

It is God's unconditional grace that leads to living a holy life that upholds the law. Paul writes that it is under grace that sin has no dominion (Rom 6:14). Grace teaches us to reject ungodliness:

> For the grace of God has appeared, bringing salvation to all, training us to renounce impiety and wordly passions, and in the present age to live lives that are self-controlled, upright, and godly, while we wait for the blessed hope and the manifestation of the glory of our great God and Saviour, Jesus Christ. He it is who gave himself for us that he might redeem us from all iniquity and purify for himself a people of his own who are zealous for good deeds. (Titus 2:11–14)

Paul asserts that we are free from the law and that godly living is a fruit of the Spirit (Galatians 5). Godly living fulfills the law but this is the fruit of the Spirit rather than our own efforts; we cannot boast of anything but the cross

---

63. J. B. T., "Covenant or Contract?," 57.
64. J. B. T., "Introduction," 6.
65. A. J. T., "The Bible as Testimony to Our Belonging," 107.

of Christ (Galatians 6). It is not law but grace that is the only way leading to authentic Christian behavior.

For the Torrances, there are no conditions placed upon humanity *for* grace, but there are obligations *of* grace. The "logic of grace," T. F. believes, is that "all of grace" does not mean nothing of man but rather "all of man."[66] Likewise, J. B. argues that although God makes the covenant for us, it demands a response from us.[67] God's claim *of* humanity places a radical claim *upon* humanity. However, it is essential to distinguish that the *obligations* of grace are not *conditions* of grace.[68] J. B. writes,

> God's grace, which certainly lays costly unconditional claims upon us, is not conditioned by considerations of worth and merit. Repentance, faith and love, are not conditions of grace, but our *response* to grace, and the way to evoke that response is to hold out to people the love of the Father, the grace of the Lord Jesus Christ, and the promises of the Spirit—and that is the road to *assurance*.[69]

God is a covenant God, not a contract God; his purposes are primarily filial over legal.[70] J. B. often asserts, "the Indicatives of grace are always prior to the obligations of law and human obedience."[71] T. F. also situates our response in relation to the fact that God has already provided the perfect human response in our place through Jesus.[72] This means that our response is a participation in a response already made, which liberates humanity from any demands to earn God's grace and allows us to offer ourselves back to God in freedom.[73]

Despite the liberating nature of unconditional grace, the fear of antinomianism, or lawlessness, can lead to people introducing conditions for salvation and also legalism. John Coffey proposes that this is the reason why seventeenth-century Federal theologian Samuel Rutherford, of whom the Torrances were so critical, taught about the conditionality of the covenant and the importance of preparations. Coffey considers that Federal

---

66. T. F. T., "The Atonement, the Singularity of Christ and the Finality of the Cross," 230; see also T. F. T., *Mediation*, 105.
67. J. B. T., "Covenant or Contract?," 55.
68. J. B. T., "Introduction," 6.
69. Ibid., 3–4.
70. Ibid., 1.
71. J. B. T., "Covenant Concept," 230.
72. T. F. T., *Theology in Reconstruction*, 131.
73. T. F. T., *Mediation*, 104.

theologians such as Rutherford held to Calvin's doctrine of *sola gratia* but, in practice, preaching focused on the necessity of human activity because of the concern that grace leads to a license to sin.[74] This serves as an example of what J. B. perceives to be the human propensity to contradict God's covenant by introducing conditions:

> The fallacy of *legalism* in all ages—perhaps this is the tendency of the human heart in all ages—is to *turn God's covenant of grace into a contract,* with the most serious consequences for preaching, worship and pastoral counselling. In the Bible, the form of the covenant is such that the Indicatives of grace are always prior to the obligations of law and human obedience. 'I am the God of Abraham, Isaac and Jacob, I have loved you and redeemed you and brought you out of the land of Egypt, out of the house of bondage, *therefore* keep my commandments.' But legalism puts it the other way round. 'If you keep the law, God will love you! If you keep the Sabbath day and carry the yoke of the Torah, the Kingdom of God will come!' The imperatives are made prior to the indicatives. The covenant has been turned into a contract, and God's grace made conditional on men's obedience.[75]

Such a contractual understanding can lead to a lack of assurance in salvation and weariness in trying to obtain it. In contrast, the affirmation of God's unconditional grace grants assurance and a freedom to respond because God has already chosen the whole of humanity for salvation and provided a response for us in Christ. Therefore, it is precisely because a response is not demanded *for* our salvation that this creates a response *to* our salvation. When a person is coerced into a contract, he does not have a true understanding of God's grace, and cannot respond with such authentic love for God. Alan J. Torrance explains this with an analogy of two husbands who must travel abroad for business. Their wives become concerned at the temptations that may arise on their trip. Margaret says, "John, never forget that if I ever find out that you have so much as nodded in the direction of another woman in the course of your travels, I shall sue you for divorce and ensure that you lose the kids, the house and a substantial portion of your salary, not to mention your reputation . . . !" On the other hand, Jane says, "David, I would just like you to know that no matter what circumstances you find yourself in and no matter what happens, I shall always be there for you and will always love you. If you make mistakes, never forget that I shall

---

74. Coffey, *Politics, Religion and the British Revolutions*, 133–34.
75. J. B. T., "Covenant Concept," 230.

always forgive you!"[76] Torrance argues that it is Jane's unconditional love that inspires a faithful response:

> Which of the two husbands is more likely to engage in the aforementioned 'untheological activities' during his trip? One suspects that it would be John for the simple reason that, as he left, his wife Margaret made it clear that she did not love him unconditionally. Contrary to the commitment inherent in their wedding vows, their relationship was a contractual one. She was, in effect, informing him that she did not really love him at all. The withdrawal of unconditional love could only serve to weaken the obligations that stem from it. The obligations on David were, by contrast, profoundly strengthened—and in a way that was both affirming of him and surely freeing. It would not only intensify the obligatory response but inspire and facilitate it.[77]

God's unconditional covenant of grace does not diminish our legal obligations but actually deeply strengthens them.[78]

Conclusion

In light of God's filial purposes for humanity as revealed through the Son, the Torrances assert that God has made a unilateral covenant with us in Christ, who has offered the perfect response to the Father in our place. For the Torrances, the proper declaration of the gospel is: "God *has* saved you. *Therefore* respond." Some argue that this message of unconditional grace leads to lawlessness and there can be a propensity to introduce conditions in order to promote lawfulness: "*If* you fulfil [a certain condition], *then* God will save you." However, as well-intentioned as this may be, it can only serve to increase lawlessness. God's gracious covenant does not diminish our legal obligations but actually strengthens them because we are able to offer ourselves back to God in freedom, knowing that the response has already been made for us in Christ.

---

76. A. J. T., "Bible as Testimony," 107.

77. Ibid.

78. The argument that grace leads to godly living raises the question of why Christians still sin. This will be explored in chapter 6 but, for now, we might affirm that although grace may not always lead to godly living, it is the *only way* to authentic godly living.

Election is Grace

Election of all in Christ

The Torrances believe that another expression of God's unconditional covenantal grace as revealed by Christ is unconditional election.[79] According to the Torrances, all of humanity is elect in Christ.[80] Paul writes to the Ephesians:

> He chose us in Christ before the foundation of the world to be holy and blameless before him in love. He destined us for adoption as his children through Jesus Christ, according to the good pleasure of his will, to the praise of his glorious grace that he freely bestowed on us in the Beloved. (Eph 1:4–6)

J. B. believes that here Paul is referring to Christ's mediatorial headship over all because God the Father sums up all things in Christ (Eph 1:10).[81] T. F. also points to Christ sustaining creation and dying for all people:

> The great fact of the Gospel then is this: that God has actually chosen us in Jesus Christ in spite of our sin, and that in the death of Christ that election has become a *fait accompli*. It means too that God has chosen all men, in as much as Christ died for all men, and because that is once and for all no one can ever elude the election of His love. In as much as no one exists except by the Word of God by whom all things were made and in whom all things consist, and in as much as this is the Word that has once and for all enacted the eternal election of grace to embrace all men, the existence of every man whether he will it or not is bound up inextricably with that election—with the Cross of Jesus Christ.[82]

God claims all of humanity in Christ: "In Christ we are all judged—and in so far as Christ died for all, then are all dead—but In Him we are all chosen by God's Grace."[83] J. B. writes, "The doctrine of election, interpreted in this Christological way, enshrines the good news that our salvation is by grace

---

79. J. B. T., "Concept of Federal Theology," 20.

80. T. F. T, "Predestination in Christ," 109.

81. J. B. T., "Concept of Federal Theology," 33. According to J. B., Calvin placed election in the context of Christ's vicarious humanity. Ibid., 20. However, T. F. believes that Calvin had a propensity towards abstracting the work of God from the work of Christ in election. T. F. T, "Introduction," *The School of Faith*, lxxviii.

82. T. F. T., "Universalism or Election?," 315.

83. T. F. T., "Predestination," 125.

alone, and is from beginning to end the one work of the one God, Father, Son and Holy Spirit. He chose us, not we him. The doctrine of election is another way of saying that all is of grace."[84]

Election is grace

According to this understanding that election *is* grace, the Torrances argue that two deterministic, logico-causal doctrines of election must be rejected: election made prior to grace, as found in Federal Calvinism, and grace made prior to election, as found in Arminianism. J. B. writes,

> The scholastic Calvinists made *election prior to grace,* beginning with the doctrine of a double decree as a major premise, and then moving on to formulate the doctrines of grace, incarnation and atonement, as God's way of executing the eternal decrees—thereby 'logically' teaching that Christ died only for the elect, to secure infallibly the salvation of the elect. The Arminians on the other hand made *grace prior to election,* so that grace means that Christ died to make all men salvable, but God, foreknowing those who would decide, elects them. This . . . grounds our salvation on our human decision. This separation of election from grace, from a proper trinitarian understanding of the being and will of God, led to the polarisation of 'Calvinists' and 'Arminians' in the seventeenth and eighteenth centuries.[85]

J. B.'s account of Federal Calvinism and Arminianism folllows in the trend of their classic polarization. Yet more recently Arminians have sought to defend their position as a misunderstood and viable evangelical option.[86] Roger E. Olsen argues that both Calvinism and Arminianism affirm the necessity of God's grace for the human response to be made possible. He argues that Calvinism and Arminianism concur that the decisive element of salvation is grace, not our human decision. Arminius affirmed a human role in salvation but not a meritorious one.[87] Olsen writes, "The only "contribution" humans make is non-resistance to grace. This is the same as accepting a gift. Arminius could not fathom why a gift that must be freely received is

---

84. J. B. T., "The Incarnation and 'Limited Atonement,'" 87.
85. Ibid.
86. See Olsen, *Arminian Theology*; Stanglin and McCall, *Jacob Arminius*.
87. Olsen, *Arminian Theology,* 14, 17–18, 33–35, 157.

no longer a gift, as Calvinists contend."[88] Therefore Olsen resists Arminianism being labelled semi-Pelagianism.[89]

Whilst the classic polarization of Calvinism and Arminianism is now less accepted, the Torrances' concern regarding the separation of election and grace should nevertheless be upheld. There is a real danger of semi-Pelagianism in *both* Calvinism and Arminianism if election is not grounded in Christ. When election and grace are separated, we lose assurance of salvation and are turned back upon ourselves to attempt to achieve it. The Torrances believe that the problem lies in answering the "how" question without first looking to the "who" question. God's self-revelation in Christ is subordinated to the projection of our own human reasoning onto God.

Arminians believe that God does not elect some for reprobation. They reason that this correspondingly entails a denial of unconditional election to salvation. Olsen writes, "According to Arminians the two are inextricably linked; it is impossible to affirm unconditional selection of some to salvation without at the same time affirming unconditional selection of some to reprobation, which, Arminians believe, impugns the character of God."[90] Therefore, Arminians consider election to be conditional: "God's electing foreknowledge is caused by the faith of the elect."[91] Whilst Olsen maintains that the faith of the elect is not meritorious, the separation of election and grace nevertheless introduces the possibility that people lack assurance of their salvation and turn to their own religious activity for evidence.

According to Federal theology, only some are elect for salvation: "Election is God's choice of particular people as recipients of his merciful grace in his Son out of the mass of condemned humanity."[92] Commenting on Romans 9, Horton argues, "everyone is in a state of condemnation and God is not bound by any necessity to save anyone (vv. 14–15)."[93] Yet, for

---

88. Ibid., 165.

89. Olsen recognizes a distinction between "Arminianism of the heart" and "Arminianism of the head." He considers that some of Arminius's heirs strayed from his teaching by following an "Arminianism of the head" which has confidence in human capacity without God's grace, thereby leading to semi-Pelagianism. Olsen, *Arminian Theology*, 17. Olsen's understanding of Arminianism as "free human participation in salvation" may come closer to the Torrances' soteriology than they may have realized.

90. Ibid., 14–15.

91. Ibid., 35.

92. Horton, *Pilgrim Theology*, 4901.

93. Ibid., 5069. T. F. understands this differently, arguing that Romans 9–11 presents election in terms of the grace and love of God that is free to all. Paul is writing of God's purpose to include the Gentiles, who were excluded, which was controversial for the Jews. Paul's intention is inclusion, not exclusion. This passage is not a portrayal of

the Torrances, this rationalizes the gospel according to an overarching legal framework and displaces Christ as the ground of election, thereby dislocating the will of the Father and the mission of the Son.[94] The Torrances are concerned that Federal Calvinists present a different God behind the back of Jesus, creating a lack of assurance in salvation which turns us back upon our own endeavors. The Torrances contend that God's self-revelation in his Son shows them to be one in their nature and mission. T. F. asserts, "Christ is Himself identical with the action of God toward men; He is the full and complete Word of God. There is therefore no higher will than Grace or Christ . . . as the express image of God He covers the whole Face and Heart of the Father."[95] Therefore T. F. argues, "There may appear to be a two-fold will of God for salvation and reprobation but at the *Parousia* we shall see that there was only one divine will for our salvation."[96]

For T. F., the election of the whole of humanity in Christ offers us assurance that we are all included in God's love.[97] David Fergusson writes,

> Included in the election of the risen Christ is the election of every man, woman and child. Each individual is thus determined by the love of God . . . The message preferred by the doctrine of predestination is no longer a mixed message of joy and terror, salvation and damnation, but a message that is unequivocally one of comfort and joy.[98]

Thus Karl Barth asserts, "The doctrine of election is the sum of the Gospel because of all words that can be said or heard it is the best."[99] People do not have to depend upon their own religious efforts to provide evidence for their salvation. Rather, we are liberated to freely devote ourselves back to God.

T. F. argues that the "pre" in "predestination" should be understood not according to logico-temporal categories but to being grounded in God

---

God's wrathful choosing of some for damnation, but the scandal of God's radical grace in choosing all for salvation. For T. F., Romans 9–11 shows God's heart to have mercy on all of humanity and his all-encompassing saving purposes. T. F. T., "Predestination," 115.

94. T. F. T., "Predestination," 109.

95. Ibid., 110.

96. T. F. T., *School of Faith*, lxxviii.

97. T. F. T., "Universalism or Election?," 316.

98. Fergusson, "Predestination," 472–73. Fergusson is writing of Barth's doctrine of election but it is applicable to that of the Torrances.

99. Barth, *Church Dogmatics* II/2, 3. Cited by Fergusson, "Predestination," 472–73.

himself.[100] When election is separated from Christ, this leads to an abstract and deterministic doctrine.[101] T. F. argues that a deterministic reading of Romans 9, whereby God chooses only some for salvation, does not appreciate that the Father's choice of Jesus makes election supremely personal.[102] T. F. contends that determinism is the result of anthropocentric thinking:

> The lapse into determinism is only possible with the employment of abstract categories of thought, such as cause, force, etc. To think of God in this way, through forms of thought that have been shaped through our interpretation of the world, is to drag God down within the abstractions of a fallen world.[103]

This is why it is imperative first of all to consider who God is in order to understand how he acts (the priority of the "who" question over the "how" question). The Torrances argue that the question of election must be guided not by a prior legal or logical framework but by God's self-revelation of his filial purposes in Christ.

Conclusion

The Torrances believe that God has elected all of humanity unconditionally in Christ. Election is not prior to grace, as found in Federal Calvinism, nor is grace prior to election, as found in Arminianism. For the Torrances, God's election and grace must not be placed within man-made logico-causal categories but rather guided by God's self-revelation of his filial purposes in Christ. This gives us assurance of salvation because we do not have to worry whether we are one of God's elect, nor do we have to wear ourselves out trying to bear fruit that is evidence of our salvation. God's election of humanity in Christ means that we are all included in his plan of redemption.

God's Sovereignty and Human Freedom

God's sovereignty

In this universal plan of salvation, all are chosen by God and reconciled in Christ, irrespective of our own will. T. F. writes of our election as a "*fait accompli*" and that "the existence of every man whether he will or no is bound

---

100. T. F. T., "Predestination," 116.
101. Ibid., 112.
102. Ibid., 113.
103. Ibid., 114.

up inextricably with that election."[104] Salvation is entirely by the grace of God, excluding any human endeavor. This is prefigured in Jesus's conception; Joseph, who is symbolic of humanity, has no part.[105] T. F. writes, "The virgin birth means that the sovereignty of man . . . has no place."[106] He perceives in this the basic gospel message: humanity is saved not by anything that we could do but by God's grace alone.[107]

Human freedom

The sovereignty of God in redemption raises the question of how we are to understand human freedom. T. F. writes of our human autonomy being set aside.[108] In their affirmation of God's universal grace, the Torrances have been criticized for undermining human freedom.[109]

In addressing this criticism, the nature of human freedom must first be examined. Maurice Bevan considers that the underlying assumption of this criticism is that we are freely self-determined individuals. Bevan argues that this perspective is a product of Western post-Enlightenment philosophy and that we are not as free as we suppose.[110] In this finite world, T. F. believes that humanity can only have a contingent freedom. Human beings are free, but in such a way that is proper to a limited and contingent existence. We are upheld by the transcendent freedom of God.[111]

What we perceive to be freedom is only a sinful self-will. Paul uses the language of being "enslaved to sin" (Romans 6). Thus we are not truly free. Our sinful self-will usurps our freedom, making it impossible to attain our own redemption.[112] "Paradoxically enough," T. F. argues, "to give man *arbitrium* over the act of his own salvation is to land him in determinism."[113]

When T. F. writes of our human autonomy being set aside, he has in mind this sinful self-will and the basis of the establishment of a true freedom. T. F. writes, "Man's will is not overridden. His self-will is certainly

---

104. T. F. T., "Universalism or Election?," 315.

105. T. F. T., *Mediation*, 100–102.

106. T. F. T., "Predestination," 131.

107. T. F. T., *Mediation*, 100–102.

108. Ibid., 100.

109. Bevan, "The Person of Christ and the Nature of Human Participation in the Theology of T. F. Torrance," 187.

110. Ibid., 188.

111. Ibid., 188–89.

112. T. F. T., "Predestination," 121–22.

113. Ibid., 118.

judged and forgiven, but it is recreated and determined by love; it is directed in the only path where it can find true freedom—and in all that it is man that wills!"[114] Therefore, God does not undermine our human freedom but rather truly establishes it because we are liberated from our enslaved, sinful condition to participate in the very life of God. Bevan argues that freedom, understood in this contingent sense, is not curtailed by the *fait accompli* of our universal election and redemption. He explains, "The human creature cannot make a free decision to accept what already sustains his or her being through grace but remains free to reject the notion that the fallen conditions of finite existence represent absolute truth."[115]

The absurdity of the criticism that our human freedom is undermined should also be considered. It is akin to being taken on a fantastic holiday but resenting it. The *fait accompli* of our redemption is to be celebrated and enjoyed! Paul uses the language of being "enslaved" in regards to both sin and righteousness (Romans 6). However, for Paul, this enslavement to righteousness is a welcome transformation:

> But thanks be to God that you, having once been slaves to sin, have come obedient from the heart to the form of teaching to which you were entrusted . . . When you were slaves of sin, you were free in regard to righteousness. So what advantage did you then get from the things of which you now are ashamed? The end of those things is death! But now that you have been freed from sin and enslaved to God, the advantage you get is sanctification. The end is eternal life. For the wages of sin is death, but the free gift of God is eternal life in Christ Jesus our Lord. (Rom 6:17; 6:20–23)

Redemption is impossible by our own endeavors because of our enslavement to the sinful self-will. Our lives being in the hands of God is fundamental to our creaturely existence. It is a comfort to know that we are in the hands of a God of everlasting love and grace, who entered our humanity in order to transform it, doing what we are incapable of doing ourselves.

It is the *fait accompli* of our redemption that establishes our freedom to decide for God. T. F. argues, "the *Biblical doctrine of election* is the very doctrine which expresses the universal action of God's grace in such a way that, far from dissolving the personal elements of choice and decision, it establishes them."[116] God's grace is not irresistible; we remain free to reject God's grace, inconceivable as this is. But for T. F., humanity can only make

114. Ibid., 120.
115. Bevan, "Person of Christ," 193.
116. T. F. T., "Universalism or Election?," 314.

a free and true decision for God because of God's prior decision for us: "It is WE who believe, and we come to believe in a personal encounter with the living Word. Faith entails a genuine human decision, but at its heart there is a divine decision, which, as it were, catches up and makes it what it is, begotten of the Holy Ghost."[117] T. F. asserts:

> There can be no doubt about it that when confronted with Jesus Christ man makes a decision—but that decision is also a double-sided act. When he decides, he finds that it has been decided already, and it is the divine decision that qualifies his decision and makes it what it is faith IN GOD. His decision is made faith through the Object of faith to which faith conforms. The possibility and the character of will and of faith do not lie in themselves but in that to which they are directed and that which determines them in that direction. And so here we have real freedom for the first time, because we have will directed by its proper Object, Jesus Christ.[118]

The relation between the divine decision already decided and the decision of the human being in response is constituted by the Holy Spirit.[119] The human decision does not have an independent existence from the divine decision. It cannot be understood according to synergistic or logico-causal categories.[120] T. F. argues, "[Election] does not mean the repudiation of human freedom but its creation, and the repudiation of bondage."[121] God's universal grace is the very means by which human freedom is established.[122]

Conclusion

God's universal plan of salvation makes our election and redemption a *fait accompli*. This raises the question of how we are to understand human freedom. The Torrances' scheme of salvation has been criticized for undermining human autonomy. However, this criticism presupposes an impossible notion of freedom whereby we are autonomous self-determined individuals. Humanity, as creatures in a finite world, has an essentially contingent freedom. God sets aside our self-will, which is enslaved to sin and ultimately

---

117. T. F. T., "Predestination," 130.

118. Ibid., 124.

119. Ibid., 127. See chapter 3 for further examination of the Holy Spirit's role in redemption.

120. Ibid., 129.

121. Ibid.

122. T. F. T., "Universalism or Election?," 314.

deterministic, but in so doing establishes for us a true freedom. God's grace is not irresistible; we remain free for the inconceivable horror of rejecting God's grace. Yet humanity can only make a free and true decision for God because of God's prior decision for us. Human freedom is not undermined but truly established by God's sovereignty.

Universal Atonement and Universalism

Universal atonement

The whole of humanity, elect in Christ, is included in Christ's atonement, according to the Torrances. T. F. points to the Apostle John's proclamation, "Herein is love, not that we loved God but that He loved us and sent His Son to be the propitiation for our sins, and not for ours only but for the sins of the whole world" (1 John 4:10; 2:2).[123] This has led the Torrances into conflict with Federal theology's doctrine of limited atonement, more recently also called "definite atonement."[124]

> The doctrine of definite atonement states that, in the death of Jesus Christ, the triune God intended to achieve the redemption of every person given to the Son by the Father in eternity past, and to apply the accomplishments of his sacrifice to each of them by the Spirit. The death of Christ was intended to win the salvation of God's people alone.[125]

Fundamental to the debate between universal atonement and definite atonement is the issue of assurance of salvation. Coffey has criticized the Torrances' scheme of universal atonement for its lack of assurance of salvation. Coffey argues that universal atonement only makes salvation a potentiality since some do not choose faith in Christ. Limited atonement is the true ground of assurance because salvation is a certainty for the elect.[126] Coffey writes,

---

123. Ibid., 316.
124. J. I. Packer prefers the language of "definite" over "limited": "*limited* is an inappropriate emphasis that actually sounds menacing." He writes, "It is as if Reformed Christians have a primary concern to announce that there are people whom Christ did not die to save, whom therefore it is pointless to invite to turn from sin and trust him as Savior." Packer, "Foreword," Kindle ed., Loc 208.
125. Gibson and Gibson, "Sacred Theology and the Reading of the Divine Word," Kindle ed., Loc 474.
126. Coffey, *Politics, Religion,* 137.

> Indeed, the whole point about limited or definite atonement was that it reinforced assurance. The Cross did not just make salvation possible or hypothetical, it made it certain; if Christ had died for a person, that person's salvation was guaranteed. The doctrine of universal atonement, on the other hand, granted no such assurance. It was cold comfort to be told that Christ had died for you, when you did not know whether Christ's atonement for you was effectual or merely hypothetical.[127]

This criticism continues to be levelled against the Torrances today. In the recent weighty tome, *From Heaven He Came and Sought Her: Definite Atonement in Historical, Biblical, Theological, and Pastoral Perspective*, David Gibson and Jonathan Gibson argue that only definite atonement offers assurance of salvation: "An atonement symbolized by the Good Shepherd who lays down his life for his sheep provides pastoral riches of motivation, joyful obedience, and perseverance for pastor and people alike."[128] They contend, "Proponents of a general, universal atonement cannot in fact, if being consistent, maintain a belief in the sincere offer of salvation for every person. All that can be offered is the opportunity or the possibility of salvation—and that not even to all in reality."[129]

Since salvation is only a possibility, and assurance of salvation is lost, it is argued that we are thrown back upon our own response as the subjective grounds for salvation. David and Jonathan Gibson contend:

> Models of the atonement that make salvation merely possible fail to provide this robust assurance and comfort. Assurance of salvation necessarily becomes detached from the secure source of what Christ has done and lodges itself in the unstable realm of our response. Atonement has been made, yes—but knowledge of it sufficient to calm our fears and assure us of our adoption is grounded in human action, not divine. We are salvation's decisive donors.[130]

Robert Letham also believes that the Torrances' scheme of universal atonement means that Christ's death is not efficacious for all and therefore becomes dependent upon our human response: "the atoning death of Christ does not of itself secure the salvation of anyone in particular, since it is

---

127. Ibid.

128. Gibson and Gibson, "Sacred Theology and the Reading of the Divine Word," Kindle ed., Loc 832.

129. Ibid., Loc 821.

130. Ibid., Loc 832.

contingent on the human response."[131] Likewise, Horton argues that Christ's work of definite atonement achieves its intention and is effective for all, but universal atonement cannot be, which means that salvation becomes dependent upon our human response.[132]

This criticism misunderstands the Torrances' scheme of universal atonement. Salvation is not a mere possibility; it is an accomplished reality. As God incarnate, Christ fulfills both sides of the covenant, God's side and our human side on our behalf. This means that our human response to what Christ has already done does not contribute anything to our salvation. Salvation is not dependent upon our human response because Christ has already provided the perfect human response. Our human response can agree and live in accordance with this reality but it does not accomplish the reality. There is arguably no greater grounds for assurance of salvation than this reality accomplished for all by Christ in our place.

It is the doctrine of definite atonement that cannot offer true grounds for assurance of salvation. Whilst it may be maintained that salvation is effective for the elect, if Christ did not die for all, this leads to the problem of people worrying whether they are one of the few for whom Christ died. This raises the potentiality for people to look to their own religious efforts and depend upon them as evidence of their salvation. This lack of assurance has indeed occurred, as T. F. observes, "For generations of people in the Kirk faith was deeply disturbed and shaken by the doctrine thundered from the pulpits that Christ did not die for all but only for a few chosen ones—assurance of their salvation withered in the face of the inscrutable decree of divine predestination."[133] The Torrances' claim that the whole of humanity is included in Christ's atonement cannot breed this lack of assurance because salvation is an accomplished reality for all and cannot be reversed unless the very atonement is to be undone.

Ultimately, the Torrances' scheme of universal atonement is misunderstood because the criticism is determined by human rational constructs of thought. Of key importance to proponents of definite atonement is that Christ's death achieves its intended efficacy.[134] If Christ dies for all, as in universal atonement, but not all are ultimately saved, Christ's work falls short

---

131. Letham, "The Triune God, Incarnation, and Definite Atonement." Kindle ed., Loc 11022.

132. Horton, *Pilgrim Theology*, Kindle ed., Loc 4172–4192.

133. T. F. T., *Scottish Theology*, 59.

134. See Letham: "This atonement is glorious, even more glorious in the knowledge that it achieves what the triune God's great plan purposed." Letham, "The Triune God, Incarnation, and Definite Atonement," Kindle ed., Loc 11435.

of God's intention.[135] The Torrances, however, subordinate such logical constructs in seeking to be faithful to the self-revelation of God in Christ.

Universalism

The Torrances' affirmation of the election of all in Christ and universal atonement has attracted the criticism that this leads logically to universalism.[136] As Fergusson expresses it, "If all are from eternity elect in Christ, does this not imply that everyone must willy nilly be gathered in at the end?"[137] The Torrances are often criticized for being universalists.[138] Myk Habets argues that, for T. F., universal atonement does not lead to universalism because of the distinction between, in the language of John Craig, "carnal" and "spiritual" union. According to this understanding, all have a carnal union with Christ by virtue of our common humanity; but only some are united by the Spirit to Christ and obtain the benefits of this union.[139] Those who have a "spiritual" union will ultimately have eternal life and those with only a "carnal" union will not.

However, it is important to note that although T. F. engages with John Craig's language of "carnal" and "spiritual" union in his introduction to *The School of Faith*, this is because his concern in this book is to summarize the core aspects of the Reformed faith.[140] T. F. does not take up this language in his own work. This language is noticeably absent from his work specifically focused on universalism and predestination.[141] In fact, T. F. perceives a problem with using this language, which may have been the reason for his not employing it in his own work. T. F. perceives the danger that distinguishing two different kinds of union could present God's grace as conditional and throw people back upon their own endeavors to accomplish the spiritual union. When T. F. comments on Craig's language, he stresses that the spiritual union is not additional to the carnal union. There is one union accomplished by Christ. The spiritual union must be understood as

---

135. Horton, *Pilgrim Theology*, Kindle ed., Loc 4192.

136. Rankin, "Carnal Union with Christ in the Theology of T. F. Torrance," 291–92; Letham, "The Triune God," Loc 11202.

137. Fergusson, "Predestination," 474.

138. Lee, *Living in Union with Christ*, 311, 313; Coffey, *Politics, Religion*, 133.

139. Habets, "The Doctrine of Election in Evangelical Calvinism," 338. See also J. B. T., "The Priesthood of Jesus," 172.

140. T. F. T., "Introduction," *School of Faith*, cvi.

141. It appears from Habets's reference to Rankin that Habets was following Rankin in employing this language. See Rankin, "Carnal Union with Christ."

a participation in this one union.¹⁴² "If the spiritual union is an additional union," he argues, "then our salvation depends not only on the finished work of Christ but upon something else as well which has later to be added on to it before it is real for us."¹⁴³ T. F. saw this conditional grace in the Westminster Catechism and the practical implications of this in the lack of assurance and burden felt by congregations. In contention with this language, T. F. writes, "As against that grave aberration it must be insisted that there is only one union with Christ, that which He has wrought out with us in His birth and life and death and resurrection and in which He gives us to share through the gift of the Holy Spirit."¹⁴⁴ Whilst this can cause confusion regarding universalism, T. F. believes that it is better to speak of one union with Christ and not make distinctions that could lead to a misunderstanding of conditional grace.

The Torrances emphatically deny the association with universalism. J. B. makes the distinction, "This is not 'universalism' but it is universal love."¹⁴⁵ Universal love is an aspect of the doctrine of universalism but it is not to be equated. For T. F., this universal love is the positive aspect of universalism; it seeks to uphold the love of God in contrast to Federal theology in which he perceives it to be subordinated to an overarching rational, legal framework.¹⁴⁶ However, T. F. argues that the doctrine of universalism is also subject to the criticism of being guided by human logical constructs of thought:

> Is the love of God to be understood abstractly in terms of what we can think about it on a human analogy, such as human love raised to the *nth* degree, or are we to understand the love of God in terms of what God has actually manifested of His love, that is Biblically? . . . The only valid analogy we have is in the life and death of Jesus Christ and there we learn where divine love was poured out to the utmost that men in unbelievable hardening of heart rejected it to the very last. Dare we go behind Calvary to argue our way to a conclusion which if we could reach by logic would make the Cross meaningless?¹⁴⁷

T. F. believes that a true appreciation of God's universal love must lead to a rejection of universalism because it does not recognize the urgency of

142. T. F. T., "Introduction," *School of Faith*, cvii–cviii.
143. Ibid., cvii.
144. Ibid.
145. J. B. T., "The Incarnation and 'Limited Atonement,'" 85.
146. T. F. T., "Universalism or Election?," 314.
147. Ibid., 310–12.

evangelism.[148] T. F. is strongly critical of universalism, arguing that it ignores the reality of hell and the necessity of mission.[149]

Essentially, universalism is flawed, for T. F., because it does not take adequate account of the fundamentally irrational fact of sin. He points to the awful and absurd reality that preaching the gospel leads to some hardening their hearts.[150] T. F. describes the rejection of God's love as inexplicable and devastating:

> To choose our own way in spite of God's absolute choice of us, to listen to the voice of His infinite love and to know that we are already apprehended by that love in the death of Jesus, and by that very apprehension of love to be given the opportunity and capacity to respond in faith and love, and still to draw back in proud independence and selfish denial of God's love, is an act of bottomless horror. If the light that is in us be darkness, how great is that darkness! To choose our own way and yet in that choice still to be chosen by God would be hell. Can we imagine anything more appalling than that a man should use the very power that God gives him to choose to contradict God, should choose to depart from God, and yet be unable to depart, because in spite of all he is still grasped by God in an act of eternal love that will not let him go?[151]

T. F. believes that God does not send the damned to hell, nor did he create the hell they experience; God loves the whole of humanity everlastingly. It is in rejecting this love that one can experience a hell of one's own creation:

> Even when a man has made his bed in hell God's hand of love will continue to grasp him there. To choose finally and for ever—unfathomable mystery of iniquity—to say "No" to Jesus is to be held in a hell of one's own choosing and making. It is not God who makes hell, for hell is the contradiction of all that is of God.[152]

---

148. Ibid., 318.

149. Ibid., 311–13. T. F. wrote this article criticizing universalism in response to Robinson, "Universalism—Is It Heretical?," 139–45.

150. Robinson, "Universalism—Is It Heretical?," 318.

151. Ibid., 316–17.

152. Ibid., 317.

This rejection of God is an absurdity. T. F. believes that the problem with the doctrine of universalism is that it attempts to rationalize the irrational mystery of sin and evil.[153]

> It commits the dogmatic fallacy of systematising the illogical. Sin has a fundamentally surd-like character. Somehow evil posits itself and cannot be rationalised. The New Testament teaches that when it speaks of the mystery of iniquity, and of the bottomless pit (*abyssos*). Evil is fundamentally discontinuity. No explanation involving only continuity or coherence can ever approach the problem, for that would be to draw the line of continuity dialectically over discontinuity. The doctrine of the atonement teaches us that no matter how much we think about it, here our reason reaches its limit. It cannot bridge the contradiction between God and man in guilt. The contradiction is resolved only by an act of God in which man in contradiction to God is reconciled and yet the terrible bottomless reality of sin is not denied.[154]

For T. F., although the doctrine of universalism can point to the possibility that all will be saved, it cannot point to the impossibility of some being lost.[155] Whether all of humanity will live reconciled with God is a mystery.[156]

Logico-causal categories

Yet if the Torrances' theology logically leads to universalism, and they deny universalism, does this not make their position incoherent? Recently, the criticism has been raised that the Torrances' theology disregards logical reasoning. Letham contends that there is an "internal incoherence" to T. F.'s belief.[157]

> It is simply incoherent for Torrance to say what he says about the definitive justification and reconciliation for all people and yet to deny universal salvation. Moreover, if it is possible for people to reject Christ and what he has done, it cannot be

---

153. Ibid., 313–14.
154. Ibid.
155. Ibid., 312.
156. Ibid., 314.
157. Letham, "The Triune God," Kindle ed., Loc 11370. See also Rankin, "Carnal Union," 291–92.

definitive and effective for them and cannot have been complete in Christ's person.[158]

For Letham, T. F.'s final recourse to mystery "appears to belittle the place of logic," coming close to "irrationalism and obsfuscation."[159] Nor is Letham satisfied with appeal to God's self-revelation in Christ over human constructs of thought:

> It simply will not do to dismiss criticism on this point by assertion that Torrance's claims stem from a center in God and that the critics have an uncrucified epistemology; this is to break down rational discourse on the basis of a privileged and precious gnosis.[160]

Here the crux of the debate is reached. The essential problem that the Torrances perceive with Federal theology is that human logical constructs are valued, no doubt unwittingly, over God's self-revelation in Christ. The Torrances maintain that we are unable to argue our way to truths about God; we rely wholly upon his self-giving in Christ. J. B. writes,

> The logic of the incarnation is not the logic of Aristotle. It seems to me a danger in 'Systematic Theology' . . . to have a neatly structured 'system' (no doubt based on biblical texts) into which we fit God and Christ and atonement 'logically,' as in pigeon holes, and fail to see that every doctrine must be seen in the light of God's self-revelation in Jesus Christ as Father, Son and Holy Spirit.[161]

The Torrances' theology is guided by the concern to look to who God is in order to understand how he acts in salvation, which means subordinating human rational discourse to what God reveals of himself in Christ. As Paul Molnar contends, "the nature of that object prescribes the manner in

---

158. Ibid., Loc 11370.

159. Ibid., Loc 11312.

160. Ibid., Loc 11382; see also Hardy, "T. F. Torrance," 173.

161. J. B. T., "Incarnation and 'Limited Atonement," 86. Paul Helm argues that if J. B. dismisses "Aristotelian logic," then J. B. ought to dismiss all argument, including his own criticism of limited atonement: "For it must not be forgotten that an argument that dismisses a theological view as the product of Aristotelian logic is still an argument, and if we throw out all argument we throw out that argument as well." However, Helm does not adequately appreciate or address J. B.'s contention. J. B. does not dismiss all use of logic. Rather, the Torrances' concern is the subordination of God's self-revelation in Christ to prior frameworks of human logic because this distorts the truth of who God is and how he relates to us in salvation. See Helm, "The Logic of Limited Atonement," 47–54.

which it is known."¹⁶² The Torrances' theology is guided by the Object of their study which means, contra Letham, that their theology is therefore profoundly internally coherent.¹⁶³

Conclusion

The election of the whole of humanity in Christ has universal implications for redemption. The Torrances affirm a universal atonement in Christ. Those who propound a definite atonement argue that, since not all are ultimately saved, universal atonement only makes salvation a potentiality and therefore we are turned back upon our own subjective response for assurance of salvation. Yet this misunderstands the accomplished reality of salvation in Christ, who offered the perfect human response for us. Definite atonement leaves people worrying whether they are one of the chosen few for whom Christ died, whereas universal atonement offers assurance that all are included in Christ's perfect response in our place.

Universal atonement is also criticized for leading logically to universalism. The Torrances reject universalism because it does not take adequate account of the irrational fact of sin and evil, whereby people choose to reject God. For T. F., the ultimate end of all of humanity remains a mystery. This is not a satisfying answer for those who value human logical constructs of thought. Proponents of definite atonement believe that Christ's death must achieve its intended efficacy. Yet the Torrances' theology is profoundly internally coherent in that it is guided by the Object of their study and this entails subordinating human logico-causal reasoning to God's self-revelation in Christ.

Conclusion

The Torrances' covenantal and filial soteriology is guided by God's self-revelation in Christ. They believe that we can only understand *how* God relates to humanity by first looking to *who* he is. Jesus is of one being with the Father and the very expression of the Father's love for humanity, showing us that his purposes are primarily filial rather than judicial. This challenges two notions: firstly, that the Father relates to humanity in merely distant, legal

---

162. Molnar, *Thomas F. Torrance*, 335. Molnar argues that, although in one sense such knowledge is privileged because it depends upon God's self-giving, in another sense it is radically inclusive because Christ died for all (336). He also contends that T. F. is not promoting irrationalism (336); see T. F. T., *God and Rationality*, 138.

163. J. B. T., "Incarnation and 'Limited Atonement,'" 86.

terms; and, secondly, that the Father is pitted against the Son in the satisfaction of his wrath. The Torrances argue that God's self-revelation in Christ shows us that the Father and Son are one in their mission to adopt the whole of humanity as children of God in order to share in the life and love of God.

The Torrances believe that God's self-giving in Christ reveals the unilateral covenant he has made with humanity, whereby Christ fulfills all the conditions in our place and on our behalf. This defies a contractual understanding of God whereby we must strive to fulfill the conditions ourselves. Preaching and teaching can advance this conditional, contractual understanding as a result of the concern that unconditional grace leads to lawlessness. However, this only serves to increase lawlessness. God's gracious covenant does not diminish our legal obligations but rather truly strengthens them because we are able to offer ourselves back to God in freedom, knowing that the covenant has already been fulfilled for us in Christ.

According to the Torrances, all of humanity is elect in Christ. To believe that God elects some for salvation and others for damnation leads to people worrying whether they are one of the few chosen for salvation. To make election prior to grace, or grace prior to election, is to displace Christ as the proper ground of election, thereby turning us back to our own endeavors for assurance of salvation. The Torrances argue that this is the result of elevating human rational systems of thought over the self-revelation of God. Looking to God's self-giving in Christ, the Torrances believe that we are all chosen for God's unconditional grace. This means that we do not have to worry whether we are one of God's chosen few, nor do we have to burn ourselves out trying to bear fruit as evidence of our salvation, because we are all included in God's universal plan of redemption.

The *fait accompli* of our election and redemption raises the question of whether our human freedom is undermined. Yet this is to presuppose an impossible notion of freedom as autonomous self-determined individuals. As creatures in a finite world, we only have a contingent freedom. God sets aside our self-will, which is enslaved to sin, in order to establish true freedom for us. The Torrances argue that we can only make a free and true decision for God because of God's prior decision for us. This is cause for celebration; human freedom is not undermined but ultimately established.

The Torrances affirm a universal atonement in Christ, resisting a doctrine of definite atonement whereby Christ died only for the salvation of some. Definite atonement leads to people worrying whether they are one of the few for whom Christ died, whereas universal atonement offers assurance that all are included in Christ's perfect response in our place. The Torrances do not believe that universal atonement leads to universalism. The irrational fact of sin and evil in the world means that people inconceivably choose to reject God. Whilst this appears inconsistent to those who believe that Christ's death must achieve its intended efficacy, the Torrances' scheme is internally coherent in that it is guided by the Object of their study. However, this entails subordinating human logico-causal reasoning to God's self-revelation in Christ.

Weariness and a lack of assurance in salvation can be the result of trying to comprehend God and his dealings with humanity within our own logical frameworks. God's universal covenant of grace resists logico-causal categories. God can only be understood in light of his self-revelation in Christ: the priority of the "who" question over the "how" question. The Torrances assert that God is a covenant God, not a contract God, with filial purposes for humanity, choosing the whole of humanity for salvation in Christ so that we might share in the life and love of the triune God of grace. This gives us assurance of salvation and freedom from the necessity of earning it by our own endeavors. Chapter 2 will further explore the Torrances' understanding of God's self-revelation in Christ and the liberating significance of Christ's vicarious humanity for our salvation.

2

The Vicarious Humanity of the Son
Ontological over External

GOD'S UNCONDITIONAL, COVENANTAL CLAIMING OF HUMANITY IN CHRIST is an ontological event for the Torrances. Salvation is worked out in the very depths of Jesus's own vicarious humanity and this transforms the very depths of our own being. The descent of Christ in the incarnation makes possible the ascension of humanity to participate in the life of God. This understanding, which is largely drawn from Patristic theology and resonates with the Eastern Orthodox tradition, brought the Torrances into disagreement with what they perceived to be external, legal categories found within their Western theological tradition.[1] The Torrances' soteriology anticipated modern re-readings of Luther and Calvin that have perceived a more participatory understanding of salvation.[2] Nevertheless, there is a strong concern today from Federal Calvinists and broader conservative evangelicals to defend the doctrine of justification conceived in terms of Christ's penal substitutionary atonement and the imputation of Christ's

---

1. John Romanides articulates the traditional Eastern Orthodox view in Romanides, *The Ancestral Sin*, 155–69. See also Kärkkäinen, *One with God*, 30, 54. For a study of *theosis* in T. F.'s theology see Myk Habets, *Theosis in the Theology of Thomas Torrance*.

2. See Mannermaa, *Christ Present in Faith*; Braatan and Jenson, *Union with Christ*; Stephen Chester, "It is No Longer I Who Live," 315–37. Habets argues that T. F. anticipated the Lutheran re-reading in conceiving of justification as more than a declaratory legal fiction but an actual making righteous by *theosis*. Myk Habets, "Reforming Theosis," 155.

righteousness to those who have faith.[3] This chapter seeks to present the significance of the Torrances' theology for the current debate.[4]

The Torrances believe that an overarching external and judicial scheme of penal substitution and imputation does not reflect God's primarily filial purposes for humanity nor does it truly transform humanity. For the Torrances, a judicial and external scheme disregards the prospective aspect of the atonement whereby we are not only forgiven but reborn to new life as sons and daughters of God to share by the Spirit in Christ's intimate relationship with the Father. The Torrances also perceive that, in practice, an external, judicial scheme requires people to respond with a decision for Christ in order to be "justified by faith." As Purves considers, "The great danger is always that at the last moment the gospel becomes its opposite, in which everything depends upon us rather than upon God—our faith, our decisions, or our works."[5] Ultimately, an external and judicial scheme turns people back upon their own endeavors in salvation. The Torrances' profoundly ontological understanding of humanity's salvation through the vicarious humanity of Christ means that humanity is liberated to freely share by the Spirit in the Son's intimate relationship with the Father.

The Latin Heresy

External

T. F. describes the Western tendency to conceptualize salvation in terms of external relations as "the Latin heresy." The term "heresy" is strong language for Western Christians who are sincere and well-meaning in their faith, yet no doubt it is fuelled by T. F.'s pastoral concern for the negative ramifications of an external soteriology. T. F. also sees a parallel with Arius's fourth-century heresy that there is only an external relation between the Father and the Son, which means that humanity cannot truly be saved.[6] An external scheme of salvation, for T. F., cannot "penetrate into our ontological depths" and transform humanity from its state of corruption to be reborn as a new

---

3. For a classic defence of Luther, see Kolb, *Martin Luther*. For a classic defense of Calvin, see Muller, *The Unaccommodated Calvin*.

4. Description of this external, forensic model of the atonement will follow T. F.'s method of tending towards caricaturization for the purposes of the argument. Examples of who exemplify these elements of an external, forensic scheme will be explored in the course of the chapter.

5. Purves, *Reconstructing Pastoral Theology*, 62.

6. T. F. T., "Karl Barth and the Latin Heresy," 473–74.

creation.⁷ Following Athanasius, who affirmed the *homoousion* in refutation of Arius, T. F. argues that salvation is not external but rather takes place within Christ's incarnate constitution:

> Since Jesus Christ is himself God and man in one Person, and all his divine and human acts issue from his one Person, the atoning mediation and redemption which he wrought for us, fall *within* his own being and life as the one Mediator between God and man. That is to say, the work of atoning salvation does *not* take place *outside* of Christ, as something external to him, but takes place *within* him, *within* the incarnate constitution of his Person and Mediator.⁸

T. F. identifies the Latin heresy in the medieval ethical conception of the atonement, as exemplified by Peter Abelard, and in the forensic conception of the atonement, as exemplified by St Anselm. These external formulations were challenged by the Reformers pointing to the Gift and the Giver as one. However, T. F. regrets that the person and work of Christ have subsequently been divided in Protestant theology, and external theories of the atonement prevail in both forensic and ethical forms.⁹

Forensic

Today the forensic model of the atonement, of which the Torrances are so critical, is exemplified when the doctrine of penal substitution commands soteriology. "The doctrine of penal substitution states that God gave himself in the person of his Son to suffer instead of us the death, punishment and curse due to fallen humanity as the penalty for sin."¹⁰ *In My Place Condemned He Stood: Celebrating the Glory of Atonement* and the large tome, *Pierced for Our Transgressions: Rediscovering the Glory of Penal Substitution,* are recent conservative evangelical defenses of the doctrine from its critics.¹¹ Penal substitution is also constitutive of Federal theology's scheme of salvation.¹²

---

7. T. F. T., *The Trinitarian Faith*, 158.

8. Ibid., 155.

9. T. F. T., "Latin Heresy," 477–78. See also J. B. T., *Worship*, 12–25.

10. Jeffery, Overy and Sach, *Pierced for Our Transgressions*, 21.

11. J. I. Packer and Mark Dever, *In My Place Condemned He Stood. Pierced for Our Transgressions* was published in support of the doctrine of penal substitution in reaction to the controversy surrounding Steve Chalke's critique in Chalke and Mann, *The Lost Message of Jesus*, 182. See also McCormack, "The End of Reformed Theology?," 46–64.

12. McGowan, "Federal theology," 43; McGowan, "The Atonement as Penal

T. F. does not deny the forensic element of the atonement in Scripture.[13] He is often misrepresented as denying any forensic element in salvation.[14] Donald MacLeod presents T. F. as having "an aversion to any forensic idea of atonement."[15] However, T. F. does contend that the New Testament never refers to the judgment which Christ bore for us as a "punishment," which T. F. believes indicates that the atonement has a profounder meaning than could be expressed by a doctrine of penal substitution.[16] Paul presents various metaphors when describing salvation, for example, taken from the lawcourt (Rom 3:24–26), temple sacrifices (Rom 3:25), adoption (Gal 4:4–7) and the slavemarket (1 Cor 7:23). Therefore, it could be argued that the forensic element of salvation should not be made absolute but remain a metaphor, expressing the ultimate ontological reality as revealed in the person of Christ.

The concern that the Torrances have is when the forensic element of the atonement is presented as the overarching framework for salvation. Whilst McGowan seeks to affirm every model of the atonement, he ultimately believes that they are subordinate to the controlling doctrine of penal substitution.[17] T. F. argues that a judicial framework of external relations does not adequately reflect that God gave of his very own Self in Christ, nor does it adequately explain how humanity is transformed.[18] It dangerously suggests, J. B. argues, a God who needs to be changed in order to accept humanity and an impersonal view of humanity as the object of justice.[19] As J. B. often asserts, God's purposes for humanity are primarily filial rather than judicial. Furthermore, in focusing upon what *God* has done for us, without an account of Christ's vicarious humanity, the human response falls upon us, so that we are turned back upon our own efforts in salvation.

Substitution"; Gibson and Gibson, "Sacred Theology and the Reading of the Divine Word," Kindle ed., Loc 484.

13. See T. F. T., "Atonement and the Moral Order," 253; T. F. T., *Scottish Theology*, 308.

14. See McGowan, "Justification and the Ordo Salutis," 14, 16; Macleod, "Dr T. F. Torrance and Scottish Theology," 67.

15. Macleod, "Dr T. F. Torrance and Scottish Theology," 67.

16. T. F. T., *Scottish Theology*, 308–9, 304.

17. McGowan, "The Atonement as Penal Substitution," 189, 206.

18. T. F. T., *Reconstruction*, 82.

19. J. B. T., "Introduction," 15; J. B. T., "Concept of Federal Theology," 35. Yet it was Adam not God who was hiding in the Garden of Eden because of sin (Gen 3:8).

Ethical

Whilst the forensic model of the atonement is typically found today in conservative evangelicalism, the ethical model of the atonement is typically found in liberal theology.[20] According to the ethical model of the atonement, Jesus's life and death are a demonstration of God's love that inspires us to follow him. However, for the Torrances, salvation comes not through our identification with Jesus but rather his identification with us. T. F. argues that the Church is not simply a group of individuals externally connected by the same moral ideals. External organization cannot transform humanity; we rely wholly upon ontological renewal in Christ.[21] Jesus did not attempt to restructure human systems of social, political, and economic power; he went to the root of the problem, healing the human heart's hostility towards God in himself and making us a new creation in union with God.[22] Moreover, if Jesus is merely an ethical example for us to follow, we have to rely upon our own endeavors to achieve salvation.

T. F. argues that moral and legal frameworks are themselves part of the broken set of affairs between God and humanity. The moral and legal order actually serves to separate God and man. Both need to be redeemed and given a new basis through the atonement. T. F. asks, according to what moral or legal order is it right for someone else to suffer and die in the place of others?[23] T. F. argues that when God is limited within human reasoning, the truth of the gospel is distorted. Our human rational faculties themselves need to be redeemed.[24] We can only know God through his self-giving in Christ and atonement can only be worked out ontologically within the incarnate constitution of the Mediator.

Conclusion

For T. F., forensic and ethical models of the atonement are indicative of "the Latin heresy," which presents salvation in external terms. However well-meaning, these models distort the nature of God and of humanity; they cannot offer a true account of humanity's salvation, and people are turned back upon their own religious efforts. T. F. calls for the atonement to be

---

20. It is outwith the scope of this book to engage in great detail with liberal expressions of theology.
21. T. F. T., *Reconstruction*, 82.
22. Ibid., 40–41.
23. T. F. T., "Atonement and the Moral Order," 249–52.
24. T. F. T., "Latin Heresy," 480.

understood not according to human reasoning but according to God's self-giving in Christ, whereby we see Christ's work inextricably bound up with his person.

Christ's Person and Work

Padah, kipper, goel

Salvation is not worked out through external relations, the Torrances maintain, but through the self-giving of God in Christ, who assumed our humanity. The Torrances call for Christ's person and work to be held together.[25] T. F. believes that the importance of this can be seen in examining the three Hebrew terms, *padah, kipper,* and *goel,* which give meaning to the word, *apolutrosis* (redemption), in the New Testament. *Padah* expresses God's mighty and dramatic act of delivering Israel from bondage; *kipper* expresses God's sacrificial offering to blot out sin; and *goel* expresses God's person as a kinsman redeemer, who restores those in need to their lost inheritance.

Whilst the Eastern Orthodox Church has a strong understanding of the incarnational, ontological aspect of the atonement expressed by the concept of *goel,* T. F. laments that it is lacking in the Western church. As is evident from forensic and moral theories of the atonement, Western theology tends to stress the act of God over his person. T. F. believes this to be a considerable problem because, when the emphasis is on the act of God, the human response is made to fall upon us, often seen in the form of having to make an existential decision for Christ. Seeking to redress this imbalance in the West, T. F. promotes the significance of the person of Christ, as our kinsman redeemer, who fulfills the human response in our place and on our behalf. For T. F., the three aspects of the atonement expressed by *padah, kipper,* and *goel,* must be held together like the strands of a rope.[26] The person of Christ is as significant as his work in redemption.

Hypostatic union

The Torrances believe that redemption is not an external act of God, but worked out ontologically within the incarnate constitution of the person of Christ. Following Athanasius's affirmation of the *homoousion,* central to their understanding of salvation is the hypostatic union in Christ: "Christ is one and the same being as God, as well as of one and the same being

---

25. J. B. sees this in Calvin. See J. B. T., *Worship,* 40.
26. T. F. T., *Atonement,* 25–59.

as ourselves."[27] Christ must have a fully divine and fully human nature in order to save humanity.

First, humanity is incapable of saving itself; only God can save humanity. Therefore, if Jesus does not have a divine nature, there can be no salvation.[28] Second, humanity is incapable of offering the perfect response to God. Therefore, it is necessary for Jesus to assume humanity and offer the perfect human response to God in our place and on our behalf. As T. F. writes, "He was the Word of God brought to bear upon man, but he was also man hearing that Word, answering it, trusting it, living by it—by faith."[29] Jesus not only embodies God's justifying act but also the human appropriation of it.[30] As both God and man, Jesus fulfills both sides of the relationship between God and humanity.[31]

For the Torrances, Jesus's assumption of humanity means that, by the Holy Spirit, humanity is able to share in everything that is his, that is, perfect union and communion with God. The hypostatic union in Christ resists an external conception of salvation, showing it to be an internal, ontological event.[32]

> The atoning mediation of Christ is thus to be expounded in terms of the *internal* relations between Christ and God and between Christ and all mankind. The expiatory and propitiatory activity of the Mediator, while deriving from the innermost being of God, is fulfilled within the ontological depths of our fallen, enslaved, depraved and guilt-laden human existence, that is, in and through the oneness of God with us in our actual condition embodied in the incarnate existence of the Mediator.[33]

Incarnation and atonement

According to the Torrances, the significance of Christ's person and of the hypostatic union means that Christ's incarnation is the beginning of the

---

27. T. F. T., *Mediation*, 124. Colin Gunton is critical of T. F.'s stress on the *homoousion* as read through Western eyes, which he believes risks flattening out the particularities of the divine persons. Gunton, *Father, Son & Holy Spirit*, 50–51.
28. T. F. T., *Mediation*, 67.
29. T. F. T., *Reconstruction*, 157.
30. Ibid.
31. T. F. T., *Mediation*, 66.
32. T. F. Torrance, *Theology in Reconciliation*, 226–30.
33. T. F. T., "Atonement and the Moral Order," 236.

atonement.[34] T. F. writes that "the atonement begins from his very conception and birth when he put on the form of a servant and began to pay the price of our redemption."[35] In the very act of the divine nature bearing upon the human nature, it could not but be transformed: "In his holy assumption of our unholy humanity, his purity wipes away our impurity, his holiness covers our corruption, his nature heals our nature."[36] Here T. F. draws upon Athanasius; whilst the Arians saw Jesus's humanity as a weakness, Athanasius considered it to be a strength. By assuming our humanity, Jesus was truly able to restore and renew us in the depths of our being.[37]

Following Athanasius and the Cappadocian fathers, the Torrances assert that Christ assumed *fallen* humanity.[38] They believe that it is essential for Christ to have assumed fallen humanity in order for it to be transformed, citing Gregory Nazianzus's maxim that "the unassumed is the unredeemed."[39] J. B. asserts, "We are not just healed 'through Christ' because of the work of

---

34. Ivor Davidson laments the neglect of the incarnation of Jesus and his humanity in modern Western theology, suggesting these diversions: "preference for experienced-based symbol; the fragmentation of biblical studies and dogmatics; the imperatives of contextual hermeneutics; and the preoccupation with methodology rather than substance" (130–31). He recognizes the necessity of the incarnation for Christ's salvific efficacy: "Since Christology is not about 'obscure metaphysics' . . . but the dramatic exposition of the encounter between God and humanity, the *enhypostasia* narrates in realistic terms the history of the reconciliation which God effects in Jesus Christ . . . Without this, talk of disclosure, and of 'solidarity' in any ultimately transformative or redemptive sense, would be meaningless, for Jesus would not truly represent God to humankind or humankind to God. It is by his obedience within the terms of his humanity, not as an ideal, that the incarnate Word deals with sin and reconciles to God." (144). Although Davidson questions T. F.'s utilization of patristic theology, he upholds him as an example of articulating the atonement in a way that upholds both the person and work of Christ (144). Davidson, "Theologizing the Human Jesus," 129–53.

35. T. F. T., "Karl Barth and the Latin Heresy," 475.

36. T. F. T., *Reconstruction*, 155–56.

37. T. F. T., *Reconciliation*, 226–30.

38. T. F. T., "Introduction," *The School of Faith*, lxxxv; J. B. T., "Christ in our Place," 47. Athanasius writes of the importance of Christ assuming the "whole man," which does not necessarily mean that he meant fallen humanity, but it would be logically consistent.

39. T. F. T., *Mediation*, 49; J. B. T., "Christ in our Place," 47. See Gregory Nazianzen, *Epistle 101*. Gregory is referring to the human mind but it would be a logical extension to extend this to the whole fallen human nature.

Christ but 'in and through Christ.'"[40] For the Torrances, the incarnation is the beginning of the ontological transformation of our fallen humanity.[41]

The Torrances' belief that Christ assumed fallen humanity is contrary to the classic Western understanding that, from the fifth century, moved away from this belief.[42] James Cassidy challenges T. F., arguing that, if Jesus is fully divine and yet assumed fallen humanity, this necessarily means affirming a sinful God. Cassidy reasons, "If Jesus Christ—in his human and divine complex—is divinized (made to be of one substance with the Father), and if one aspect of that complex is sinful humanity, then would it not follow that God—at the incarnation—becomes sinful?"[43] Yet Christ's assumption of fallen humanity does not necessitate a sinful God. Fallen humanity is transformed in the very act of the incarnation, as the holiness of Christ's divinity bears upon unholy humanity. Therefore it can be affirmed that Christ assumed fallen humanity and yet God was not sinful. The Torrances are also defended by Dawson, who points to Jesus's cry on the cross, "My God, my God, why have you forsaken me?" (Matt 27:46), and his last words, "Father, into your hands I commit my Spirit" (Luke 23:46). Dawson argues that these words indicate Jesus plumbing the depths of our fallen humanity and setting it aright through his perfect faithfulness to the Father.[44]

In affirming the significance of Christ's incarnation for the atonement, the Torrances are criticized for presenting a merely physical account of the atonement; Christ's work becomes redundant. Letham contends that the atonement is "conflated into the incarnation" which makes the cross unnecessary.[45] Habets believes that T. F.'s emphasis on the incarnation does lend towards a physical theory.[46] However, Gunter Pratz argues that this is a misinterpretation, which unnecessarily polarizes atonement by the incar-

---

40. J. B. T., "Christ in our Place," 47.

41. T. F. T., *Mediation*, 73, 82. Bevan criticizes T. F. for failing to properly explain the nature of this ontological transformation. Bevan, "The Person of Christ," 212–14. Richard Muller criticizes T. F.'s ontological understanding. Richard Muller, "The Barth Legacy," 673–704.

42. According to the Torrances, exceptions to the popular Western view in this regard include Martin Luther, Edward Irving, Karl Barth, and H. R. Mackintosh. T. F. T., "Latin Heresy," 477; J. B. T., "Christ in our Place," 47.

43. James Cassidy, "T. F. Torrance's Realistic Soteriological Objectivism and the Elimination of Dualisms," 193.

44. Dawson, "Far as the Curse is Found," 73.

45. Letham, "The Triune God," Kindle ed., Loc 11324. See also Watson, "Did Christ die as our Substitute?" Watson argues that, if reconciliation commences at the hypostatic union, this is difficult to unite with the necessity of Christ's passion.

46. Habets, *Theosis*, 194.

nation of Christ and atonement by his death. Pratz argues that the person and work of Christ are inseparable, as the Torrances maintain.[47] T. F. clearly expresses that he does not believe that the incarnation alone effects salvation.[48] He also upholds the importance of Christ's obedient life and sacrifice on the cross, seeking to reflect the three aspects of the atonement expressed by *padah, kipper,* and *goel*.[49] Christ's person and work are each necessary and inseparable.[50]

Conclusion

The Torrances believe that salvation cannot be worked out through external relations, but only through the self-giving of God in Christ, who assumed our humanity. T. F. argues that the three Old Testament aspects of redemption, *padah, kipper,* and *goel,* must be held together, and in particular the incarnational, ontological reality expressed by *goel* which has been overlooked by external, forensic, and moral paradigms. According to the Torrances, the hypostatic union in Christ enables Jesus to fulfill both sides of the relationship between God and man. In the very act of God assuming fallen human nature, humanity is being transformed. Jesus assumes humanity in order to plumb the depths of our fallen nature and turn it back to right relationship with God. Therefore, for the Torrances, the incarnation is integral to the atonement; Jesus's person must be held together with his work.

Vicarious Humanity

Life and death

The Torrances understand Christ's death on the cross in an ontological way. By virtue of Christ assuming human flesh, all of humanity is included in his death. T. F. writes, "In Jesus Christ we have been crucified, have died and

---

47. Pratz, "The Relationship between Incarnation and Atonement in the Theology of Thomas F. Torrance."

48. T. F. T., *Trinitarian Faith,* 156. T. F. has been misrepresented on this subject in Macleod, "Dr T. F. Torrance and Scottish Theology," 67, and Cassidy, "T. F. Torrance's Realistic Soteriological Objectivism," 185, 192.

49. T. F. T., *Trinitarian Faith,* 156.

50. Furthermore, it is the Torrances' very emphasis on the incarnation that is vital in order to decry a physical theory. God's assumption of humanity in Jesus leads to humanity being brought to its fullest reality; Jesus is the "personalising Person" and the "humanising Man." See T. F. T., *Mediation,* 78–79. This does not fit with a physical theory of redemption that immortalizes humanity.

have been buried."[51] In support of this ontological relation, J. B. points to Paul's assertion, "one has died for all; therefore all have died" (2 Cor 5:14).[52] The cross is an ontological event because, in Christ's death, our old humanity dies, and the whole body of sin and death is destroyed.[53]

Not only Christ's death, but his whole life is of atoning significance. In everything that Christ does, he is turning the human nature from its corruption back to a perfect relationship with God:

> Throughout the whole course of his human life Jesus Christ was at work healing, sanctifying and humanising the human nature which he assumed from our fallen, dehumanised state, converting it from its estrangement from the Creator back to its proper relation to him.[54]

This is an unconvincing scheme for Letham. He argues that Christ's humanity does not have any effect on our humanity; Christ only affects his own humanity.[55] The Torrances might have contended with this argument by pointing to the priority of the "who" question over the "how" question. The inconceivable mystery of the hypostatic union whereby Christ is fully God and fully man resists human rational categories of thought. The Torrances believe that we must subordinate our human rational categories of thought as to how God works in the atonement to his self-revelation in Christ. For the Torrances, this means affirming Christ's vicarious humanity, whereby his life in human flesh heals and transforms our humanity.

---

51. T. F. T., *Atonement*, 134.

52. J. B. T., "The Priesthood of Jesus," 172.

53. T. F. T., *Reconstruction*, 203.

54. T. F. T., *Mediation*, 81. Although the Torrances emphatically affirm the salvific efficacy of the whole life of Christ, they do not engage in a comprehensive exposition of the gospel accounts of his life. Gunton comments on T. F., "While the humanity of Christ is affirmed and used theologically in Torrance's work, it is surprising how little interest is shown in the *Christusbild*, the detailed Gospel presentations of the life, death, resurrection and ascension of Jesus." Gunton acknowledges that it is a large project and he hopes that it might be undertaken by later generations. Gunton, "Being and Person," 132–33. An example of this already being undertaken by a later generation can be seen in Deddo's discussion of the story of the feeding of the five thousand. Deddo, "The Christian Life," 148–50. However, as Molnar points out, "Torrance also believed that focusing on the details of Jesus' human life without seeing the depth dimension of that life was problematic; it was not Jesus' religious experience that was of interest to the biblical authors and to Torrance, but the fact that he himself was and is God's Word acting toward us and for us within history." Molnar, *Thomas F. Torrance*, 343.

55. Letham, "The Triune God," Kindle ed., Loc 11337.

The Vicarious Humanity of the Son   59

In affirming the salvific efficacy of Christ's person and life, the Torrances have been the subject of criticism by theologians such as Letham for not taking seriously enough Christ's death on the cross and human sin and guilt.[56] Yet such a criticism reflects a superficial reading of the Torrances. First, T. F. and J. B. describe the cross as the supreme pinnacle of the atonement. J. B. writes, "The whole life of Jesus is a life of self-offering to the Father on behalf of the world, culminating in the one true sacrifice of love and obedience on the cross."[57] T. F. asserts, "It was his whole life, and above all that life poured out in the supreme sacrifice of death on the Cross, that made atonement for sin, and constituted the price of redemption for mankind."[58] A key Pauline teaching for T. F. is 1 Corinthians 2:2: "For I decided to know nothing among you except Jesus Christ, and him crucified." He reflects, "The Cross of Christ surely lies at the heart of our faith and of the mission of the Gospel. It is the centre of the Christian Gospel."[59] T. F. takes sin seriously, believing that the gospel of grace reveals the depth of sin and depravity in humanity.[60] J. B. often affirms that God's grace demands a response and that Christ's death leads us to repentance.[61] The Torrances therefore do take seriously Christ's death and human sin and guilt.

Second, it is the Torrances' articulation of both the person and work of Christ in this way that ultimately takes Christ's death and human sin and guilt more seriously than their critics. David W. Torrance argues,

> Emphasis upon the vicarious humanity of Christ and the fact that we are saved through his life as well as his death, has troubled many evangelicals. They mistakenly believe that speaking of Christ's vicarious humanity detracts from what took place on the cross. The very reverse is the case. By speaking of Jesus's vicarious humanity we are actually magnifying what Christ did in reconciling us to God.[62]

D. W. contends that, in rejecting the significance that T. F. and J. B. place on Christ's whole life, evangelicals are just as erroneous as liberal theologians.[63] When Christ's death is abstracted from his person, it becomes an

---

56. Ibid., Loc 11324. See also Watson, "Did Christ die as our Substitute?"
57. J. B. T., *Worship*, 71.
58. T. F. T., *Trinitarian Faith*, 169.
59. T. F. T., "Preaching Jesus Christ," 23.
60. T. F. T., *Scottish Theology*, 142.
61. J. B. T., "Covenant or Contract?," 55, 57.
62. D. W. T., "Introduction," 5.
63. Ibid. This is not to deny that some critics do seek to take account of Christ's

external remedy for sin that does not truly save humanity in its depths.[64] For T. F., although an exclusive focus on the cross rightly highlights Jesus's substitutionary death, it does not recognize the radical nature of Jesus's substitution for us that spans his whole life.[65] Death is a consequence of the corruption of humanity and therefore a part of human life that Jesus has to assume in order to redeem. Christ not only saves us through his death, but *from* death. The Torrances emphasize Christ's person in order to counteract this focus on Christ's work in abstraction from his person. They perceive this abstraction to render the atonement as an external transaction between God and humanity that fails to effect a true transformation of the corrupt human nature.

Resurrection, Ascension, Pentecost

Today, within conservative evangelicalism, atonement can tend to be presented *exclusively* in terms of Christ's death. Leon Morris' *The Atonement: Its Meaning and Significance* and John Stott's *The Cross of Christ* have been influential in this regard.[66] Stott describes Christ's incarnation simply as a means to his death, and the cross is presented as an external, legal transaction whereby God is conditioned to forgive humanity. For Stott, the function of the resurrection is to serve as proof that our sins have been dealt with by Christ's death on the cross: "what the resurrection did was to vindicate the Jesus whom men had rejected, to declare with power that he is the Son of God, and publicly to confirm that his sin-bearing death had been effective for the forgiveness of sins."[67]

Whilst such a scheme of salvation has virtuous intentions, the Torrances believe that it is a deficient presentation of the atonement.[68] Not only is the cross limited to a forensic scheme, but the significance of Christ's broader life, resurrection, ascension, and Pentecost is not fully appreciated. The incarnation is not simply the means to the cross; humanity's salva-

---

earthly life. Allen upholds the significance of Christ's earthly life of faith. However, the Torrances would be dissatisfied with how it seems to be understood within a primarily legal rather than filial framework. See Allen, *Justification and the Gospel*, 73–77.

64. Ibid., 6.
65. T. F. T., "Preaching Jesus Christ," 24.
66. Morris, *The Atonement*; Stott, *The Cross of Christ*.
67. Stott, *The Cross of Christ*, 238.
68. Douglas Campbell and Michael Bird are also critical of the tendency to minimize the significance of Christ's life. Campbell, *Deliverance*, 211–12; Bird, *The Saving Righteousness of God*, 40.

tion depends upon our ontological union with Christ inaugurated by his birth into our humanity. Yet the union of God and man is not ontologically complete at the incarnation; rather it depends upon Christ's life, death, resurrection, ascension, and Pentecost.[69] Christ's resurrection is not simply confirmation of the forgiveness of sins, but the new birth of a righteous humanity in Christ. For T. F., the cross alone is not the grounds of our justification because Paul writes that Christ "was raised for our justification" (Rom 4:25).[70] T. F. asserts, "This means that the mighty act of God in the resurrection belongs to the very essence of atonement."[71]

The ascension is the indispensable counterpart to Jesus's descent in the incarnation.[72] At Christ's ascension, our new humanity is raised up in Christ to share by the Spirit in his perfect relationship with the Father.[73] J. B. writes, "The Son of God takes our humanity, sanctifies it by his vicarious life in the Spirit (John 17:17–18), carries it to the grave to be crucified and buried in him, and in his resurrection and ascension carries it into the holy presence of God."[74] T. F. therefore argues, "Ascension is not just an addendum to the story of Jesus, a bringing down of the curtain of his earthly life, but it is one of the great essential salvation events."[75]

Today the ascended Christ continues his vicarious ministry, in our place and on our behalf. He offers worthy worship, which we are unable to do, so that we might be included in his perfect relationship with the Father.[76] J. B. regrets that Christ's continuing ascended high priesthood has been much neglected.[77] He writes:

> That life of worship and communion with the Father which Jesus fulfilled in our humanity, did not end in death. Having offered for us a life of perfect obedience to the Father, culminating in the one perfect self-offering for all people and all nations, Jesus rose from the dead and returned to the Father to intercede for us (Rom. 8:34) as our great High Priest (Heb. 4:14). As the eternal

---

69. T. F. T., *Scottish Theology*, 14; J. B. T., "Priesthood of Jesus," 157.

70. T. F. T., *Atonement*, 127.

71. T. F. T., "Karl Barth and the Latin Heresy," 474.

72. T. F. T., *Space, Time and Resurrection*, 123.

73. T. F. T., *Theology in Reconstruction*, 151.

74. J. B. T., "Prayer and the Priesthood of Christ," 62. See also Farrow, *Ascension Theology*; Farrow, *Ascension and Ecclesia*.

75. T. F. T., *Reconstruction*, 151.

76. J. B. T., "Christ in our Place," 45.

77. Ibid., 62. See also Dawson, *Jesus Ascended*; Purves, *Reconstructing Pastoral Theology*, 105–26.

Mediator of an eternal covenant, he now appears on our behalf in the presence of God that we might be accepted as sons and daughters (Eph. 2:13ff., 1 Tim. 2:1–6, Heb. 4:14; 9:24; 7:25).[78]

Pentecost too is essential to the atonement, according to the Torrances. In his earthly life, Jesus receives the Spirit in order that, when he has ascended to heaven, he might pour it out upon humanity. J. B. considers that it is necessary for us to have the Spirit in order to participate in the divine life: "He pours out his Spirit on the Church at Pentecost to lift us up into that life of communion with the Father that we might participate in his glorified life."[79] Thus T. F. writes, "Pentecost must be regarded, not as something added on to atonement, but as the actualisation within the life of the Church of the atoning life, death and resurrection of the Saviour."[80] This means that Christ's death is not the sum of the atonement: "We are saved, therefore, not only by the death of Christ which he suffered for our sakes, but by his life which he lived in our flesh for our sakes and which God raised from the dead that we may share in it through the power of the Spirit."[81]

Retrospective and prospective

A further contention with looking exclusively to Christ's death is that this can lead towards a tendency to affirm the retrospective aspect of the atonement but overlook the prospective aspect. Purves considers, "This latter aspect especially has not always been seen to be part of the doctrine of the atonement, yet it is the heart of the nature of the atonement and the basis for living the Christian life."[82] For the Torrances, salvation has both a retrospective and prospective aspect because humanity was included not only in Christ's death, but also in his resurrection, ascension, and Pentecost. This means that salvation involves not only a retrospective forgiveness of sins but also a prospective sharing by the Spirit in Jesus's relationship with the Father. We are a new creation as sons and daughters of God.[83] We have been

---

78. J. B. T., *Worship*, 72.

79. J. B. T., "Prayer and the Priesthood of Christ," 58. See also T. F. T., *Trinitarian Faith*, 258.

80. T. F. T., *Trinitarian Faith*, 190.

81. Ibid., 155.

82. Purves, *Reconstructing Pastoral Theology*, 63.

83. T. F. T., *Atonement*, 133. See also McLeod Campbell's filial understanding of the prospective aspect of the atonement. McLeod Campbell, *Nature of the Atonement*, 151–91.

adopted into Christ's filial relationship to the Father.[84] God created us not for external, legal relations but for intimate communion with him. T. F. asserts, "It is not atonement that constitutes the goal and end of that integrated movement of reconciliation but union with God in and through Jesus Christ in whom our human nature is not only saved, healed and renewed but lifted up to participate in the very light, life and love of the Holy Trinity."[85]

T. F. writes of an "atoning exchange" which is "worked out within the saving economy of the incarnation, and in the ontological depths of the humanity which he made his own, and therefore reaches its appointed end and fulfillment through his transforming consecration of us in himself and through his exaltation of us as one body with himself into the immediate presence of the Father."[86] Christ takes what is ours, sinful humanity, and gives us what is his, a perfect relationship with the Father. We are not only forgiven but, in Christ and by the Spirit, raised up to participate in the inner relations of God's life.[87] "Jesus received the Word of forgiveness for us from the Father, not only that our past sins might be wiped out," wrote J. B., "but in order that we might receive the Spirit of adoption, and be restored to the status of sonship by a life of union with Christ."[88]

T. F. believes that this perspective is faithful to the theology of the early church. Athanasius teaches that Christ has a twofold ministry: he mediates the things of God to man, and the things of man to God. He comes down to earth and assumes our humanity in order to raise humanity up to God by the Spirit.[89] Athanasius's famous dictum proclaims, "He became man that man might become god."[90] Similarly, Irenaeus declares, "Out of his measureless love our Lord Jesus Christ has become what we are in order to make us what he is himself."[91] T. F. believes that Western Latin theology has lost sight of Nicene theology in this regard:

> The atoning exchange lies at the heart of Nicene theology, wherein the death and resurrection of Christ were neither separated nor treated in isolation from one another. Redemption was considered to have taken place not only through the death of Jesus Christ but also through the resurrection and ascension,

---

84. T. F. T., *Reconciliation*, 156.
85. T. F. T., *Mediation*, 77.
86. T. F. T., *Trinitarian Faith*, 179–81.
87. T. F. T., *Mediation*, 74–77.
88. J. B. T., "Christ in our Place," 50.
89. T. F. T., *Mediation*, 83.
90. St Athanasius, *De incarnatione verbi dei*, VIII:54.
91. T. F. T., *Trinitarian Faith*, 179.

so that redemption is not only release from death, bondage, and judgement but also the pathway to new life and freedom in God.[92]

For the Torrances, an external, judicial scheme which focuses upon Christ's death neglects the profoundly filial nature of the prospective aspect of the atonement whereby God adopts us as sons in order to enjoy an intimate relationship with him. Thomas Smail reflects upon his personal experience of this:

> Many of us have known a sin-soaked guilt-ridden evangelicalism where there has been a great deal of talk about the cost of our atonement in the blood of Christ and very little upon the free and loving grace of the Father who in his intense desire for the homecoming of sinners gave his Son. The God people have been shown is the righteous judge who requires the propitiation which Jesus alone can offer, and who in response to it can just manage to restrain his wrath against us provided those redeemed by Christ continue to behave in a moral and religious way. In such a context which is of course parody, but one that many people have absorbed as gospel, the ability to answer the grace and freedom of God's forgiveness with a free and joyful heart . . . was one that to put it mildly did not come easily, and their confidence and expectation towards God was about as great as that of a man who expected a life sentence but has been put on probation for life instead. In such a context atonement has the smell of law fulfilled rather than of grace poured out.[93]

Conclusion

The Torrances believe that Jesus's whole life is of atoning significance, including the events of his death, resurrection, ascension, and Pentecost. His life of perfect faithfulness to the Father turns our humanity back to right relationship with God. In Christ's death, the old human nature dies; in his resurrection, humanity is reborn to new life; in his ascension, we are raised up to heaven in him; and at Pentecost, we receive the Spirit so that we might share by the Spirit in Jesus's perfect relationship with the Father. This resists human rational categories of thought, but the Torrances believe that it is faithful to God's self-revelation in Christ. Whilst the Torrances are criticized for not taking seriously enough Christ's death and human sin and guilt, it is

92. Ibid., 180.
93. Smail, *The Forgotten Father*, 127.

their broader account of Jesus's substitution that takes these most seriously. The Torrances argue that an external, judicial scheme of salvation which looks narrowly to Christ's death and the forgiveness of sins does not offer a filial account of the prospective aspect of the atonement, nor does it effect a true transformation of humanity.

Christ is our Righteousness

Active and passive obedience

Today the predominant understanding of atonement in Western Protestant theology "consists of a specific conception of justification as the forgiveness of sins supplemented by the imputation of Christ's righteousness to the believer."[94] An example can be seen in Jeffery, Overy and Sach's defense of the doctrine of penal substitution, where the significance of Christ's life is depicted in terms of his fulfillment of the law so that his righteousness might be imputed to believers.[95] The Torrances believe that we share in Christ's righteousness on account of his active and passive obedience, yet they understand this in primarily personal, filial, and ontological terms, as opposed to what they perceive as abstract and external judicial terms.

For the Torrances, Christ's active obedience is fulfilled in his obedience to the will of God and the law in perfect filial faithfulness, love, praise, trust, and thanksgiving: "By *active obedience* of Christ is meant the positive fulfillment in the whole life of Jesus of his Sonship."[96] Christ's passive obedience is fulfilled in his submission to God's judgment, ultimately leading to his death on the cross: "By *passive obedience* is meant the submission of Jesus Christ to the judgment of the Father upon our sin which he assumed in our humanity when he was 'made under the Law' in order to bear it in our name and on our behalf."[97] Whilst the incarnational union deals with original sin, Christ's obedience in life deals with our actual sins. However, the distinction between active and passive obedience is not a separation; they both begin in the incarnation and are led to fulfillment in Christ's death and resurrection.[98] The Torrances believe that, on account of the hypostatic union, humanity shares in Christ's active and passive obedience and therefore his righteousness.

94. Bird, *Saving Righteousness of God*, 6.
95. Jeffery, Overy and Sach, *Pierced for our Transgressions*, 212–13.
96. T. F. T., *Reconstruction*, 154.
97. Ibid.
98. Ibid., 154–56.

However, Jesus's obedience to the law has been criticized for being a legalistic concept. N. T. Wright argues that, if Jesus fulfilled the law for us, this is works-righteousness, thus validating legalism. Wright proposes that Jesus's obedience was not to the law but to God's commission to bless the world.[99] The believer partakes in Christ's death and resurrection but not his righteousness.[100] Rather, we ourselves fulfill the righteous demands of the law by means of the indwelling Spirit (Rom 8:4).[101]

Wright's perspective certainly highlights the danger of perceiving Christ's obedience in legalistic terms. This is a problem that T. F. recognizes in his own Scottish Reformed tradition:

> this notion of justification as a legal fulfilling of the contractual requirement of the covenant in respect of God's eternal law, rather than as a gracious manifestation of the faithfulness of God embodied in the person of Christ, had a moralising effect upon the life and theology of the Kirk, which was particularly evident in the overwhelming attention given to the law, in comparison to the Gospel, and the call of the *Larger Catechism* for a detailed fulfilment of divine commandments.[102]

However, a legalistic perspective is a misunderstanding of Christ's obedience. For the Torrances, Jesus was not obedient to the law in order to earn righteousness; he was obedient to the law in joyful response to the grace of God. His obedience should be understood in personal and filial terms rather than legal and conditional terms.[103] Furthermore, for the Torrances, Christ's righteousness is not gained through external transaction; his obedience does not merit righteousness. His vicarious perfect obedience transforms the humanity which he assumes, turning it back to a right relationship with God: "through his obedient Sonship he converted our disobedient human being back into true filial relation to the heavenly Father."[104] T. F. writes of Christ's fulfillment of the law in ontological terms, liberating humanity from evil:

---

99. Wright, *Justification*, 114.
100. Ibid., 205.
101. Ibid., 208.
102. T. F. T., *Scottish Theology*, 144–45.
103. Alister McGrath considers that the Hebrew word for "righteousness" has no English equivalent and has been understood in absolute, impersonal standards of justice and morality yet it has a much more personal, relational meaning. McGrath, *Justification by Faith*, 24.
104. T. F. T., "Karl Barth and the Latin Heresy," 476.

He came to fulfil all righteousness and to fulfil every jot and tittle of the law, acknowledging to the fullest extent the divine sanction in the law. He submitted himself under the law and was wholly obedient to the Father's will in the life he lived on earth and in Israel. By his very holiness and perfect obedience sin had no power over him, and it was therefore as the holy one in entire fulfilment of the holy will of God that he invaded the domain of evil and redeemed us out of the power of darkness by his holy life and his holy submission to the Father's will even unto the death of the cross.[105]

Therefore, although it is possible to misinterpret Jesus's fulfillment of the law, it cannot be equated with legalism. In fact, if Jesus's fulfillment of the law is denied, it is this which can lead to legalism because we are turned back upon ourselves to achieve it for ourselves.[106]

In Christ

The Torrances' personal, filial, and ontological understanding of Christ's righteousness is in contention with the notion of external, forensic imputation. In recent years, the notion of imputation has been hotly debated. Whilst some are concerned to maintain an external concept, some wholly dismiss the doctrine, some seek to affirm it in more personal, participatory terms, and others dismiss the *language* of "imputation."

For Allen, an external concept of imputation is important for reflecting that God is due the glory in salvation. He writes, "the doctrine of imputation testifies to the externality of human being and, thus, its gracious roots in the person and works of Jesus Christ."[107] Robert Gundry, on the other hand, dismisses the doctrine of imputation, arguing that Paul never explicitly supports it. Gundry argues that Paul usually attributes righteousness to God rather than Christ (except for 2 Pet 1:1). Humanity must live its own obedient life of righteousness, Gundry insists, because there will be a final judgment of our works.[108] D. A. Carson has responded to defend the notion of imputation, which he affirms in more personal, participatory terms. Carson argues that the antithesis between the righteousness of God and Christ

---

105. T. F. T., *Atonement*, 31–32.

106. Guy Prentiss Waters and John Piper argue that Wright's view ultimately leads to the notion of salvation by works. Waters, *Justification and the New Perspectives on Paul*, 171, 174, 188; Piper, *The Future of Justification*, 128.

107. Allen, *Justification and the Gospel*, 154.

108. Gundry, "The Nonimputation of Christ's Righteousness," 17–45.

is unnecessary for "in Christ God was reconciling the world to himself" (2 Cor 5:19). Although Paul does not explicitly write of imputation, "in Christ" language pervades his letters. In fact, Paul asserts that "Christ has become for us . . . our righteousness" (1 Cor 1:30).[109]

Mark A. Seifrid argues that the *language* of "imputation" is deficient. It suggests a mere juridical declaration that makes justification a portioned out, isolated gift which detracts from Christ.[110] Seifrid believes that this is far from the teaching of the Reformers and of Paul himself, who wrote in personal, Christological terms: "we are justified by the redemption which is 'in Christ Jesus' (Rom. 3:24); his resurrection is our justification (4:25); through Christ we receive 'the gift of righteousness', the 'justification which is life' (5:17, 18); Christ himself is our righteousness (1 Cor. 1:30); we become the righteousness of God in him (2 Cor. 5:21)."[111] Therefore, Seifrid argues, "It is not so much *wrong* to use the expression 'the imputed righteousness of Christ' as it is *deficient*."[112]

Similarly, Michael Bird considers the language of "imputation" to be misleading because it suggests a detached declaration that is external and abstracted from Christ. Whilst Bird argues that "imputation" may be legitimately used to express the forensic aspect of justification, it must be recognized that the word itself is not used in the New Testament, where union with Christ is presented as the overarching framework to understand justification.[113] In order to better reflect the "in Christ" language of Paul, Bird proposes the term "incorporated righteousness."[114]

T. F. uses the language of "imputation" yet understands it in personal, filial, and ontological terms.[115] He argues that God does not give us abstract benefits; he gives us his very self: "Grace is to be understood as the impartation not just of something from God but of God Himself. In Jesus Christ and in the Holy Spirit God freely gives to us in such a way that the Gift and the Giver are one and the same in the wholeness and indivisibility of

---

109. Carson, "The Vindication of Imputation," 76–77.
110. Seifrid, *Christ, Our Righteousness*, 174.
111. Ibid.
112. Ibid., 175.
113. Bird, *Saving Righteousness of God*, 70.
114. Ibid., 2–5, 60 85.
115. T. F. T., *Atonement*, 136. Marcus Johnson uses the language of imputation but with the qualification that Christ's righteousness is imputed to us on account of our participation in Christ's person. He warns of separating the gifts from the Giver, arguing that Christ does not merely perform the atonement; he *is* the atonement. Johnson, "The Highest Degree of Importance," 225–30. However, to avoid the problems articulated, it might be better to avoid the language altogether.

His grace."[116] Paul asserts that Christ *is* our righteousness (1 Cor 1:30). We receive righteousness not through an external imputation of the benefits of Christ but through a personal participation in Christ's very self.[117]

The Torrances fall within Allen's critique of Michael Gorman, Douglas Campbell and others who present the notion of participation is contention with an external, federal doctrine of justification.[118] Yet Allen's conception of the relationship between justification and participation is only "mutually enforcing," as he describes it, because he significantly qualifies the notion of participation in the scheme of salvation.[119] For Allen, justification is an exclusively forensic doctrine, which *leads* to participation.[120] He argues, "*While participation in God is the goal of the gospel, justification is the ground of that sanctifying fellowship.*"[121] Allen presents the earthly analogies of marriage and adoption in support:

---

116. T. F. T., *Reality and Evangelical Theology*, 14–15. From his exegesis of Galatians 2, Wiard Popkes argues that salvation should be understood in personal and participatory terms. Paul writes of being "in Christ" and of Christ "in us" (Gal 2:20). Salvation therefore is not an external transaction but a person in whom we participate: "Christ is not just a saviour in the sense of helping out of a need. Rather, he is the very content of salvation; for Christ means life in its eternal quality of glory and love." Popkes, "Two Interpretations of "Justification" in the New Testament Reflections on Galatians 2:15–21 and James 2:21–25," 129–46.

117. McGowan questions whether theologians such as T. F. should even be called Reformed when they present justification in terms of sharing in Christ's righteousness rather than in external, forensic terms. McGowan, "Justification and the Ordo Salutis," 14–17. See also Cassidy, "T. F. Torrance's Realistic Soteriological Objectivism," 184. However, first, modern re-readings of Luther and Calvin have perceived a more participatory understanding of salvation in contrast to a simple external, judicial interpretation. Second, even if these are to be disputed, a fundamental tenet of the Reformed church is "*ecclesia semper reformanda est*" (the church is always to be reformed). Alasdair Heron observes that T. F. does not follow people merely for the sake of tradition, according to his understanding of theology as "not the slavish following of any teacher or tradition, however brilliant or venerable, but the bringing of the mind into grateful subjection to the glorious revelation of the truth and reality of God in the light of him who for us and for our salvation came down . . . and was made man." Heron, "T. F. Torrance in Relation to Reformed Theology," 44.

118. Allen, *Justification and the Gospel*, 35–37. See also Campbell, *Deliverance of God*; Gorman, *Inhabiting the Cruciform God*. Gorman argues, 'The judicial image must be understood within a wider covenantal, relational, participatory, and transformative framework" (25).

119. Allen, *Justification and the Gospel*, 37.

120. Ibid., 51, 61–67. See also Horton, *Pilgrim Theology*, Kindle ed., Loc 5541–5553, 5650.

121. Ibid., 37.

> The marriage precedes the married life, while the adoptive declaration founded the familial ties. But the marriage is for the sake of a life together, and the adoption proceedings aim solely at genuine commitment to daily household existence. It would be foolish to suggest that life together makes one married or that household proximity equates with adoption per se.[122]

The difficulty here is that earthly marriage and adoption are an inferior reflection of the way in which God relates to humanity. To project these earthly institutions onto God is limiting and fails to appreciate the profoundly intimate nature of salvation as revealed in the incarnation of Christ. God is similarly limited when Allen believes that "Eden is the symbol" of the participation that believers have once they are justified.[123] This is consistent with his understanding of participation as "covenant fellowship" rather than as a true sharing in Christ.[124] Yet it does not adequately reflect Christ's considerably more intimate purposes for humanity. Christ came not only so that humanity may have close fellowship with God, but so that we might share by the Spirit in the Son's intimate communion with the Father.

Ontological

In reaction to the Roman Catholic belief that justification involves an infused moral transformation, Protestant theology established a forensic doctrine of imputation whereby the believer is declared to have an alien righteousness. Horton expresses it as "a declaration that is pronounced solely by virtue of Christ's imputed righteousness, while the believer is actually unrighteous in himself/herself."[125] To Roman Catholics, this external doctrine of imputation can appear to be a "legal fiction."[126] Some Protestant theologians are advocating a doctrine of imputation that is transformative, understanding

---

122. Ibid., 70.

123. Ibid., 38.

124. Ibid., 15, 45.

125. Horton, *God of Promise*, Kindle ed., Loc 5640. See also Piper, *Counted Righteous in Christ*.

126. Roman Catholic and Eastern Orthodox theology typically understand salvation in transformative rather than external, legal terms. Roman Catholic theology typically understands the transformation in moral terms and Eastern Orthodox theology in ontological terms. See Kärkkäinen, *One with God*, 33. Horton argues that imputation is not a legal fiction "since the justified do in fact possess in Christ the status of those who have perfectly fulfilled all righteousness." Horton, *God of Promise*, Kindle ed., Loc 5868.

God's declaration as a creative act.[127] The Torrances argue from the vicarious humanity of Christ that righteousness is not an external, legal status, but involves a true transformation.[128]

The notion of imputation is empty, T. F. insists, unless it is understood in terms of transformative, ontological union.[129] The work of Christ cannot be separated from his person. The hypostatic union in Christ shows justification to be a real ontological event rather than an external, legal status. Justification is transformative because humanity is included in Christ's resurrection. T. F. points to the story of the healing of the paralyzed man; Jesus forgives his sins, commands him to rise and walk, and the man is healed (Mark 2:1–12). "Justification is not only a declaratory act," T. F. argues, "but an actualization of what is declared. When Christ said to the paralysed man that his sins were forgiven, they *were forgiven*—as the word of healing made clear."[130] T. F. believes, "When, therefore, the Protestant doctrine of justification is formulated only in terms of forensic imputation of righteousness or the non-imputation of sins in such a way as to avoid saying that to justify is to make righteous, *it is the resurrection that is being bypassed*."[131] For T. F., the resurrection is evidence that justification is a creative event.[132] Humanity is raised to new life in Christ, which means that there is a real ontological transformation. T. F. argues that an external, forensic notion of justification fails to effect a true re-creation of humanity through Christ's death and resurrection.

Bruce McCormack seeks to uphold a judicial and transformative understanding of Christ's righteousness without recourse to the Torrances' notion of participation in Christ's vicarious humanity. McCormack supports the forensic doctrine of imputation but argues that the ontology is underdeveloped: "At its heart, forensicism is deeply ontological."[133] He seeks to show how a judicial understanding of imputation can be transformative without the Torrances' ontology of participation in Christ's humanity.[134] McCormack contends, "I do not participate in the historical humanity of Christ

---

127. Mark Garcia identifies this in Lutheran theology but argues that a creative declaration compromises what he perceives to be the exclusively forensic nature of justification. Garcia, "Attribution," 415–27.

128. J. B. T., "Priesthood of Jesus," 172.

129. T. F. T., *Space, Time and Resurrection*, 63.

130. Ibid., 62.

131. Ibid., 63.

132. Ibid.

133. McCormack, "What's at Stake in Current Debates over Justification?," 115.

134. Ibid., 84.

... rather I participate in the *kind* of humanity which Jesus instantiated and embodied through his life of obedience."[135] For McCormack, union with Christ should be understood as "a union of wills." Our life conforms to Christ's as far as our will corresponds to his. McCormack explains, "The being of the Christian "in Christ" is to be construed along the lines of the conformity of my life to his life of obedience, which brings about his likeness in me."[136] The ethical is ontological, he argues, because our being is constituted in part by what one does.[137] McCormack writes, "A judicial act for God is never merely judicial; it is itself transformative."[138]

The Torrances perhaps would not be satisfied with McCormack's scheme because it seems to present union with Christ as something that comes about by our own action. We are not "in Christ" on account of our own obedience; Paul writes of being united to Christ in his death and resurrection (Romans 6), which indicates that our union with Christ does not depend upon our own activity. By no action of our own are we able to birth ourselves. There is also the question of how our actions are able to conform to Christ's if our very being has not first been transformed. For the Torrances, an external, ethical or judicial framework fails to offer an adequate account of the transformation of humanity.

Conclusion

T. F. uses the Reformed language of Christ's active and passive obedience and the imputation of his righteousness, but he understands it in profoundly personal, filial, and ontological terms. Christ's obedience is not an external transaction that merits righteousness; his perfect faithfulness transforms the humanity that he assumes vicariously, turning it back to a right relationship with the Father. The person and work of Christ must be held together; God does not give us abstract benefits, but his very self. We receive righteousness not as an external, legal status but by participating in Christ himself. This means that we have a true righteousness. The hypostatic union in Christ shows justification to be a real ontological event. Justification is transformative because humanity is included in Christ's resurrection and reborn to new life. For the Torrances, an external, forensic understanding of Christ's obedience and the imputation of his righteousness prioritizes the judicial over the filial and fails to offer a true transformation of humanity. Without

---

135. Ibid., 110.
136. Ibid.
137. Ibid., 113.
138. Ibid., 107.

the Torrances' understanding of the vicarious humanity of Christ and our participation in his righteousness, there is the danger of being thrown back upon ourselves to make ourselves righteous.[139]

Justified by Faith

Existential decision

The gospel calls us to receive by faith this salvation objectively achieved by Christ. In the oft-proclaimed words of John, "For God so loved the world that he gave his only Son, so that everyone who believes in him may not perish but may have eternal life" (John 3:16). When Jesus is asked, "What must we do to perform the works of God?," he answers, "This is the work of God, that you believe in him whom he has has sent" (John 6:28–29). Paul writes of being "justified by faith" (Rom 3:28; 5:1; Gal 2:16; 3:24; Eph 2:8), asserting, "if you confess with your lips that Jesus is Lord and believe in your heart that God raised him from the dead, you will be saved. For one believes with the heart and so is justified, and one confesses with the mouth and so is saved" (Rom 10:9–11).

This gospel call is distorted by preaching and teaching today which makes faith a *condition* of salvation.[140] Douglas Campbell articulates the distortion in this way: "If you exercise faith *then* you will be saved. If not, however, then this contract is not activated and its obligations will not be honoured by God."[141] Campbell perceives that, according to this perspective, God's grace is unmerited rather than unconditional. Justification by faith, as opposed to works, is considered incredibly gracious of God and yet this understanding still presents faith as a condition for salvation.[142]

---

139. This danger is arguably seen in Gundry, Wright, and McCormack.

140. T. F. T., *Mediation*, 103; J. B. T., "Introduction," 3–4.

141. Campbell, *The Quest for Paul's Gospel*, 159.

142. Campbell, *The Deliverance of God*, 26–27. Campbell proposes that this is more reflective of modern Western culture than biblical thought. He argues that its "powerful commitments to individualism, to rationalism, and to consent, these being organized in turn by an overarching contractual structure" are "also fundamental components within Western history and culture" (7). For example, this perspective displays a striking resemblance to John Locke's individual contractualism whereby religion is a matter of individual choice and belief which establishes a contract with God (302–3). Campbell argues that it is only by rescuing our reading of the Bible from modern cultural presuppositions that it will be better able to speak to our culture. He asks, "Indeed, in a supreme irony, could it be that a reading that lays claim to being a construal of the Pauline gospel is in fact a projection of essentially modern European cultural values into the Pauline texts and into their ostensible construal of salvation

Allen argues that Campbell contends with "a historical bogeyman that does not exist as such" and that his criticism is "based entirely on a debunked reading of a historical movement (post-Reformation Protestant theology, largely in its scholastic form) that finds scholarly backing in the work of one man, James Torrance."[143] However, Allen's impassioned rebuttal does not take serious account of the reality within the church today, where God's acceptance of us can be made conditional upon the strength of our faith, the sincerity of our repentance, the passion of our worship, the quality of our prayer, and more.[144] J. B. exercised meticulously thought-out, analytic theology that engages with the reality of the popular practice of the church. Whilst there is a rich theological tradition that upholds salvation by God's grace alone, nevertheless practice within the church demonstrates the Torrances' and Campbell's concern.[145] It is expressed, for example, in this well-intentioned evangelistic call:

> God has done His part. Jesus gave His own life as a punishment for OUR sin. We didn't deserve it. It wasn't 'fair' but that's how much God loves you. But now you have to decide if you want to accept this gift of forgiveness, this promise of eternal life. If you want to be free from the punishment you brought on yourself by not doing things God's way, you need to decide to surrender to God and do things His way from now on. You need to believe that He exists, that He loves you and that He died for you.[146]

Another example, from popular theology, may be seen in Wayne Grudem's description of "saving faith":

---

itself, and is therefore at bottom an idolatrous exercise—a mere pandering to the Western Zeitgeist? Have such interpreters constructed Paul at these points—and through him God's relationship to humanity—in their own image?!" (8).

143. Allen, *Justification and the Gospel*, 42–43. Allen asserts that "Campbell misconstrues classical Protestant teaching regarding Christian faith: it is unequivocally not construed as a work." Allen, *Justification and the Gospel*, 122.

144. Furthermore, Allen's criticism of Campbell, and of Gorman (150–51), displays a contemptuous derision that only serves to undermine his argument. Allen's ungraciousness leads one to question his understanding of God and, thereby, the accuracy of the Federal scheme which he seeks to promote.

145. McGrath writes, "The doctrine of justification came to be seen as dealing with the question of what an individual had to do in order to be saved." McGrath, *Historical Theology*, 185. Hays writes, "This doctrine has always carried with it the risk of turning faith into another kind of work," such as "intellectual assent to propositionally-formulated dogma." Hays, *The Faith of Jesus Christ*, 139. Eberhard Jüngel observes that faith is often understood in terms of making a "decision for God." Jüngel, *Justification*, 238.

146. "Point 4" of "The 4 Points": http://www.the4points.com/INT/about_the4points.php?page=PT4.

> There must be some basic knowledge or understanding of the facts of the gospel. There must also be approval of, or agreement with, these facts. Such agreement includes a conviction that the facts spoken of the gospel are true, especially the fact that I am a sinner in need of salvation and that Christ alone has paid the penalty for my sin and offers salvation to me. It also includes an awareness that I need to trust in Christ for salvation and that he is the only way to God, and the only means provided for my salvation. This approval of the facts of the gospel will also involve a desire to be saved through Christ. But all this still does not add up to saving faith. That comes only when I make a decision of my will to depend on, or put my trust in, Christ as my saviour.[147]

According to Grudem's scheme of salvation, our faith conditions God into responding with forgiveness: "God must respond to our faith and do what he promised."[148]

T. F. calls this "the modern notion of salvation by *existential decision*," which perceives our faith and decision to be the means to secure salvation.[149] He observes that "Evangelical Protestantism has developed a way of preaching the Gospel which distorts and betrays it by introducing into it a subtle element of co-redemption."[150] Salvation is presented as a potentiality that can only be actualized by our faith. When our faith is necessary to secure our justification, "this is to make the effectiveness of the work of Christ conditional upon what the sinner does, and so at the crucial point it throws the ultimate responsibility for man's salvation back upon himself."[151] This is an immense burden that can lead to weariness and a lack of assurance in salvation.

Vicarious faith

The Torrances understand the gospel call to faith in relation to the vicarious humanity of Christ. Justification is not a potentiality to be actualized by our faith; salvation is an accomplished reality in Christ:

> In Jesus Christ God has actualised his unconditional love for you in your human nature in such a once for all way that he cannot go back upon it without undoing the Incarnation and

147. Grudem, *Systematic Theology*, 713, 722.
148. Ibid., 722.
149. T. F. T., *God and Rationality*, 58.
150. Ibid.
151. Ibid.

the Cross and thereby denying himself. Jesus Christ died for you precisely because you are sinful and utterly unworthy of him, and has thereby already made you his own before and apart from your ever believing in him. He has bound you to himself by his love in a way that he will never let you go, for even if you refuse him and damn yourself in hell his love will never cease.[152]

Therefore, salvation is not dependent upon our believing or faith. "It is not faith that justifies us," T. F. asserts, "but Christ in whom we have faith."[153]

This does not mean that the Torrances diminish the gospel call for us to respond with faith.[154] Rather, it means that faith cannot be understood according to logico-causal categories. Our response of faith is a participation in a response already made in our place and on our behalf by Christ. J. B. writes, "Our response in faith and obedience is a response to the Response already made for us by Christ to the Father's holy love, a response we are summoned to make in union with Christ."[155] Indeed, our response is only made possible by Christ's all sufficient response. Our decision for Christ is a response to Christ's prior decision for us, a "yes" to Christ's "yes" to God on our behalf.[156] As J. B. puts it, "He chose us, not we him."[157]

In his vicarious humanity, Christ has faith *for* us, so that we are liberated from the impossible task of trying to work up enough faith for ourselves. Christ lives a life of perfect faithfulness to the Father in our place and on our behalf and continues to intercede for us as our ascended high priest.[158] T. F. asserts,

> Jesus Christ is not only the Word of God become flesh, He is also Believer, but Believer for us, vicariously Believer, whose very humanity is the embodiment of our salvation. In Him who is Man of our humanity, we are graciously given to share, and so to participate in the whole course of His reconciling obedience from His birth to His death. That He stood in our place and gave to God account for us, that He believed for us, was faithful

---

152. T. F. T., *Mediation*, 103–4.

153. T. F. T., *God and Rationality*, 58.

154. T. F. T., *Mediation*, 105; J. B. T., "The Priesthood of Jesus," 172; "Introduction," 14.

155. J. B. T., "Christ in our Place," 48.

156. T. F. T., *Incarnation*, 26. Jüngel writes of faith not as an independent, determining decision for God but as an acknowledgement that the decision has already been made for humanity in Christ. Jüngel, *Justification*, 241–45.

157. J. B. T., "The Incarnation and 'Limited Atonement.'" 87.

158. J. B. T., *Worship*, 18.

for us, and remains faithful even when we fail Him again and again, is the very substance of our salvation and the anchor of our hope.[159]

We are called to have faith, but it is not an autonomous, independent act. T. F. writes, "Faith in Christ involves a polar relation between the faith of Christ and our faith, in which our faith is laid hold of, enveloped and upheld by his unswerving faithfulness."[160]

Πίστις Χριστοῦ

There is ongoing debate in scholarship as to how to translate the occurrences of Πίστις Χριστοῦ in the New Testament.[161] The genitive case may be translated as the "faith of Christ" or "faith in Christ." T. F. holds to a subjective genitive translation of Galatians 2:20, an immensely significant verse for him: "It is no longer I who live, but it is Christ who lives in me. And the life I now live in the flesh I live by the faith *of* the Son of God, who loved me and gave himself for me." For T. F., the subjective genitive reflects the centrality of Christ's faithfulness, which is the foundation for ours.[162] He also examines the words for "faith" in both the Old and New Testament, finding that their meaning points to humanity's dependence upon the steadfastness of God.[163] He concludes, "God draws man within the sphere of His own faithfulness and righteousness and gives man to share in it, so that his faith is embraced by God's faithfulness."[164]

The debate over translation is significant because an objective genitive (faith *in* Christ) can encourage the notion of salvation by existential

---

159. T. F. T., "One Aspect of the Biblical Conception of Faith," 114.

160. T. F. T., "Preaching Jesus Christ," 25.

161. For recent perspectives on both sides of the debate, see Bird and Sprinkle, *The Faith of Jesus Christ*. For arguments for an objective translation, see Dunn, "Once More, Pistou Christou" 61–81; Dunn, "Pisteos," 351–66; Matlock, "Detheologizing the pistis Christou Debate," 1–23; Dunn, "The Rhetoric of *pistis* in Paul," 173–203. For arguments for a subjective translation, see Hays, *Faith of Jesus Christ;* Hooker, "Πίστις Χριστοῦ," 165–84; Campbell, *Deliverance of God*.

162. C. F. D. Moule criticizes T. F.'s subjective genitive translation because he sees it to disparage the response of the human will. Moule argues that our faith is necessary to subjectively lay hold of our objective justification. See Moule, "The Biblical Conception of 'Faith,'" 157. This is a misunderstanding of T. F. because he does not disparage the human act but rather argues that our response is only made possible by Christ's all-sufficient substitution in our place and on our behalf.

163. T. F. T., "One Aspect," 111–14.

164. Ibid., 113.

decision, whereby people are dependent upon their own quality of faith for salvation.[165] Stephen Chester seeks to defend the objective genitive translation of Πίστις Χριστοῦ from this criticism. He argues that the objective genitive does not necessarily lead to an anthropocentric soteriology because Luther holds to the objective genitive whilst also offering a thoroughly Christological account of faith.[166] In response to Chester, it may be affirmed that the notion of "faith *in* Christ" is not wrong in itself.[167] The Torrances are emphatic about the necessity of our own faith. The problem is that a Christological account of faith can be neglected in preaching and teaching, which means that an objective genitive translation can serve to further a false notion of salvation by existential decision. When our faith is abstracted from Christ's vicarious faith in which we participate, there is the danger of an anthropocentric soteriology.

Furthermore, there are compelling reasons for translating Πίστις Χριστοῦ as a subjective genitive. Richard B. Hays has considered the significance of the whole framework of Paul's thought for the Πίστις Χριστοῦ debate.[168] Paul's theological language is rooted in a narrative substructure: the story of Christ.[169] This story is presupposed and also developed throughout his writing to include Paul and his churches in a progressing narrative.[170] This narrative framework has often been overlooked because Paul's letters are "manifestly non-narrative texts."[171] Yet the narrative framework, argues Hays, provides an underlying direction to Christ's faith, rather than our own.

---

165. It is notable that Grudem, whose description of "saving faith" presents faith as a condition of salvation, assumes an objective genitive translation of Galatians 2:20: "And the life I now live in the flesh I live by faith *in* the Son of God." Grudem, *Systematic Theology*, 56. An objective genitive translation here seems implausible in light of its context. The context provides no support for the belief that Paul is referring to humanity's faith in Christ. Rather, the centrality of Christ's redemptive work and the dismissal of human endeavor is clear: "I have been crucified with Christ; and it is no longer I who live, but it is Christ who lives in me" (2:19–20).

166. Chester, "It is No Longer I Who Live," 334.

167. For T. F., verses such as Galatians 2:16, 20 and 3:22 should not be presented in terms of an either/or debate between Christ's faith or ours. The issue is the primacy of Christ's faithfulness to man's faith, which answers and participates in it. T. F. T., "One Aspect," 113.

168. Hays, *Faith of Jesus Christ*, 1.

169. Ibid., 73–74.

170. Ibid., 266.

171. Ibid., 247.

> Because justification hinges upon this action of Jesus Christ, ... it is a terrible and ironic blunder to read Paul as though his gospel made redemption contingent upon our act of deciding to dispose ourselves towards God in a particular way. The "grammar" of Paul's gospel—more precisely, of the gospel's topical sequence—places humanity in the role of "Receiver."[172]

Hays's argument is supported by Campbell's interpretation of Πίστις Χριστοῦ in Romans 3:21–22 which, he argues, evokes the gospel narrative of Christ's death and resurrection. Campbell believes that it is functionally equivalent to other references to the passion in terms of language. He argues that Paul is therefore referring to Christ's faithfulness even to death in order to reveal God's righteousness. Campbell translates Romans 3:21–22: "But now, irrespective of the law, the righteousness of God has been disclosed and it is attested by the law and the prophets, the righteousness of God through the faith of Jesus Christ for all who believe."[173] Campbell's interpretation is compelling when considering the wider context of the passage. Paul continues, "Then what becomes of our boasting? It is excluded" (Rom 3:27). This appears to point to the insufficiency of our own endeavors and our dependency upon Christ.[174]

---

172. Ibid., 240.

173. Campbell, *Deliverance of God*, 612–13.

174. Another disputed passage is Galatians 3:22, which Hays translates as follows: "But the Scripture has imprisoned all things under the power of sin, so that what was promised through the faith of Jesus Christ might be given to those who believe." Hays, *Faith of Jesus Christ*, 247. He argues that the wider context supports this translation; Paul writes that Christ "gave himself for our sins to set us free" (1:4), which recalls the notion of recapitulation in Romans 5. This underlines the belief that Jesus's faith is not merely an example for us to emulate but actually salvifically efficacious (248). Earlier Paul asks, "Did you receive the Spirit by doing the works of the law or by believing what you heard?" (Gal 3:2). This is exegetically ambiguous because Paul may have meant that the Spirit is received by faith rather than works, or he may have meant that the Spirit is received by neither faith nor works. Hays contends for the latter interpretation because the juxtaposition of works and faith is not as credible as works and law. It is more convincing that Paul is contrasting human activity with God's activity rather than one human activity with another. It is also supported by 3:5, where the syntax indicates that the prepositional phrases are modifiers of God's action (143–47). The emphasis is on God's action, not human capability. Paul also writes, "Now it is evident that no one is justified before God by the law; for 'The one who is righteous will live by faith'" (Gal 3:11). "The one who is righteous" takes a singular adjective and it may have been used by Paul as a title for the Messiah (cf. Acts 3:14; 7:52; 1 Pet 3:18; 1 John 2:1). Paul also asserts in Galatians 3:23–26 that Christ is the answer to the problem of humanity's unfaithfulness (173). Paul is quoting Habakkuk 2:4, which was interpreted messianically by the LXX translation (150–51). This indicates that 3:11 is

Morna Hooker makes six key observations about the occurrences of Πίστις Χριστοῦ in the New Testament: (1) all of the passages refer to Jesus, evoking his earthly ministry; (2) they refer to Πίστις Χριστοῦ as the ground of existence for the believer; (3) they also refer to the believer's faith, which would make a second reference to "faith in Christ" redundant; (4) the passages contrast righteousness based on the Law with righteousness based on Πίστις Χριστοῦ and the logical antithesis to works of the Law in us is the faith of Christ; (5) they concern being in Christ; and (6) they also concern the death of Christ.[175] This seems to suggest that Paul is referring to the salvific efficacy of the "faith of Christ," in which we participate.

Hooker also draws upon Paul's theology in other passages to support the argument that our faith is a sharing in Christ's faith. In 2 Corinthians 1:17–22, Paul defends himself against an accusation of faithlessness, arguing that he shares in the faithfulness of God through Christ, the very embodiment of God's faithfulness. Leading up to 2 Corinthians 4:13, Paul writes that his ministry involves participation in Jesus's death and resurrection,

---

highlighting the significance of Christ's faith in contrast to our incapacity to earn our justification. Paul stresses Christ as the only heir to God's promise to Abraham and that we participate in this inheritance "in Christ Jesus" (Gal 3:14–16) (153). We are all justified through Christ's faith (157). The Πίστις Χριστοῦ references in both Galatians 3:22 and Romans 3:26 have a clear parallel to the faith of Abraham in Romans 4:16. Logically, it is incoherent to affirm that believing in Jesus is the basis of the promise to Abraham. It is more cogent to affirm that Jesus's faith is the basis of the promise (164). Elsewhere, Paul considers Jesus's obedience to have salvific efficacy for us (Rom 5:19; Phil 2:8) (166). Hooker observes that there is no reference to the faith of the believer when Paul writes of righteousness established by Christ in Romans 5:19. Hooker, "Πίστις Χριστοῦ," 336. In the next chapter, Paul asks, "Now, however, that you have come to know God, or rather to be known by God, how can you turn your back again . . . ?" (Gal 4:9). Paul initially depicts the Galatians as active knowing subjects but then revises his words to place the emphasis on God, perhaps as an intentional rhetorical device. Thus Hays argues that those who believe depend upon the believing of Christ. Hays, *Faith of Jesus Christ*, 240. As Paul asserts, "Everything is from God, who reconciled us to himself through Christ" (2 Cor 5:18). Hooker considers that Paul teaches that we become sons of God because Christ is Son of God (Rom 8; Gal 4); that our righteousness and holiness is dependent upon Christ's righteousness and holiness (2 Cor 5:21; 1 Cor 1:30); and that the spiritual gifts, including faith, depend upon life in Christ (Gal 5:22). Thus she concludes that it follows that our faith is also dependent upon his. Hooker, "Πίστις Χριστοῦ," 324. Campbell provides support for Hays in observing the grammatical singularity in Galatians 3:23: "Now before faith came, we were imprisoned and guarded under the law until faith would be revealed." The single event of coming in relation to a single subject supports the interpretation that Paul is referring to the faith of Christ, not the faith of all believers. Campbell, *Deliverance of God*, 879.

175. Hooker, "Πίστις Χριστοῦ," 336–37.

and then he writes that he shares in the "same spirit of faith" as Jesus.[176] Hooker writes,

> In Paul's view, Christians owe everything to the fact that they are in Christ: they are nothing and they have nothing, except by virtue of being in him. Christian faith is always the response to what God has done in Christ and to what Christ is. It seems, then, that they need the faithfulness of Christ—for how are they to have even faith, except by sharing in his?[177]

Therefore, there are significant arguments to affirm a subjective genitive translation of Πίστις Χριστοῦ. It is a relevant debate because the subjective genitive points to the centrality of the faith *of* Christ, and thereby challenges an external, anthropological notion of salvation by existential decision.

Conclusion

The gospel call to receive our salvation by faith can be misunderstood as presenting faith as a condition of salvation. T. F. calls this "salvation by existential decision," whereby our faith is deemed an autonomous, independent act that brings about our justification. Yet justification is not a potentiality to be actualized by our faith; salvation is an accomplished reality in Christ. Humanity has been saved in Christ prior to any decision of our faith. According to the Torrances, Christ has faith for us, in his vicarious humanity, and our faith should be understood as a participation in his perfect faithfulness.

There are compelling arguments to translate the occurrences of Πίστις Χριστοῦ in the New Testament as a subjective genitive, which reflects the centrality of Christ's faithfulness as the foundation for ours. This debate is important because an objective genitive translation can advance the pervasive notion of salvation by existential decision, whereby people are turned back upon themselves to work up enough faith for salvation. In affirming the vicarious faith of Christ, we are liberated from striving to have faith and worrying that our faith is not adequate enough to be saved; rather we are free to joyfully participate by the Spirit in Christ's perfect faithfulness to the Father.

---

176. Ibid., 334–35
177. Ibid., 337–38.

Conclusion

The Torrances present God's claiming of humanity as an ontological event within the incarnate constitution of Jesus. Christ assumes humanity to plumb the depths of our fallen humanity and turn it back to right relationship with God. The hypostatic union in Christ enables Jesus to fulfill both sides of the relationship between God and man. Thus the incarnation is integral to the atonement; Jesus's person is essential to his work. This challenges external models of the atonement that distort the nature of God and of humanity and fail to offer an adequate account of the transformation of our very being. People are thrown back upon themselves to attempt to earn their salvation, which can lead to weariness and a lack of joy and assurance.

For the Torrances, Jesus's whole life is of atoning significance, including the events of his death, resurrection, ascension, and Pentecost. Although the Torrances are criticized for not taking seriously enough Christ's death and human sin and guilt, it is their broader account of Jesus's substitution that takes these most seriously. In Christ's death, the old human nature dies; in his resurrection, humanity is reborn to new life; in his ascension, we are raised up to heaven in him; and at Pentecost, we received the Spirit so that we might share in Jesus's perfect relationship with the Father. Whilst this resists human rational categories of thought, the Torrances call for the atonement to be understood not according to human reasoning but according to God's self-giving in Christ. The Torrances' understanding also challenges an external, forensic scheme that tends to look exclusively and narrowly to Christ's death and the forgiveness of sins. Without this wider conception of the atonement, an external scheme fails to offer a true transformation of humanity or this profoundly filial account of the prospective aspect of the atonement.

The Torrances offer a personal, filial, and ontological understanding of Christ's righteousness. Christ's life of perfect faithfulness is not an external transaction which merits righteousness; rather it transforms the humanity that he assumes vicariously, turning it back to a right relationship with the Father. His resurrection is the rebirth of a new humanity, which challenges the notion of an external imputation of Christ's righteousness. The Torrances believe that the difficulty with this is that it prioritizes the judicial over the filial and fails to offer a real righteousness to humanity. The Torrances argue that we are righteousness not in terms of an external, legal status but by participating in Christ himself, which means that we are truly made righteous.

The gospel call to faith is understood by the Torrances as a participation in Christ's prior response on our behalf. Christ has faith for us, and our faith is included and upheld in his continuing perfect faithfulness. This challenges the notion of salvation by existential decision whereby faith is understood as an autonomous, independent, logico-causal act that brings about our justification. This makes people dependent upon their own efforts to make a decision for Christ or work up enough faith. The Torrances contend that salvation does not depend upon the adequacy of our own faith; rather we are set free to enjoy the reality of our inclusion in Christ and his perfect relationship with the Father by the Spirit.

Justification is not a potentiality to be actualized by our faith; salvation is an accomplished reality in Christ:

> In Jesus Christ we have been crucified, have died and have been buried—and so the old age, the power of darkness and the sovereignty of evil are already defeated. In Christ Jesus we have been resurrected, made alive; we are already justified and sanctified and redeemed for he has been made our wisdom, righteousness, sanctification and redemption; already we have been reconciled to God; already have peace with God, already our life is hid with Christ in God, and already we have been granted all things necessary for life and godliness that we might have participation in the divine nature.[178]

This is a profoundly objective view of the atonement that gives us assurance of salvation and rest from trying to obtain it ourselves. Yet it also raises questions regarding the elusive role of the Holy Spirit and of our subjective human participation that will be explored as the Spirit comes into greater focus in the next chapter.

---

178. T. F. T., *Atonement*, 134–35.

3

Drawn to Participate by the Holy Spirit

Objective over Subjective

THE TORRANCES' SCHEME OF SALVATION IS RADICALLY CHRISTOCENTRIC. Everything pertaining to our salvation has been accomplished in the vicarious humanity of Christ, even our response to God and our faith. The Torrances' understanding of salvation is also radically objective. Redemption is wholly an act of God, which sets our human autonomy aside. This objective, Christocentric scheme of salvation is a radical claim that does not go uncontested. It raises the question of whether salvation is reduced to a noetic concept whereby epistemology essentially defines what it means to be saved. Furthermore, in the recent rise of Western interest in the Holy Spirit, some theologians have sought to give greater attention to the Spirit, and believe that the Spirit in turn grants humanity an important, subjective, autonomous role in salvation. They seek to affirm a greater salvific role for the Spirit and for humanity in our response of faith and in our works in anticipation of final judgement.

In the Torrances' scheme of salvation, the Holy Spirit has a pervasive but elusive role, often expressed in the simplest of terms: "by the Spirit." It is "by the Spirit" that Jesus lived a vicarious life of perfect faithfulness to the Father in our place, and it is "by the Spirit" that humanity is brought to share in Jesus's communion with the Father.[1] For the Torrances, this is appropriate to the self-effacing nature of the Spirit, whose role ultimately is to draw us up in Christ to participate in God's triune life. This personal, relational, and participatory scheme of salvation defies the Spirit being utilized to promote any autonomous human activity, which can only lead to us being thrown back upon our own resources. However, it also raises the question

---

1. J. B. T., "Introduction," *Nature of the Atonement*, 15; "Christ in our Place," 51; *Worship*, 55; T. F. T., *Atonement*, 129; *Reconstruction*, 121–22.

of whether this confuses the Creator and the creature. For the Torrances, the Holy Spirit is the means by whom humanity is unconditionally adopted into the divine life, with liberating, intimate, and transformative implications.

The Spirit of Christ

Christocentricity

Whilst the Eastern Orthodox tradition has a strong pneumatological underpinning, both the Protestant and Catholic traditions are considered to be more Christologically focused.[2] This Christological focus is true to affirm of the Torrances' theology, which has the vicarious humanity of Christ at its center:

> Everything in the message of the Gospel, and everything in the doctrine of the Holy Trinity, hinges upon the concrete mediatorial activity of Christ in space and time, for it is through the incarnate *parousia* of the Son of God in Jesus that the activity of God in its nature and reality is revealed to us and its saving power is actualised among us in the Spirit whose coming to us is made possible on the ground of Christ's atoning and reconciling work.[3]

This raises the question of whether the Torrances' scheme of salvation is too Christocentric, to the detriment of their pneumatology. Rankin argues that T. F. is subject to the charge of Christomonism.[4] This is an unfair charge because the Torrances present an unmistakably Trinitarian scheme of salvation whereby humanity is drawn by the Spirit to participate in Christ's intimate relationship with the Father.[5]

The Torrances' scheme of salvation is certainly Christocentric, yet T. F. is unapologetic of this because he believes that Christ is the appropriate axis of theology as the revelation of who God is and that this is faithful to Nicene theology.[6] He writes,

---

2. Kärkkäinen, "Introduction to Pneumatology," xix.

3. T. F. T., *The Christian Doctrine of God*, 196.

4. Rankin, "Carnal Union with Christ in the Theology of T. F. Torrance," 289.

5. Kye Won Lee defends T. F. against this criticism, arguing that it is based upon a failure to understand his theology. Lee, *Living in Union with Christ*, 315. Dick Eugenio has recently examined the Trinitarian nature of T. F.'s soteriology. See Eugenio, "Communion with God." Molnar contends that T. F. is *Christocentric*, not Christomonist. Molnar, *Thomas F. Torrance*, 325.

6. T. F. T., *Trinitarian Faith*, 62–63.

> It is the incarnation of the Word which prescribes to dogmatic theology both its matter and its method, so that whether in its activity as a whole or in the formulation of a doctrine in any part, it is the Christological pattern that will be made to appear. That does not mean that all theology can be reduced to Christology, but because there is only one Mediator between God and man, the Man Christ Jesus, in the orderly presentation of the doctrines of the Christian faith, every doctrine will be expressed in its inner coherence with Christology at the centre, and in its correspondence to the objective reality of God's revelation in Jesus Christ who is true God and true Man.[7]

This Christocentricity does not detract from the Holy Spirit, but rather upholds the significance of the Holy Spirit. J. B. writes,

> It is as if the whole purpose of the Incarnation, Death, Resurrection and Ascension, is in order that we might receive the Holy Spirit, that the Triune God of grace might bring to fulfilment the purposes of creation in sanctifying our humanity in Christ, that we might be brought into a life of holy communion, a life of prayer.[8]

Thus T. F. asserts, "It is in and through the humanity of Christ in all that he has done for us that the Holy Spirit is conveyed to us, so that the Holy Spirit is given along with the incarnation of the Son a place of central significance in the structure of Christian theology."[9] Therefore, whilst the Torrances' scheme of salvation is Christocentric, concentrated upon the vicarious humanity of Christ, this is appropriate to the method of their theology and actually serves to uphold rather than diminish the significance of the Holy Spirit.

Mutual mediation

Christ and the Spirit are inseparable in the Torrances' scheme of salvation. T. F. writes of a "mutual mediation" of Christ and the Spirit. Christ mediates the Holy Spirit to humanity by vicariously receiving the Spirit in human flesh at his baptism and then pouring out the Spirit upon humanity

---

7. T. F. T., *Reconstruction*, 128–29.
8. J. B. T., "Prayer and the Priesthood of Christ," 59.
9. T. F. T., *Trinitarian Faith*, 63–64; see also *Reconciliation*, 253. Deddo writes, "For Torrance, a proper Christocentricism makes pneumatology no less central." Deddo, "The Holy Spirit in T. F. Torrance's Theology," 84.

at Pentecost.[10] Yet the Holy Spirit also mediates Christ because it is by the Spirit that Christ assumes human flesh, vicariously lives a life of perfect faithfulness, offers his life as a perfect sacrifice, resurrects our humanity and ascends to heaven.[11] The Spirit is "the Spirit of Christ" who unites humanity to Christ and lifts us up to participate in God's triune life.[12] This means for T. F. that to be "in the Spirit" is the same as to be "in Christ."[13]

Commentators are divided as to whether this is an adequate account of the Spirit's role in salvation. Some extol T. F. for having a rich pneumatology.[14] Kye Won Lee asserts, "The Spirit is the hero behind the curtain of Torrance's theological stage."[15] Yet others seek a fuller pneumatological account. Whilst in support of the Torrances' Christology, Ivor Davidson calls for "a more overt statement of the Spirit's action in, upon and towards the human Jesus."[16] Habets makes a similar call, arguing that without an adequate account of the Spirit's action upon Jesus's humanity, T. F. runs the risk of the docetic or Apollinarian heresy:

> By positing too great an emphasis on the agency of the divine Word on the human nature of Jesus, as opposed to a relation mediated by the Holy Spirit, Torrance implicitly makes the

---

10. T. F. T., *Reconstruction*, 245–46. Regarding the gap between Christ's baptism and Pentecost, T. F. believes that humanity was becoming accustomed to bear the Holy Spirit but was not ready until atonement was completed: "Jesus Christ was himself the Bearer in our human nature of the fullness of the Spirit, but the Spirit in this his new mode of presence and activity could not be transmitted to others when they were yet in their sins or be received by others until atonement for sin was completed and the Mediator took his place on the throne of God in his consecrated and glorified Humanity." (247)

11. Ibid., 246–47.

12. Ibid., 221; J. B. T., "The Priesthood of Jesus," 172; "Covenant or Contract?," 75.

13. T. F. T., *Christian Doctrine*, 61. Jürgen Moltmann writes, "What Paul calls the new creation in Christ, John calls the new birth from God's Spirit" and "God makes new people of us through the work of reconciliation, and out of the Spirit of God we are reborn as if from a mother . . . The being-in-Christ and the new life-from-the-Spirit are two sides of the same thing, but they express something different." Moltmann, *Jesus Christ for Today's World*, 136. Kärkkäinen argues that to be "in Christ" and to be "in the Spirit" are "virtually synonymous" for Paul. Kärkkäinen, "Introduction to Pneumatology," xiv. This critically questions the separation of the Spirit from Christ in the Pentecostal-Charismatic movement.

14. Gatewood, "Alive to God in Christ: The Spirit and the Church in the Torrance Tradition." See also Elmer Colyer, "Thomas F. Torrance on the Holy Spirit," 160, 164; and Deddo, "The Holy Spirit," 103.

15. Lee, *Living in Union with Christ*, 316.

16. Davidson, "Theologizing the Human Jesus," 130–31, 150–51.

human nature of Christ merely instrumental. It would be too much to suggest that Torrance's christology is docetic or Apollinarian, but his lack of pneumatology in this area does risk bringing him to the brink of such a failing.[17]

A fuller discussion of the Spirit's action upon Jesus's humanity would be beneficial for a better awareness and understanding of the Spirit's action upon our own humanity today. J. B. believes that "As Christ was anointed by the Spirit in our humanity to fulfil his ministry for us, so we are united by the same Spirit to share his ministry."[18] A closer exploration of the Spirit's action upon Jesus would aid and empower us in this ministry.[19] This may be the benefit of a Spirit Christology.[20] As Clark Pinnock considers, "While Logos Christology highlights how different we are from Jesus, Spirit Christology underlines how like him we can be. The Father sends us as he sent Jesus, filled with the Spirit. The power that was at work in Jesus is at work in us."[21] A more detailed examination of the Spirit's action upon Jesus's humanity would be a welcome endeavor.

There have also been calls to answer the "how" questions of the Spirit's role in salvation. Bevan argues that a fuller account of the role of the Spirit is needed to explain how humanity is ontologically transformed in Christ.[22] Similarly, Habets argues that T. F.'s articulation of *theosis* lacks a sufficient discussion of the role of the Spirit: "He does not go far enough in articulating the actual dynamics of how the Holy Spirit 'deifies' believers in practice."[23]

Deddo recognizes this unsatisfying gap of knowledge regarding pragmatics but he argues that, for T. F., such "how" questions are incoherent. We simply cannot know, for example, *how* Jesus was conceived by the Spirit in

---

17. Habets, *Theosis*, 71.

18. J. B. T., "Christ in our Place," 51.

19. Smail writes, "It is when we think of the humanity of Jesus in terms of the operation of the Holy Spirit, that we can see its possibilities for us who, from the same fleshly starting point, and by the same power, can be made wholly new men in Christ." Smail, *Reflected Glory*, 71.

20. For example, Clark Pinnock seeks to highlight how the Spirit actively works in every aspect of Christ's life and mission. Pinnock, *Flame of Love*. A compelling Spirit Christology is also advanced by Myk Habets, who proposes a fuller account of the Spirit that does not diminish the place of Christ but complements it. He advocates the work of Moltmann, Smail, Ralph del Colle, David Coffey and Gary Badcock. Habets, "Spirit Christology," 199–234.

21. Pinnock, *Flame of Love*, 111.

22. Bevan, "The Person of Christ," 212.

23. Habets, *Theosis*, 196; see also 152.

Mary's womb. The ultimate answer that can be given to such "how" questions is that it is "by the Spirit."[24] Deddo writes,

> Referring to the agency of the Holy Spirit as the ultimate answer goes against the grain of modern Western habits of mind which seeks impersonal, causal, or instrumental means as explanation. For the most part agency has been eliminated from the category of being essential to explanation. But for Torrance the Triune agency in perichoretic communion is the ultimate explanation.[25]

The self-effacing Spirit

Western theology has been subject to the criticism that it has an underdeveloped pneumatology.[26] T. F. himself asserts, "It may be admitted that the doctrine of the Holy Spirit is the weakest of all the doctrines of the Church, for it has never been given the disciplined attention it requires."[27] Karl Barth dreamed of:

> The possibility of a theology of the third article, a theology where the Holy Spirit would dominate and be decisive. Everything that one believes, reflects, and says about God the Father and God the Son in understanding the first and second articles would be demonstrated and clarified basically through God the Holy Spirit, the *vinculum pacis* between the Father and the Son.[28]

However, in recent years, there has been a rise of Western interest in the doctrine of the Holy Spirit.[29] With a "theology of the third article," Lyle

---

24. Deddo, "The Holy Spirit," 105–6.

25. Ibid., 106.

26. Moltmann, "The Trinitarian Personhood of the Holy Spirit," 302; Smail, *The Giving Gift*, 42; Macchia, "Justification and the Spirit," 5. I. John Hesselink proposes that the inadequate pneumatology in Protestantism is the consequence of straying from the initial teaching of the Reformation. He argues that Luther and Calvin had a rich pneumatology. Hesselink, "The Charismatic Movement and the Reformed Tradition," 377–84.

27. T. F. T., "Introduction," *The School of Faith*, xcv.

28. Karl Barth, *The Theology of Schleiermacher*, 278.

29. Kärkkäinen, "Introduction to Pneumatology," xix. He proposes that the surge of pneumatological studies is due to a better awareness and understanding of Eastern Orthodox theology and of the Pentecostal-Charismatic movement (xi). For example, see Welker, *The Work of the Spirit: Pneumatology and Pentecostalism*; and Macchia, *Justified in the Spirit: Creation, Redemption and the Triune God*.

Dabney has called for what has been put *last* in the creed to be put *first* in modern theological enterprise. Dabney perceives a theology of the first article of the creed in medieval Scholasticism, which had great confidence in the capacity of our created nature to attain knowledge of God. He perceives the sixteenth-century Reformation to have then inaugurated a theology of the second article, by protesting this Scholastic belief in an innate *capax Dei* and affirming that right relationship with God is established only by grace through Christ. Dabney argues that the current age, having changed culturally, socially, and intellectually, has rejected Scholasticism's created rationality and finds the Reformation's protest meaningless. To address this post-Christendom age, Dabney calls for a theology centered on the Holy Spirit.[30]

However, a theology centered on the Holy Spirit would be at odds with T. F.'s account of the person and work of the Spirit. For T. F., the Holy Spirit is ineffable and self-effacing, pointing away from himself to Christ and the Father:

> Like Christ the Holy Spirit is one in being and of the same being as the Father, but unlike Christ the Holy Spirit is not one in being and of the same being as we are, for he incarnated the Son but does not incarnate himself, he utters the Word but does not utter himself. He directs us through himself to the one Word and Face of God in Jesus Christ in accordance with whom all our knowledge of God is formed in our minds, knowledge of the Spirit as well as of the Father and of the Son. This is the diaphanous self-effacing nature of the Holy Spirit who hides himself, as it were, behind the Father in the Son and behind the Son in the Father, but also the enlightening transparence of the Spirit who by throwing his eternal Light upon the Father through the Son and upon the Son in the Father, brings the radiance of God's Glory to bear upon us.[31]

This self-effacing nature of the Spirit may be the reason why, according to critics, a satisfactory pneumatology has not been articulated in Western theology in general or in T. F.'s theology more specifically.[32] For T. F., the lack

---

30. Dabney, "Why Should the Last be First?," 240–61.

31. T. F. T., *Christian Doctrine*, 66. In his understanding of the Spirit's self-effacing nature, T. F. follows Athanasius. See T. F. T., *Reconstruction*, 214.

32. Perhaps this is the reason why, as Habets has observed, pneumatology has been the least examined aspect of T. F.'s theology. Habets, *Theosis*, 140.

of a more comprehensive pneumatology in his work reflects his belief in the ineffable nature of the Spirit.[33]

Conclusion

Although some have criticized the Torrances' scheme of salvation for being too Christocentric to the detriment of the role of the Spirit, the Torrances believe that Christ is the appropriate axis of theology and this actually serves to uphold rather than diminish the significance of the Holy Spirit. According to the Torrances, there is a mutual mediation of Christ and the Spirit to humanity. Christ mediates the Holy Spirit through his baptism and Pentecost; the Holy Spirit mediates Christ by empowering his life and uniting us to him.

In one sense the Torrances' pneumatology is rich for the Spirit is integral to every aspect of salvation, yet more could certainly be articulated regarding the Spirit's action upon Jesus's humanity. This would aid a better understanding of the Spirit's action upon our own humanity today. However, T. F. believes that the Holy Spirit is ineffable and self-effacing, pointing away from himself to Christ and the Father. This means, for T. F., that practical specifics regarding the Spirit are essentially indefinable.

Our Human Response

Onto-relational

The radical objectivity and Christocentricity of the Torrances' account of salvation raises questions regarding our human response by the Spirit. According to the Torrances, the whole human race has been united to Christ on account of his vicarious humanity. This incurs the criticism that this negates the subjective actualization of our union by the Spirit.

James Cassidy contests the Torrances' belief that a person could be united to Christ without his own subjective contribution of faith by the Spirit.[34] For Cassidy, a person is united to Christ only when he has made a response of faith by the Spirit.[35] Similarly, Paul Helm believes that justification only occurs when a person has faith: "Men are justified *by faith*. The implication is clear. Until a person believes, he is not justified, even though

---

33. This same suggestion has been made by Deddo and confirmed by T. F. See Deddo, "The Holy Spirit," 103–4; T. F. T., "Thomas Torrance Responds," 312.

34. Cassidy, "T. F. Torrance's Realistic Soteriological Objectivism," 181–82.

35. Ibid., 187.

Christ has rendered satisfaction for sin. A person is not justified before he believes, but *upon* believing."[36] Cassidy contends, "For [T. F.] Torrance, "union *with* Christ" is swallowed up by "union *in* Christ." The *unio mystica* disappears into *unio hypostasia* and the *ordo salutis* is collapsed into the *historia salutis*."[37]

Likewise, Rankin argues that the Torrances' objective understanding of union with Christ does not do justice to our human activity or the activity of the Spirit.[38] In so doing, Rankin foresees the repercussion that Christ becomes "relevant to everybody and meaningful to none."[39] He writes,

> Especially in our day and age, will a doctrine including a constraint of nature, which to many ears might smack of determinism, touch modern women and men isolated and abandoned in our overcrowded cities? Do they not want to hear that God in the flesh is there for them, choosing to love them, volunteering to save them, personally and individually, rather than by a doctrine that involves a contingent necessity of nature? Will that make them feel like merely one of the herd?[40]

However, this critique fails to recognize the significance of the Torrances' objective account of union with Christ. If union with Christ depended upon subjective human appropriation, this would throw us back upon ourselves to achieve salvation, an impossible task. T. F. is acutely aware of this problem, which he perceives in the Westminster Catechisms:

> In the Westminster theology the main focus of attention is upon man's appropriation of salvation through justifying faith . . . Ultimately the main content of these Catechisms is concerned with man's action, man's obedience, man's duty toward God, man's duty to his neighbour, and man's religion, although undoubtedly all that is directed upward in a most astonishing way to the glory of God. But it is *man's* glorification of God that occupies most of the picture.[41]

In addition, this union with Christ is essential in order for humanity to be ontologically transformed and therefore truly saved from the depths of our

---

36. Helm, *Calvin and the Calvinists*, 77–78.
37. Cassidy, "T. F. Torrance's Realistic Soteriological Objectivism," 193.
38. Rankin, "Carnal Union," 286.
39. Ibid., 293.
40. Ibid.
41. T. F. T., "Introduction," *The School of Faith*, xvii–xviii.

corruption. Christ can only really be meaningful if we have been united to him in this ontological and objective way.

From this essential objective basis, the Torrances do distinguish between an ontological relation to Christ and a pneumatological relation to Christ.[42] We are in ontological relation to Christ on account of his incarnation and vicarious humanity. However, an ontological relation alone leads to universalism. J. B. believes that universalism is precluded by the New Testament call for a human response of faith by the Spirit.[43] Thus he writes of the necessity of a pneumatological relation to Christ in order to enjoy our ontological relation to Christ:

> On the grounds of our ontological relation to Christ, our Second Adam, we are called through the Holy Spirit into union with Him. Without Pentecost and without the sealing of the Holy Spirit in faith, we cannot regard ourselves as members of Christ's Body and partakers of His blessings.[44]

There is one union with Christ but two modes of relating to Christ. Our ontological union with Christ is a *fait accompli*; we cannot reverse its reality. However, we can live in ignorance or denial of this or we can live in agreement with it and enjoy its reality. For the Torrances, it is the role of the Spirit to open us up within our subjectivities for Christ so that we live out of ourselves and in him.[45] T. F. believes that humanity's *objective* union with Christ is *subjectively* actualized in us by the Spirit.[46] J. B. writes, "Therefore we have to hold two things together. First, he has *already* taken our humanity into the Holy of Holies, the presence of the Father in his own person. Second, he comes to us *today* by the Holy Spirit to take us with him into the Holiest of All."[47] J. B. follows Calvin in identifying three "moments" of the one work of salvation by God:

> The confession of faith of the believer is to say that our salvation is made actual by the work of the one God, Father, Son and Holy Spirit. It is from beginning to end entirely the work of God's grace, but within that one work there are three great 'moments'—the moment of eternity, the eternal love of the

---

42. Note the language here of "relation" rather than "union." The significance of not distinguishing between different unions is explored in chapter 1.

43. J. B. T., "The Priesthood of Jesus," 172.

44. Ibid.

45. T. F. T., *Reconstruction*, 238.

46. T. F. T., *Mediation*, 77.

47. J. B. T., "Prayer and the Priesthood of Christ," 58.

Father; the moment of history, when Christ died and rose again nineteen hundred years ago to fulfil for us in time God's eternal purpose, so that (in Calvin's phrase) 'all parts of our salvation are complete in Him'; the moment of experience when the Holy Spirit unites us to Christ and brings us to personal faith and repentance.[48]

Therefore, the *unio mystica* is not indistinguishable from the *unio hypostasia* and the *ordo salutis* is not collapsed into the *historia salutis*.[49] Yet there is unity in the distinction because if there is not only one work of salvation, we are thrown back upon our own efforts to achieve it for ourselves. For the Torrances, the believer's activity of faith by the Spirit is imperative, yet it depends upon the prior ontological union made by Christ. As Timothy Dearborn writes:

> Salvation is onto-relational. It is neither solely ontological, as if it were an automatic, impersonal intrinsic encounter with God either through his cosmic presence . . . Nor is it solely relational, as if it were an extrinsic encounter through faith without any ontological change in people in Christ. Both the ontological and the relational dimensions must be affirmed for an adequate understanding of salvation.[50]

Participatory

The Torrances believe that a response of faith by the Spirit is necessary for the subjective actualization of our objective ontological union in Christ. However, in order to show that this is not a burdensome task for humanity, they emphasize that Christ has already made this response of faith by the Spirit vicariously in our place. For some, this appears to diminish our

---

48. J. B. T., "The Incarnation and 'Limited Atonement,'" 83–84.

49. Colin Gunton writes, "Our union with the person of Christ, which Calvin called an *unio mystica*, presupposes the hypostatic union, but does not reduplicate it." Gunton, "Being and Person," 147. "Two possible mistakes need to be avoided here. One is to reduce the *unio hypostatica* downwards to the *unio mystica*. This is the typical mistake of modern liberal theology. The other moves in the opposite direction by dissolving the *union mystica* upwards into the *unio hypostatica*. This is the typical mistake of various high sacramental ecclesiologies. By seeing the *unio hypostatica* as absolutely *sui generis* and the *unio mystica* as pertaining to our union with the person of the incarnate Son by virtue of our participation in his vicarious humanity, Torrance preserves their proper distinction, and so the proper unity-in-distinction (and distinction-in-unity) between Christ and his Church" (159).

50. Dearborn, "God, Grace and Salvation," 290.

own human response by the Spirit and the Torrances have been criticized for not giving this adequate appreciation.[51] As Letham expresses it, "[T. F.] Torrance has an uncompromisingly objective doctrine of justification. However, its decisive finality in the person of Christ for each and every person would appear to render faith superfluous."[52]

Thomas Smail argues for a greater appreciation of our own human response by the Spirit to Christ's response for us. In so doing, Smail is keen to avoid semi-Pelagianism, and does not wish to suggest that we are co-authors of our salvation. He writes, "We have to believe *for* ourselves, but we cannot believe *by* ourselves. The freedom to believe is the work and gift of the Spirit in his incorporating others into what Christ has done."[53] With much modern Christianity overemphasizing our human response, Smail commends T. F. for showing that our response is wholly dependent upon Christ's prior response on our behalf.[54] However, Smail wishes to emphasize that the Spirit enables us to make our own response to Christ.[55]

Smail is critical of T. F. for diminishing the role of the Holy Spirit and the effect that this diminishment has on the value of our human response.[56] He argues that, whilst the Spirit is the Spirit of Christ who effects in humanity what is achieved in Christ, the Spirit also has his own personal action apart from Christ, calling forth one's own personal response to Christ. Christ receives the Spirit from the Father and responds to the Father in the Spirit; we too receive the Spirit from Jesus and respond in the Spirit to the Father through Jesus. Smail asserts that, for the human response to be authentic, it must be our own. Peter's confession of Christ depends upon Jesus's prior response to God, yet it is nevertheless true that Peter makes the confession himself (Matt 16:13–20). Therefore Smail argues that Christ's response alone is not enough; we must respond for ourselves through the Spirit. Simi-

---

51. Moltmann has made this criticism more generally of the Reformed tradition. He proposes that the personal decision of faith is a crucial pneumatological counterpart to Reformation Christocentricism. He argues that the Reformation doctrine of justification lacks an adequate account of humanity's role through the Holy Spirit. Its Christological focus limits the work of the Holy Spirit to merely conveying the knowledge of salvation. Wishing to uphold the necessity of freedom in the Spirit, Moltmann proposes a greater stress on the human response of faith. Moltmann, *The Spirit of Life*, 149–50, 116.

52. Letham, "The Triune God, Incarnation, and Definite Atonement," Kindle ed., Loc 11370.

53. Smail, "Third Person Singular—The Trinitarian Spirit."

54. Smail, *Giving Gift*, 109–11.

55. Ibid., 174.

56. Ibid.

larly, Allen contends, "The mediator does exercise faith on our behalf, but this does not absolve the believer of the responsibility to believe."[57] Smail argues that the failure of T. F. to differentiate between Christ's response and our own response is a consequence of a further failure to differentiate the work of Christ and the Spirit. He believes that T. F. emphasizes what Christ does objectively *for* us at the expense of what the Spirit does *in* us so that we are able to subjectively appropriate our salvation.[58]

This criticism by Smail and Allen appears to be founded on a logico-causal misunderstanding of T. F.'s profoundly participatory scheme of salvation. Christian D. Kettler defends T. F. from Smail's criticism, suggesting that Smail mistakenly understands the human response according to the Newtonian principle of cause and effect. Smail conceives of our response by the Spirit as the result of Christ's response. Yet for T. F., our response by the Spirit is not simply the result but a very participation in Christ's response for us. Christ and the Spirit cannot be so easily separated. The Spirit enables us to participate *in* Christ's response. Kettler considers that Christ's radical substitution is difficult to accept because it is thought to deprive us of freedom. However, he argues that the objectivity of Christ and the Spirit does not displace our humanity, but rather truly establishes it.[59] As T. F. asserts, "Far from crushing our creaturely nature or damaging our personal existence, the indwelling presence of God through Jesus Christ and in the Holy Spirit has the effect of healing and restoring and deepening human personal being."[60]

Although Smail wishes to avoid semi-Pelagianism, there is an inherent danger in stressing our own autonomous human response in logico-causal terms. This can lead to the belief that our human response has salvific efficacy, which makes people dependent upon their own endeavors. The Torrances' emphasis on Christ's all-sufficient response in which we participate by the Spirit excludes any subtly synergistic notion of co-redemption.

Whilst a greater appreciation of the Spirit is often championed by those who wish to see more of an emphasis on our human response, the Spirit does not enable us to make our own autonomous response to Christ, but to participate in Christ's response for us.[61] Frank Macchia promotes an emphasis on the Spirit *over against* an emphasis on our human response

---

57. Allen, *Justification and the Gospel*, 108.

58. Smail, *Giving Gift*, 108–12.

59. Kettler, *The Vicarious Humanity of Christ and the Reality of Salvation*, 139–41. See also Molnar, *Thomas F. Torrance*, 336.

60. T. F. T., *Trinitarian Faith*, 230.

61. See, for example, Moltmann, *The Spirit of Life*, 149–50, 116.

of faith.[62] Like the Torrances, he conceives of our human response in participatory terms.[63] Macchia argues that "pneumatology has the potential to help us see how justification can be both theocentric and open to creaturely participation."[64] Thus a greater appreciation of the Spirit's role actually counteracts an autonomous, anthropological emphasis.

The sacraments

The Torrances understand our human response by the Spirit as a participation in Christ's perfect response on our behalf, rather than as an autonomous, logico-causal act. Yet this concept of participating in Christ's response has also been questioned, for it challenges our human rationality.[65] Rankin has expressed dissatisfaction with Kettler's response to Smail, arguing that it does not get to the root of the problem of how our human response relates to Christ's response. Rankin argues that T. F. "fails to articulate a proper relation between the response of human beings and Christ's vicarious response for them."[66] Kye Won Lee reflects,

> There seemingly remains something like an enigma, even if it is not [T. F.'s] genuine intention, in regard to the relation between the objective realities which God has once and for all accomplished for all of humanity in Jesus Christ and our subjective response to or acceptance of them.[67]

It is true that there is "something like an enigma" regarding how our human response is a participation in Christ's vicarious response. Yet the Torrances would not find this troubling because it is a consequence of their seeking to be faithful to God's self-revelation in Christ. For the Torrances, God's self-giving takes priority over human rational thought. Furthermore, whilst T. F. does not explain this enigma, he does write very practically about how we participate in Christ's vicarious response. The sacraments of

---

62. Macchia, *Justified in the Spirit*, 98–99.
63. Ibid., 230.
64. Ibid., 217.
65. For David Brondos, the notion of participating in Christ is absurd. It is logically impossible to participate in a human being who existed in a different time and place. In fact, it is an impossible notion to participate in a human being at all. Brondos rather presents Christ as an ethical example to follow and believes that salvation involves "an *ethical decision and commitment* on the part of believers." Brondos, *Paul on the Cross*, 155–66, 179.
66. Rankin, "Carnal Union," 286.
67. Lee, *Living in Union with Christ*, 313.

baptism and the Eucharist are tangible expressions of our participation in Christ. Of the Eucharist, T. F. writes:

> This union of Jesus Christ with us in body and blood by virtue of which he became our Priest and Mediator before God demands as its complement our union with him in his body and blood, in drawing near to God and offering him our worship with, in and through Christ, while his continuous living presentation of us before the Father on the ground of his one perfect all-sufficient sacrifice calls for our continuous living communion with him as the Son. It is in this union and communion with Christ the incarnate Son who represents God to us and us to God that the real import of the Lord's Supper becomes disclosed, for in eating his body and drinking his blood we are given to participate in his vicarious self-offering to the Father.[68]

The sacraments of baptism and the Eucharist point to the objective reality of salvation by God's grace alone.[69] Baptism is indicative of Christ's once-for-all finished work of death and resurrection, whilst the Eucharist is indicative of our continuing participation in Christ.[70] Both rule out any notion of human co-operation in salvation. George Hunsinger writes,

> No secondary form can do anything more than manifest, attest, mediate, and participate in the one central form, precisely because Christ's finished work of salvation, being once for all, perfect, and all-sufficient, allows for no supplementation, repetition or increase. In its perfection, however, the finished work of Christ (*opus perfectus*) does allow for secondary forms of self-manifestation, self-attestation, and self-mediation (i.e., Word and Sacrament) which participate in the central form without becoming confused with or changed into it (*operatione perpetuus*).[71]

Thus the sacraments bring to expression our participation in Christ's all-sufficient response.

---

68. T. F. T., *Reconciliation*, 111.
69. J. B. T., *Worship*, 65.
70. T. F. T., *Mediation*, 100–101.
71. Hunsinger, "The Dimension of Depth," 155.

Conclusion

The radical objectivity and Christocentricity of the Torrances' account of salvation attracts the criticism that it diminishes the role of the Spirit and our human response. If the whole human race has been united to Christ on account of his vicarious humanity, this raises the question of whether subjective actualization by the Spirit is negated. However, the Torrances have an onto-relational understanding of salvation. They strongly believe that the believer's activity of faith by the Spirit is imperative, yet they perceive that it depends upon the prior ontological union made by Christ. For the Torrances, this radically objective union is the basis of our ontological transformation and is essential in order to avoid being turned back upon ourselves to achieve salvation.

If Christ has offered the perfect response of faith by the Spirit in our place, this raises the question of whether our own human response by the Spirit is diminished. However, whilst a greater appreciation of the Spirit is often championed by those who wish to see more of an emphasis on our human response, the Spirit does not enable us to make our own autonomous response to Christ, but to participate in Christ's response for us. The difficulty with an autonomous logico-causal response is that this also throws people back upon themselves to earn salvation. The Torrances understand our human response by the Spirit as a *participation* in Christ's response, rather than as an autonomous, logico-causal act. This participatory scheme, rather than diminishing our humanity, truly establishes it.

The notion of our human response as a participation by the Spirit in Christ's response may appear to be somewhat of an enigma. Yet it is essential to the liberation of humanity from attempting to earn salvation, so that we can freely share by the Spirit in Christ's relationship with the Father. Whilst it may not be comprehensible, it comes to tangible expression in the sacraments of baptism and the Eucharist, whereby we participate in Christ's once-for-all (baptism) and continuing (Eucharist) vicarious response.

Works and Final Judgment

Final judgment

The Torrances' objective, Christocentric view of salvation raises the question of whether this diminishes the significance of our human works by the Spirit for the last judgment. In the Torrances' scheme of salvation, full judgment has already taken place in Christ. In his perfect obedience, Jesus submits to God's judgment against sin.[72] The hypostatic union in Christ means that he is both "God the judge judging sin" and "man the judged submitting perfectly to God's holy judgement."[73] T. F. describes this judgment in absolute terms:

> It was the full realisation of the holy will of God in our human nature, the full meting out of the divine condemnation against sin, the full outpouring of the divine love into and upon human nature. But in Christ Jesus all that was also gladly suffered and endured for our sakes, so that in him there was achieved in judgement, in complete and final justification, a judgement, a union between God and humanity which death and hell itself could not break or in any way surrender. Nothing could isolate Jesus as man from God, not even the final judgement of God, for Jesus as man was God himself come as man.[74]

This is a very real and total judgment, which exposes humanity's guilt, yet it involves a profoundly "positive act of acceptance" in that God chooses to be on humanity's side in Christ and reconcile us to Himself.[75] T. F. writes, "That if you like is the paradox of the cross: that the divine assumption of our judgment is our most complete judgment, and yet it is in no sense a rejection of humanity, but its very reverse, an entire acceptance of man for Christ's sake, in the blood of Christ."[76]

The Torrances believe that this acceptance of humanity is irrevocable: "To reverse it would be to bring Christ back to the cross again, and to deny the reality of what he has already done."[77] Since God has taken the rejection upon himself in Christ, now "there is no positive act of rejection or judgement extended toward any human being, but only the act of acceptance."[78] This means that those who are in hell are there of their own volition. God has accepted them but, inconceivably, they have refused to acknowledge his acceptance.[79] Since all of humanity is unconditionally accepted by God, according to the Torrances' scheme, this raises the question of whether this diminishes the significance of our works by the Spirit.

---

72. T. F. T., *Atonement*, 123; J. B. T., "The Priesthood of Jesus," 172.
73. Ibid., 124.
74. Ibid., 125.
75. Ibid., 155–56.
76. Ibid., 156.
77. Ibid., 157–58.
78. Ibid., 156–57; See also J. B. T., "The Priesthood of Jesus," 170.
79. T. F. T., *Atonement*, 157.

Works

Paul writes to the Corinthians, "For all of us must appear before the judgement seat of Christ, so that each may receive recompense for what has been done in the body, whether good or evil" (2 Cor 5:10). Paul writes to the Romans that "[God] will repay according to each one's deeds" (Rom 2:6) and to the Galatians that "you reap whatever you sow" (Gal 6:7). In recent years proponents of the New Perspective on Paul have stimulated debate by arguing that our works by the Spirit are a necessary condition for final justification.[80]

Wright argues that there has been a neglect of Paul's teaching on a final judgment according to works (Rom 2:6, 13; 8:1, 13; 14:10–12; 1 Cor 6:9; 2 Cor 5:10; Gal 3:4f.; 5:19–21).[81] Wright, who believes that the notion of Jesus fulfilling the law for us is essentially works-righteousness, contends that we ourselves must fulfill the demands of the law by the Spirit.[82] Humanity has an active and essential role to play in faith and works, inspired by the Spirit (Phil 2:12, 3:12, 4:13; Col 1:29).[83]

Wright also perceives a neglect of the Holy Spirit in the Reformed doctrine of justification. He argues that, if the role of the Spirit is overlooked, the burden falls upon human striving for assurance.[84] Wright insists that we cannot add our own works to the finished work of Christ.[85] He writes, "Please note: this is not the logic of merit. It is the logic of love . . . Within the logic of love is the rich, theological logic of the work of the holy spirit."[86] In

---

80. For a taxonomy of the numerous different perspectives on the relationship between our works and final judgment, see Ortlund, "Justified by Faith, Judged According to Works," 323–39.

81. Wright, *Justification*, 159–61.

82. Ibid., 208. For a refutation of Wright's belief that Jesus's fulfillment of the law is works-righteousness, see chapter 2.

83. Ibid., 129–30, 33. Paul Rainbow argues that works are not simply the outworking of initial justification, as held by the Reformers, but an instrumental ground for final justification. He draws upon E. P. Sanders's argument that, for Paul, obedience to the law is a condition for staying in the covenant. For Rainbow, we must fulfill the "dual condition" of faith and obedience: "Christian obedience may be called a subcondition for the culminating moment of justification. It is a second condition in its own right besides faith, because God requires holiness just as surely as he requires faith for our salvation, and will use good works at the judgment as the index of faith's authenticity." Rainbow, *The Way of Salvation*, xvii–xx, 206, 264.

84. Wright, *Justification*, 210.

85. Ibid., 165.

86. Ibid., 163.

Wright's scheme, the Spirit is at work through a person, who paradoxically at the same time acts in freedom (1 Cor 15:10).[87]

Although Wright wishes to avoid a merit-based salvation, stressing our empowerment by the Spirit, there is nevertheless the danger of throwing people back upon their own efforts by the idea that our works are a condition for final justification.[88] If we await a final justification dependent upon our works, this runs the risk of breeding a lack of assurance because there is an element of uncertainty regarding our salvation. People then turn away from Christ and in upon themselves to examine whether they are bearing enough fruit to be accepted by God.

Bird perceives the essential problem of this perspective to be that "it shifts the material cause of eschatological justification from Christology to pneumatology."[89] Bird contends that salvation must be understood in Christocentric terms; the works of obedience that God requires were accomplished by Christ's faithfulness and the final judgment was accomplished in his death. This means that justification is not a two-stage event where the final end can be in doubt. All those who place their faith in Christ have assurance of salvation because "the verdict awaited at the final judgment has been declared in advance."[90]

This is the merit of the Torrances' objective, Christocentric scheme of salvation: assurance of salvation and freedom from having to earn it ourselves. T. F. asserts, "In God there is no Yes and No, but only Yes. It is upon the Yes of God's eternal love for us that our salvation rests."[91] He points out that the New Testament word *"parousia"* is singular, indicating the continuity between Christ's first and second coming.[92] Since our judgment is

---

87. Ibid., 167–68. For similar views to Wright see Dunn, *The Theology of Paul the Apostle*, 365–66, 636–37; and Watson, *Paul, Judaism, and the Gentiles*, 209–16.

88. Guy Prentiss Waters argues that Wright's perspective is essentially Semi-Pelagianism because justification is based upon our performance, which leads to a lack of assurance and a denial of grace. Waters, *Justification and the New Perspectives on Paul*, 171, 174; Bird criticizes a similar viewpoint in E. P. Sanders, arguing that the notion of getting in the covenant by grace but staying in by works is merit-theology. Bird, *Saving Righteousness of God*, 91, 95.

89. Bird, *Saving Righteousness of God*, 173.

90. Ibid., 174–75.

91. T. F. T., *Christian Doctrine*, 246. A difficulty that T. F. perceives with Federal theology's doctrine of limited atonement is that it separates the cross from final judgment, and Christ from the Father, leading to the belief that there is still an unknown judgment to be poured out at the *eschaton*. T. F. T., *Atonement*, 185.

92. T. F. T., *Space, Time and Resurrection*, 144.

complete in Christ and we are fully accepted by God, the last judgment is an unveiling of this permanently positive verdict:

> He will come again in the fullness of his humanity and deity to judge and renew his creation, but that will not be another work in addition to his finished work on the Cross or in the resurrection, so much as the gathering together of what the cross and resurrection have already worked throughout the whole of creation and the unveiling of it for all to see, and therefore an unfolding and actualization of it from our point of view.[93]

Indicative and imperative

If our works by the Spirit are not a necessary condition for final justification, because the last judgment is an unveiling of God's unconditionally positive verdict, the question remains as to the place of our works by the Spirit. For the Torrances, our works by the Spirit are a *response* to God's grace, rather than a means to earn it. J. B. often asserts that "the indicatives of grace are always prior to the obligations of law and human obedience."[94] This is made clear in God's giving of the Ten Commandments, which are preceded by a statement of his covenantal faithfulness and grace: "I am the Lord your God, who brought you out of Egypt, out of the land of slavery" (Ex 20:2). J. B. considers that it is on this basis that the law is given; "*therefore* keep my commandments."[95] Our works by the Spirit are in joyful, obedient response to God's unconditional grace.[96]

Moreover, for the Torrances, this response by the Spirit to God's unconditional grace cannot be understood in abstraction from Jesus's vicarious response on our behalf. Our response by the Spirit is a participation in Christ's perfect obedience.[97] Our works by the Spirit cannot be understood according to logico-causal categories whereby our works earn a final justification.[98] In the Torrances' scheme of salvation, our works by the Spirit

---

93. Ibid., 152.
94. J. B. T., "Covenant Concept," 230.
95. Ibid.
96. J. B. T., "Introduction," 14.
97. Ibid.
98. Ortlund writes, "Justification and judgment are linked not so much in cause-and-effect or linear progression as they are organically unified . . . Justification and obedience both sprout from the seed of union with Christ . . . Those who are justified will, for reasons other than any kind of earning, do the law." Ortlund, "Justified by Faith," 338. Bird writes, "Justification is not the result of the empowerment of the Spirit

are the fruit of participating in Christ. Rather than being turned in upon ourselves, worrying about whether we are bearing enough fruit for final justification, J. B. encourages the believer to fix his eyes upon Jesus. Christ has lived a life of perfect obedience in our place, taking full judgment upon himself and securing our acceptance, so that as we participate in him in freedom and joy, we might bear the fruit of the Spirit. J. B. writes, "As we look to him in faith, we know that the righteous requirements (*dikaiomata*) of the law and the ordinances of worship have not only been fulfilled for us by Christ, but are fulfilled in us as we live in the Spirit (Rom. 8:1–4)."[99]

Conclusion

A greater appreciation of the Holy Spirit is perceived to be the answer not only by those who have wished to see a greater emphasis on our human response of faith, but also by those who wish to see a greater emphasis on our human works. For proponents of the New Perspective on Paul, the Holy Spirit has an essential role in inspiring us to good works in order to be justified at the final judgment. Yet the difficulty with a final justification dependent upon our works, regardless of empowerment by the Spirit, is that it posits a last judgment that is uncertain and thus turns us inwards upon ourselves to examine our works for assurance of salvation. Essentially, it disregards the total judgment already made in Christ.

According to the Torrances' scheme of salvation, Christ lived a vicarious life of perfect obedience by the Spirit, submitting to God's judgment upon sin, which means that an unconditionally positive verdict has been made upon humanity. The last judgment will be a full unveiling of this irrevocable decision. This gives us assurance of salvation and freedom from having to earn it ourselves. Although the Torrances do diminish works by the Spirit understood according to merit-based, logico-causal categories, they uphold our works by the Spirit in their proper place: the fruit of participating in Christ's communion with the Father which he has objectively established for us.

---

in the life of the believer . . . Ultimately, obedience and faithfulness are functions of believing in Christ and flow from the work of Christ operating in the believer through the Spirit." Bird, *Saving Righteousness of God*, 183.

99. J. B. T., *Worship*, 109; See also "Prayer and the Priesthood of Christ," 61.

Knowledge and Experience

Spirit of truth

The Torrances' objective, Christocentric view of salvation raises questions as to the significance for humanity of knowledge of God, relationship with God and experience of God. Since our salvation is a finished work in Christ, our knowledge of this objective reality has an essential place in the Torrances' scheme of salvation. T. F. describes humanity's reception of salvation in terms of a "realization" that it has already been accomplished for us in Christ:

> Our adoption, sanctification and regeneration have already taken place in Christ, and are fully enclosed in his birth, holy life, death and resurrection undertaken for our sakes, and proceed from them more by way of realisation or actualisation in us of what has already happened to us in him than as new effect resulting from them.[100]

Knowledge of God does hold an essential place in the biblical witness. Paul often prays that the early Christians would come to a deeper knowledge of God's truth (Eph 1:18–20; 3:14–19; Phil 1:9–10; Col 1:9–10). Paul urges the Romans to "be transformed by the renewing of your minds" (Rom 12:2). The Greek word for "repentance," *metanoia*, which has come to be understood in terms of acts of confession and penance, is better translated as "a change of mind."[101] This indicates the significance of what we believe for the actualization of salvation in us.

However, the importance of knowledge of God in the Torrances' soteriology raises the questions as to whether this makes salvation dependent upon intellectual capacity or correct theological knowledge. These questions are significant because this would suggest that some are unfairly excluded from salvation on these grounds.[102] However, the Torrances are not susceptible to this problem because they affirm that our "realization" is not dependent upon our own intellectual capacity or knowledge of the

---

100. T. F. T., *Reconciliation*, 89. Whilst this perspective is profoundly liberating because it reflects that there is nothing that humanity can contribute to salvation, it is cause for criticism by Horton: "the necessity of faith for receiving this justification is denied. Faith simply acknowledges the status that pertains objectively to every person." Horton, *Pilgrim Theology*, Kindle ed., Loc 5790.

101. T. F. T., *Atonement*, 3.

102. This is a further difficulty with the notion of "salvation by existential decision" which is discussed in chapter 2. See also Campbell, *Deliverance of God*.

truth, but upon the revelation of the Holy Spirit.[103] The Holy Spirit is "the Spirit of truth" (John 14:7; 16:13), who reveals the reality of our salvation in Christ.[104] T. F. writes,

> The mission of the Spirit sent from the Father in the name of the Son as the Spirit of truth is to convict people of the truth as it is in Jesus, in judgement and mercy, to enlighten, inform and strengthen the Church through serving the centrality of Christ and deepening its understanding of his teaching and person as the incarnate Son of the Father, the one Lord and Saviour of humanity.[105]

For the Torrances, our reception of the objective reality of salvation is also a thoroughly objective event because it is a work of the Holy Spirit.

Spirit of adoption

If we receive salvation by realizing that we have already been redeemed, this raises the question of whether the Torrances reduce salvation to a noetic concept. As Kye Won Lee considers, "What is at stake, for [T. F.] Torrance, is the reduction of the soteriological fact or reality into the realm of our cognition, even though he argues for pneumatological epistemology in which this cognition is given as the gift by the Holy Spirit."[106] Bevan considers what this means for human faith, which may be understood "too narrowly as

---

103. The Torrances' objective scheme of salvation is radically inclusive because all of humanity is unconditionally included in God's filial purposes. See Molnar, *Thomas F. Torrance*, 336. As T. F. wrote, "Those outside the Church are to be regarded in the sphere where this reconciliation has not yet been subjectively actualized but is nevertheless objectively accomplished for them in Jesus Christ." T. F. T., "Introduction," *The School of Faith*, cxvii. A Federal view whereby God is related to only some of humanity as Father runs a high risk of not extending grace to those who do not share the same theology (on account of the belief that God himself may not have intended them for salvation). Nevertheless, there is still the danger, despite holding the Torrances' theology of inclusive grace, of having an ungracious attitude towards others who have not yet benefited from this revelation. Although a person's legalistic or contractual thinking may be wrong, it is appropriate for the one who has come to a better understanding of God to demonstrate grace and patience. A lack of grace perhaps can arise from having a knowledge of grace without a more intimate relationship with the giver of Grace. The Spirit is not only the Spirit of truth but also the Spirit of adoption.

104. J. B. T., *Worship*, 75; T. F. T., *God and Rationality*, 167.

105. T. F. T., "The Christ Who Loves Us," 19.

106. Lee, *Living in Union with Christ*, 315.

Drawn to Participate by the Holy Spirit 107

an intellectual act."[107] Habets has also perceived that T. F. is subject to the criticism that epistemology essentially defines what it means to be saved.[108]

The theology of the Torrances does not reduce salvation to a noetic concept. The anhypostatic movement of the Spirit revealing the truth of God to humanity is accompanied by the enhypostatic movement of the Spirit raising humanity up to participate in God's triune life. As J. B. writes, "There is a God-humanward movement of the Spirit, in creating, in revealing . . . But there is also a human-Godward ministry of the Spirit of leading us to the Father through Christ . . . lifting us up into communion with God, into the very life of the Triune God."[109] The Spirit, J. B. argues, must not be conceived of as a mere impersonal, instrumental cause; the Spirit is the bond of union between the Father and the Spirit who draws humanity up to share in their communion.[110]

The Holy Spirit is not only the Spirit of truth but "the Spirit of adoption" (Rom 8:15). By the Spirit, humanity is enabled to cry "Abba, Father," sharing in Jesus's relationship with the Father.[111] Habets argues, "For [T. F.] Torrance, "knowing" is a participatory knowledge in which one indwells the subject, hence for Torrance "knowing" moves well beyond the merely noetic."[112] Trevor Hart writes of this as a "personal knowing," the difference between "knowing" God or just "knowing about" God.[113] Thus salvation is not reduced to a noetic concept; the Torrances' articulation of the enhypostatic movement whereby humanity is drawn by the Spirit into God's triune life is profoundly personal and relational.

Nevertheless, it does seem that whilst the Torrances were of one mind theologically, they had different emphases personally and practically. Whilst they both affirmed that the Spirit brings humanity knowledge of God and draws us up to participate in God's triune life, there can be seen in T. F. an emphasis on the noetic aspect of salvation, whilst in J. B. an emphasis on the relational aspect.

T. F. spent much of his time reading and writing in his study and he published prolifically. Appreciative testimonies of T. F. point to his noetic

---

107. Bevan, "The Person of Christ," 212.

108. Habets, "There is no God behind the back of Jesus Christ," 190.

109. J. B. T., "Christ in our Place," 51.

110. J. B. T., "Strengths and Weaknesses of the Westminster Theology," 53.

111. T. F. T., *Christian Doctrine*, 154; *Trinitarian Faith*, 231.

112. Habets, "There is no God behind the back of Jesus Christ," 190; See also Habets, "The Doctrine of Election," 348.

113. Trevor Hart, "Atonement, the Incarnation, and Deification: Transformation and Convergence in the Soteriology of T. F. Torrance," 83.

concern for the truth of the gospel as expressed in preaching and teaching. His brother, David W. Torrance, considers that T. F. described himself primarily as "a preacher of the gospel" and reflects, "He was passionately concerned that ministers should understand the Word of God and be faithful in proclaiming and teaching it."[114] Habets writes, "Perhaps the greatest accolade one might pay [T. F.] Torrance, and one that he himself would certainly welcome, is that he was at heart a Christian, a figure who was utterly persuaded by the truth of the gospel and who sought to persuade others of that same truth."[115]

J. B. published comparatively little but devoted much of his time to his students. His former student, Heron, reflects that he was an academic teacher who engaged both his mind and his heart, "a man of faith whose goal and interest was above all the nurturing and guiding of others in the way of that same faith."[116] The thrust of J. B.'s academic work was to correct an impersonal, contractual view of God, showing that he is a covenantal God with primarily filial purposes for humanity. J. B. often wrote of how humanity in Christ is "drawn by the Spirit into communion with the Father."[117] He was concerned to affirm this enhypostatic movement which he perceived to have been so neglected in his church tradition:

> We need a recovery of the doctrine of the Priestly ministry of the Spirit. Christ as the One Mediator alone represents God to man and man to God. The Spirit as the Spirit of Christ is *speaking Spirit* and *interceding Spirit* (Romans ch. 8). As speaking Spirit He mediates God's Word to men . . . As interceding Spirit, He lifts us up into heavenly places in Christ. He puts the prayer of Jesus into our lips—'Abba, Father' . . . Perhaps in Presbyterianism we have emphasised speaking Spirit at the expense of the interceding Spirit.[118]

Spirit of communion

If salvation is an objective reality in Christ that we can realize and share in by the Spirit of truth and adoption, this leads to questions regarding our

114. D. W. T., "Interview," 25.
115. Habets, "T. F. Torrance," 91.
116. Heron, "James Torrance: An Appreciation," 2.
117. J. B. T., *Worship*, 55.
118. J. B. T., "Covenant or Contract?," 75–76. J. B. is writing here specifically about worship but it has wider implications. The Presbyterian emphasis on "speaking Spirit" perhaps explains T. F.'s noetic accent.

personal experience of this union and communion. The Torrances' account of being drawn by the Spirit into the triune life is personal and relational, which suggests that intimate experience of God follows as a direct consequence. The Torrances write of the joy and peace produced by this communion but experience of God is not discussed much further than that.[119]

Habets considers, "It can be argued that [T. F.] Torrance tends to undermine his commitment to a theology of union and communion between God and humanity, emphasizing cognitive union to the relative neglect of mystical and spiritual union."[120] T. F. is critical of mysticism, which he understands in the sense of "intuitive knowledge" or "non-logical knowing that arises under the constraint of reality upon the mind."[121] However, Habets argues that T. F.'s criticism of mysticism is based upon an unfair assessment of mysticism as a whole. Habets proposes that T. F.'s theology is actually harmonious with the essential nature of mysticism, which concerns the experience of intimacy with God.[122] Furthermore, whilst the essence of mysticism is experiential, it depends upon knowledge. Mysticism and theology are bound up with one another, as can be seen in the example of Athanasius. Considering that Athanasius is a seminal figure for T. F., Habets finds T. F.'s complete denunciation of mysticism surprising.[123] Habets argues,

> By rejecting mysticism *tout court*, Torrance's articulation of the Christian life, theology, and spirituality is weakened if not obfuscated. It is apparent that Torrance has adopted an inaccurate definition of mysticism, which leads him to an *a priori* exclusion of mystical elements within his own theology at precisely the points at which it should be evident.[124]

The Torrances' theology would be complemented by attention to the mystical and experiential aspects of the Christian life, as seen in the Eastern

---

119. T. F. T., *Incarnation*, 115; J. B. T., *Worship*, 9–10.

120. Habets, "T. F. Torrance," 102. According to Heiko Oberman, mysticism has been misunderstood by Protestants. Heiko Oberman, *The Reformation*, 80. Julie Canlis observes that Calvin's background of the medieval and mystical theological tradition is more recently being appreciated. She argues that Calvin's mysticism is rooted in Christ and his ascent, which defies notions of spiritual stages. Canlis, *Calvin's Ladder*, 46–48.

121. Ibid., 101. For T. F.'s criticism of mysticism, see T. F. T., "Thomas Torrance Responds," 324, 28–29.

122. Ibid., 101–2.

123. Ibid., 102. T. F.'s suspicion of mysticism may perhaps be influenced by his esteem for H. R. Mackintosh. See Mackintosh, *Divine Initiative*, 110–11.

124. Ibid.

Orthodox Church and the Pentecostal-Charismatic movement.[125] Edmund Rybarczyk considers that these traditions "Both emphasize that the human person was created for a transforming fellowship with God."[126] Although in form these two traditions are extremely different, both embrace intimate experience of God and *charismata*, in contrast to the established beliefs of the Torrances' own Reformed tradition.[127]

The personal, intimate encounters with God that are experienced by the Pentecostal-Charismatic movement could be seen to be the direct consequence of being drawn by the Spirit into God's triune life.[128] J. B. was less reserved about the Pentecostal-Charismatic movement than T. F., although J. B. never wrote about it whereas T. F. was openly critical.[129] Their younger brother, David W. Torrance, is of one mind with them theologically yet finds it consistent to be an active proponent of the Pentecostal-Charismatic movement. Smail is another example, affirming both the Torrances' theology and the experiences of the Pentecostal-Charismatic movement. Whilst Smail's Barthian and Torrancean schooling had made him suspicious of mystical experience, he was personally impacted by new experiences of God at the dawn of the Pentecostal-Charismatic movement in Britain.[130] Smail came to believe that his experience of God complemented his theological belief: "What the Holy Spirit was doing was to take what I had always affirmed of Jesus and make some of it actually happen in me, so that at least to some degree my experience of God began to reflect his, the way a mirror reflects the object at which it is directed."[131] Smail came to believe that an intellectual

---

125. One of T. F.'s great achievements is the theological dialogue he initiated between Reformed and Orthodox churches. See T. F. T., *Theological Dialogue: Volume 1*; *Theological Dialogue: Volume 2*.

126. Rybarczyk, *Beyond Salvation*, 350. This has been hindered by Western external, legal concepts of atonement that fail to offer a true transformation of humanity. Rybarczyk also observes, "Curious by evangelical Christian standards, neither the Orthodox nor the Pentecostals have *traditionally* been concerned about rebutting any attacks on their respective experiential characters." Rybarczyk has suggested that the Pentecostal movement has not needed to intellectualize its faith because people are impacted at the deepest existential levels. Rybarczyk, *Beyond Salvation*, 257.

127. Robeck, "Foreword," xii–xvii.

128. Jim Purves argues that T. F. fails to see merit in the Pentecostal-Charismatic movement because his pneumatology is controlled and subsumed by Christology. Purves, *The Triune God and the Charismatic Movement*, 203.

129. D. W. T., "Interview," 25.

130. Smail, "A Renewal Recalled," 8–16.

131. Ibid., 15. See also Nettles: "Revival is the application of reformation truth to human experience." Nettles, "A Better Way—Reformation and Revival," 29.

faith without intimate experience of God is insufficient.[132] Thus attention to the mystical and experiential aspects of the Christian life arguably would complement the Torrances' theology.

Conclusion

Knowledge of God holds an essential place in the Torrances' scheme of salvation. Since salvation is a finished accomplishment in Christ, all that remains for humanity to enjoy it is to realize this objective reality. The Holy Spirit is "the Spirit of truth" who reveals the reality of our salvation in Christ. This objective activity by the Spirit precludes any suggestion that salvation is dependent upon our own intellectual capacity or correct theological knowledge.

T. F. does place an emphasis on the noetic aspect of salvation, yet salvation is not reduced to epistemology in the theology of the Torrances. The anhypostatic movement of the Spirit revealing the truth of God to humanity is accompanied by the enhypostatic movement of the Spirit raising humanity up to participate in God's triune life. The Holy Spirit is "the Spirit of adoption," by whom we participate in Jesus's relationship with the Father.

This personal, relational, and participatory scheme of salvation indicates a God whom humanity can not only know but experience intimately. The Torrances refer to the fruits of the Spirit such as joy and peace but experience of God is not discussed much further. Their account of being drawn

132. Smail writes, "But a truth that is only intellectual and objective . . . does not have the power and the means to effect that which it longs for . . . A gospel that remains in the realm of intellectual orthodoxy . . . cannot but fail to grasp the dynamism of the Spirit to come and by his mighty acts realise the kingdom again among us." Smail, *Reflected Glory*, 101–2. "The theological enterprise that mattered so much to me, and still does, is secondary to that, because how can you know what to say about God if you do not know the God of whom you are speaking? And how can you serve him and his kingdom if you are not in touch with the king you claim to be serving and lack the spiritual energy to fulfil his purposes, once you have discovered them?" Smail, "A Renewal Recalled," 15. See also Pinnock, who perceives merit in the Pentecostal-Charismatic movement for its expectancy that salvation is relational and affective, bringing humanity into intimate relationship with God. Pinnock, *Flame of Love*, 149, 171. Pinnock argues that personal experience of God is a necessary corollary to knowledge of God: "We must know God experientially, not just cognitively. We need to be empowered for mission, freed from fear, able to speak, full of praises. We need a breakthrough in the realm of the Spirit, an awakening to the presence and power of God. There may need to be a release of the Spirit, a flowering of grace in experience, an openness to the full range of the gifts" (170). In fact, the vulnerability inherent in Pentecostal-Charismatic experience may even be an antidote to the danger of intellectual snobbery.

by the Spirit into God's triune life would be complemented by attention to the mystical and experiential aspects of the Christian life, as seen in the Eastern Orthodox Church and the Pentecostal-Charismatic movement.

Theosis

In the Spirit, through the Son, to the Father

In the Torrances' personal, relational, and participatory scheme of salvation, the descent of the Spirit is in order to lift humanity up to God. T. F. argues that both sides of the patristic formulation of the movement of the Spirit must be upheld: "*From the Father, through the Son, in the Spirit* and *in the Spirit, through the Son, to the Father.*"[133] The Spirit draws us up as adopted sons of God to participate in Christ's relationship with the Father.[134]

From this basis, T. F. is critical of the Pentecostal-Charismatic movement for a preoccupation with experiences of the Spirit at the expense of the Spirit's enhypostatic movement that leads us to relationship with the Father through the Son:

> The Holy Spirit is sent to us in the name of the Son not in order to concentrate our attention upon our own experiences, either inwardly or outwardly, but to lift up our vision and enable it to embrace a transcendent reality that extends infinitely above and beyond us . . . A deeper recognition of this all-important movement of the Spirit through the Son to the Father could do much for the Pentecostalists, for it would help them to direct the focus of their attention away from the phenomena that so often fascinate and absorb them to the mystery of God himself.[135]

This same criticism is made by Smail, whilst also upholding the importance of Charismatic experience. Smail strongly supports the necessity

---

133. T. F. T., *Reconciliation*, 290.

134. J. B. T., *Worship*, 55.

135. T. F. T., *Reconciliation*, 292. Moreover, T. F. is suspicious of charismatic experiences themselves, concerned about "the open and uncircumscribed character of these forms which extend beyond normal and controlled experience which constitutes their potential danger, for they are open to all kinds of extraneous forces and aims which may invade and pervert them" (290). However, he does not discuss this much further. Deddo observes that T. F. makes "suggestive comments" to the Pentecostal-Charismatic movement but most of his dialogue partners are dead church fathers, and so Deddo has expressed that he wishes that T. F. had engaged more with modern issues raised by the Pentecostal-Charismatic movement. Deddo, "The Holy Spirit," 107–8.

of the Spirit making real in our experience what is promised in Christ.[136] Yet he too recognizes the problem of "a narrow pursuit of charismatic experiences and manifestations" and argues that there needs to be a "discovery of Abba Father."[137] He points to the Spirit's role in the New Testament as inspiring within humanity the declarations of "Abba Father" (Rom 8:15; Gal 4:6) and "Jesus is Lord" (1 Cor 12:3).[138] Smail argues, "The work of the Spirit is defined by the fact that in it the Father calls us into a sharing of life with himself and his Son (1 John 1:3)."[139] Smail writes,

> But it is the business of the Holy Spirit to take the things of Jesus and open them up to us, so that we in our way become participant in them. That is the basis of all the particular charismata, the gifts of grace. And it is also the basis of this central gift of grace, that the Spirit opens up to us the holy of holies and bids us enter, and become sharers in Jesus' relationship to the Father.[140]

David W. Torrance, reflecting on the early days of the Charismatic movement, perceives a preoccupation with experience over against the intimacy of relationship with the triune God. He remembers being in a meeting of Charismatics who were asked to share what the new experiences of the Spirit essentially meant to them. D. W. was disappointed that the majority of answers focused on experiential feelings, such as joy and peace, because he believed that the Holy Spirit essentially leads us to participate more fully in Christ.[141] This is still a problem within the Pentecostal-Charismatic movement today.[142] However, there are Pentecostal-Charismatics who are discovering more fully what it means to participate by the Spirit in Jesus's relationship with the Father.[143]

---

136. Smail, *Reflected Glory*, 34.

137. Smail, *Forgotten Father*, 45. This is the essential thesis of and reason for his book.

138. Ibid., 13, 30.

139. Ibid., 98.

140. Ibid., 42.

141. D. W. T. in personal conversation. "All three of us [brothers] agreed with Rev. Tom Smail, a theological leader in the charismatic movement and a friend of ours, that the Holy Spirit makes us more aware of Jesus Christ and leads us to participate more fully in Christ's death and resurrection." D. W. T., "Interview," 25.

142. See also Macfarlane, "The Role of the Holy Spirit in Revival," 46.

143. For example, John Crowder, *Sons of Thunder*; David Vaughan and Joanne Gravell, *The New Ecstatics*; Godfrey Birtill, "It's a Wonderful Dance," https://www.youtube.com/watch?v=0LIasj5fU04.

Whilst charismatic and mystical experience is an indispensable aspect of a personal, relational, and participatory scheme of salvation, it is possible to misunderstand experiential manifestations as an *end* in themselves. Jesus declared that people would do miracles in his name yet not truly know him (Matt 7:22–23). The ultimate end of God's saving purposes is seen in the Torrances' account of the enhypostatic movement of the Spirit, whereby humanity is drawn up to participate in Christ's intimate relationship with the Father:

> By his very nature the Holy Spirit not only proceeds from the Father but lifts up to the Father; he is not only the Spirit sent by Christ but the Spirit of response to Christ, the Spirit in whom and by whom and with whom we worship and glorify the Father and the Son. Not only is he God descending to us, the Spirit by whom God bears witness to himself, but God the Holy Spirit lifting up all creation in praise and rejoicing in God, himself the Spirit of worship and witness by whom the Church lives and fulfils its mission to the glory of God.[144]

Theosis

The Torrances' personal, relational, and participatory scheme of salvation whereby humanity's ultimate end is to be drawn by the Spirit to share in the Son's intimate relationship with the Father is closer to Eastern Orthodox theology than the external, legal doctrine characteristic of their own Protestant Reformed tradition. It has been proposed that T. F.'s soteriology is best encapsulated by the doctrine of *theosis*.[145] T. F. urged the Reformed tradition in his time to be more receptive to this Eastern Orthodox doctrine.[146]

The notion of participation in the divine is considered by many not to be a Reformed category.[147] *Theosis* is suspected of wrongly confusing humanity with God.[148] Allen argues that it weakens the distinction between

---

144. T. F. T., *Reconstruction*, 242.

145. Hart, "Atonement, the Incarnation, and Deification," 90. Habets has written a monograph on T. F.'s doctrine of *theosis*. See Habets, *Theosis in the Theology of Thomas Torrance*.

146. T. F. T., *Theology in Reconstruction*, 243.

147. Canlis, *Calvin's Ladder*, 13. Canlis gives the example of John Webster, *Holiness*, 62. However, the translation of Eastern Orthodox texts along with re-readings of Luther and Calvin which identify participatory modes of thought are attributed to drawing greater attention to *theosis* in the West. See Habets, "Reforming Theosis," 151.

148. Habets, *Theosis in the Theology of Thomas Torrance*, 196. For example, John

Creator and creature.[149] A classic statement of *theosis* is Athanasius's dictum, "[God] became man that man might become god."[150] However, T. F. understands *theosis* in terms of communion with God rather than a change in our being, appreciatively citing Georges Florovsky:

> The term *theosis* is indeed embarrassing, if we would think of it in 'ontological categories.' Indeed, man simply cannot become 'god.' But the Fathers were thinking in 'personal' terms, and the mystery of personal communion was involved at this point. *Theosis* means a personal encounter. It is the ultimate intercourse with God, in which the whole of human existence is, as it were, permeated by the Divine Presence.[151]

T. F. writes, "we are adopted and made sons of God in [Christ], and in that respect, as those who through union with Christ receive the grace and light of his Spirit, are said to be *theoi* (in Greek)."[152] His understanding of *theosis* is Christocentric, rooted in the mediation of Christ:

> In the ascension of the Son of Man, New Man in Christ is given to partake of divine nature. There we reach the goal of the incarnation, in our great *Prodomos* or Forerunner at the right hand of God. We are with Jesus beside God, for we are gathered up in him and included in his own self-presentation before the Father.[153]

T. F. is aware of "the danger of *vertigo*" and is very careful to make clear that *theosis* does not mean that humanity *becomes* God. Although humanity is united to Christ and shares in the divine life, we retain our creatureliness, just as Jesus's humanity is not deified by its union with his divine nature:

Webster considers that Eberhard Jüngel rejects the notion of human participation in the divine because he perceives it to compromise our humanity. John Webster, "Introduction." However, although it is indeed wrong to confuse humanity with God, the offense taken at the notion of such an intimate relationship with the divine may be symptomatic of the wider problem within the church that we have a poorer view of ourselves than God does, which will be explored in part 2 of this book. Looking at the reality of the church today, the problem of a poor view of humanity is arguably exceedingly wider than the problem of people confusing themselves as divine.

149. Allen, *Justification and the Gospel*, 46–47.
150. Athanasius, *De incarnatione*, 54:3.
151. Florovsky, *Bible, Church, Tradition*, 96.
152. T. F. T., *Trinitarian Faith*, 139.
153. T. F. T., *Space, Time and Resurrection*, 135.

> The hypostatic union of the divine and human natures in Jesus preserves the human and creaturely being he took from us, and it is in and through our sharing in that human and creaturely being, sanctified and blessed with him, that we share in the life of God while remaining what we are made to be, humans and not Gods.[154]

T. F. also does not adopt the doctrine of *theosis* unquestioningly, rejecting the Palamite distinction between God's essence and energies, and preferring not to use the language of "deification" for the reason that it does not adequately reflect the Creator–creature distinction.[155]

Habets argues that whilst T. F. does not provide a comprehensive doctrine of *theosis*, he nevertheless lays a good foundation, articulating how humanity remains as creatures yet communes with God, on account of being united to Christ by the Spirit.[156]

Like Christ

Whilst it is necessary to maintain the distinction between God and humanity, Smail argues that to deny the similarity would be to dishonor God and his grace and to make him irrelevant.[157] As sons of God, we should have the confidence to enjoy our inheritance.[158] Smail perceives merit in the Pentecostal-Charismatic movement for appreciating that we have been made "fellow heirs with Christ, the New Adam, the ultimate man, whose new humanity spills over in the Holy Spirit to us so that we become new men and signs of the new creation."[159]

Theosis is defined as a transformative concept by Gorman: "Theosis is transformative participation in the kenotic, cruciform character of God through Spirit-enabled conformity to the incarnate, crucified, and resurrected/glorified Christ."[160] Paul exhorts the Corinthians to follow his exam-

---

154. Ibid., 136. T. F. is critical of this danger of vertigo in mysticism.

155. T. F. T., *Christian Doctrine*, 187–88. However, not all Orthodox follow this Palamite distinction. Habets describes T. F.'s doctrine of *theosis* as "at once deeply respectful of Eastern Orthodoxy and indelibly Reformed." Habets, "Reforming Theosis," 167.

156. Habets, "Reforming Theosis," 152, 157.

157. Smail, *Forgotten Father*, 133–34.

158. Ibid., 129.

159. Ibid., 138. Although at the same time Smail is cautious of an over-realized eschatology (142).

160. Gorman, *Inhabiting the Cruciform God*, 7.

ple, as he follows the example of Christ (1 Cor 11:1). Conformity to Christ, Gorman points out, is an essential aspect of *theosis*.[161]

In writing of Christ's atoning exchange, T. F. cites Gregory Nazianzen:

> Let us become like Christ, since Christ became like us. Let us become divine for his sake, since he for ours became man. He assumed the worst that he might give us the better; he became poor that we through his poverty might be rich; he took upon himself the form of a servant that we might receive back our liberty; he came down that we might be exalted; he was tempted that we might conquer; he was dishonoured that he might glorify us; he ascended that he might draw us to himself, who were lying low in the fall of sin. Let us give all, offer all, to him who gave himself a ransom and reconciliation for us.[162]

However, the emphasis of T. F.'s theology is upon *Christ* taking our humanity and it would be complemented by a greater appreciation of that which humanity has received and is called to in Christ. The two must be held together. Christ's vicarious humanity is the indispensable foundation which prevents our likeness to Christ from becoming a burdensome task which we must achieve ourselves. This is expressed well by J. B. when he calls for humanity to become by the Holy Spirit who we *already* are in Christ:

> The Kingdom of God as God's will for man has been realized for us intensively in the humanity of Jesus, and what has been realized intensively for us *in Christ* must be worked out extensively *in us* in the world, by the Holy Spirit, through the mission of the Church. Through the preaching of the Gospel we are called to become now in ourselves what we already are in Christ.[163]

Therefore, whilst it is imperative to make a proper distinction between God and humanity, it is also important to take proper account of the likeness to which God calls us through participating in Christ by the Holy Spirit.

Conclusion

Theosis is the ultimate end of the Torrances' personal, relational, and participatory scheme of salvation. Whilst charismatic and mystical experience is an indispensable aspect, it is not an end in itself. It serves God's greater filial purpose of drawing us up by the Spirit to participate in Christ's intimate

---

161. Ibid., 23.
162. T. F. T., *Trinitarian Faith*, 180–81; citing Gregory Nazianzen, *Oration 1.5*.
163. J. B. T., "The Priesthood of Jesus," 165–66.

relationship with the Father. In so doing, humanity does not lose its humanness, but we are transformed to become more like Christ. The Torrances' theology would be complemented by a greater appreciation of what humanity has received and is called to in Christ.

Conclusion

The Torrances' soteriology presents a Father with covenantal and filial purposes who elects all of humanity in his Son; a Son who intimately assumes our humanity in order to transform it ontologically in himself by the Spirit; and a Holy Spirit who draws us as adopted sons and daughters to participate in Jesus's relationship with the Father and to share in the triune life of love.

This radically objective, Christocentric scheme of salvation has been criticized for focusing on Christ at the expense of the Spirit. However, the Torrances believe that, as the God-man, Christ is the appropriate axis of theology and this serves to uphold rather than diminish the role of the Holy Spirit. There is a mutual mediation: Christ mediates the Holy Spirit to humanity by vicariously receiving the Spirit and pouring him out; the Holy Spirit mediates Christ because it was by the Spirit that Christ was incarnated and lives a vicarious life, and it is by the Spirit that humanity is united to Christ and lifted up to share in God's triune life. The Spirit is therefore integral to every aspect of salvation. A more detailed exposition of the Spirit's action upon Jesus's humanity would aid a better understanding of the Spirit's action upon us today. However, T. F. believes that there is an inherent mystery to pneumatology for the nature of the Holy Spirit is to point away from himself to Christ and the Father.

The objectivity of the Torrances' soteriology has been considered to diminish the significance of both the Spirit and our human response. The objective union of Christ with humanity is thought to negate its subjective actualization in us by the Spirit. However, whilst the believer's activity of faith by the Spirit is imperative, it is only made possible on account of the prior ontological union in Christ. This radical objectivity is essential for our ontological transformation and to avoid being thrown back upon our own efforts. There is also the further concern that Christ's perfect response on our behalf is thought to negate our own human response by the Spirit. However, the Spirit does not enable us to make our own logico-causal, autonomous response to Christ, which would only throw us back upon ourselves again, but to participate in Christ's response for us. The Torrances' participatory scheme comes to tangible expression in the sacraments of baptism and the Eucharist and, rather than devaluing our humanity, truly establishes it.

The objectivity of the Torrances' soteriology has also been considered to diminish the significance of our human works by the Spirit for final judgment. However, a final judgment dependent upon works, despite empowerment by the Spirit, makes the last judgment uncertain and turns humanity in upon itself in search of assurance of salvation. An objective, Christocentric view of judgment is essential to provide assurance of salvation and freedom from having to earn it ourselves. According to the Torrances, Christ's vicarious life of perfect obedience by the Spirit, whereby he submits to God's judgment upon sin, means that an irreversibly positive verdict has been made upon humanity. Whilst this diminishes the significance of logico-causal, merit-based human works, it upholds the significance of works by the Spirit that are the fruit of freely participating in the Son's intimate communion with the Father.

Such an objective scheme of redemption can appear to reduce salvation to a noetic concept. Since salvation has been decisively achieved in Christ, the Torrances believe that all that remains for humanity to enjoy it is to realize this objective reality. The Holy Spirit is "the Spirit of truth" who reveals the reality of our salvation in Christ. This objective activity is important in disallowing any notion that salvation is dependent upon our own intellectual capacity or correct theological knowledge. However, the Holy Spirit is also "the Spirit of adoption," by whom we participate in Jesus's relationship with the Father. Salvation is not reduced to epistemology in the Torrances' scheme because the anhypostatic movement of the Spirit revealing the truth of God to humanity is accompanied by the enhypostatic movement of the Spirit raising humanity up to participate in the triune life. This is a profoundly personal, relational, and participatory understanding of salvation that indicates a God whom humanity can not only know but experience intimately. A greater openness to and consideration of the mystical and experiential aspects of the Christian life would therefore complement the Torrances' soteriology. Mystical experience is not an end in itself but serves God's greater filial purpose of drawing us up by the Spirit to enjoy Christ's intimate relationship with the Father. In so doing, we do not lose our humanity, but are transformed to become more like Christ. A greater appreciation of what we receive in Christ would strengthen the Torrances' understanding of the atoning exchange.

Theosis is the ultimate end of the Torrances' personal, relational, and participatory scheme of salvation, yet so much more can be explored in this regard. Habets considers,

> Because [T. F.] Torrance emphasises the objective elements of salvation his articulation of the subjective elements remain

largely undeveloped. Thus his theology promises more than it delivers as it contains little by way of clearly articulated practical application. This is not to imply that his theology is impractical ... but rather, that he has not elaborated on many of these points in detail.[164]

Part 2 of this book will seek to constructively extend the implications of the Torrances' soteriology to the doctrine of sanctification and the outworking of sanctification in our lives today.

---

164. Habets, *Theosis*, 152.

PART 2

Sanctification and Human Participation

Christ Is Our Holiness
Objective over Subjective

THE PURPOSE OF PART 2 OF THIS BOOK IS TO MORE FULLY EXTEND THE liberating implications of the Torrances' soteriology to the doctrine of sanctification. Part 1 explored the profoundly objective dynamics of the triune God of grace in the Torrances' scheme: the Father elects all of humanity in his Son, the Son becomes flesh to transform us ontologically in himself by the Spirit, and the Spirit now draws us to participate as adopted sons and daughters in Jesus's communion with the Father. The objectivity of this account enables us to freely enjoy the reality of our salvation, liberated from the burden of attempting to achieve it ourselves.

This chapter seeks to argue that, according to the Torrances' scheme, humanity is not only set free from the burden of attempting to achieve salvation, but also from the burden of attempting to achieve sanctification. Whilst there is a lack of emphasis on the subjective nature of sanctification in the Torrances' theology, the objectivity of their account of salvation offers a valuable foundation for a liberating understanding of sanctification. This is a significant contribution for, having been justified by faith, it is often supposed that it is the Christian's task to work out his own sanctification. As Deddo considers,

> What I have observed so often in the Christian Church is that whether conservative or liberal, traditional or contemporary, emergent or mega-church, Christians basically live as if saved by grace but sanctified by works. We depend on our own efforts, choices, accomplishments or zeal. Grace is where we start the Christian life but often we somehow end up 'thrown back upon our own resources' and feeling under a great burden. Then we

become first unimpressed, then perhaps depressed, and finally even coldly cynical about the whole Christian life itself.[1]

This burden is created when sanctification is separated from its ground with justification in Christ and made a subsequent stage in the *ordo salutis*. Humanity is then turned back upon its own resources to attempt to achieve sanctification. The Torrances affirm the liberating reality that sanctification is rooted definitively with justification in the vicarious humanity of Christ. It is the vicarious humanity of Christ, Barth considers, that is the key to releasing humanity from a contractual conception of sanctification:

> It has not always been taken with sufficient seriousness that He took our place and acted for us, not merely as the Son of God who established God's right and our own by allowing Himself, the Judge, to be judged for us, but also as the Son of Man who was sanctified, who sanctified Himself. Far too often the matter has been conceived and represented as though His humiliation to death for our justification by Him as our Representative were His own act, but our exaltation to fellowship with God as the corresponding counter-movement, and therefore our sanctification, were left to us, to be accomplished by us. "All this I did for thee; what wilt thou do for me?" The New Testament does not speak in this way.[2]

The subjective outworking of sanctification can also become a burden when it is conceived of as an external, logico-causal response whereby the Christian must apply Christ's benefits with the aid of the Spirit. As Deddo considers,

> The grace of God can begin to seem merely as if it provided us with a new potential. We can end up thinking: 'By grace God made the Christian life possible by forgiving our sins and giving us a new status of being in right relationship with him. Now all

---

1. Deddo, "The Christian Life," 138–9; See also Smail: "We have been saved in the power of his blood, but have to live the Christian life out of our own resources of our own humanity, by pious dedication and consecration, or by organised religions, evangelistic or social activism—so that instead of the principle of grace covering the whole of our life, we behave as if we had been saved by grace, but have to live by our own works." Smail, *Reflected Glory*, 60–61. For a taxonomy of evangelical Reformed, Wesleyan, Keswick and Charismatic perspectives on sanctification, see David Bebbington, "Holiness in the Evangelical Tradition."

2. Barth, *Church Dogmatics*, IV/2, 516.

we have to do is appropriate, apply or actualize that new potential life that God has graciously given us.³

In contrast, according to the Torrances' soteriology, the outworking of sanctification can be conceived in radically liberating terms of a free and joyful participation by the Spirit in what God has already objectively accomplished in Christ.

This is widely significant with regards to attitudes within the church today, but it is also particularly relevant in the light of the current movement within Federal theology and conservative evangelicalism to recover Puritan theology.⁴ Joel R. Beeke and Mark Jones's extensive tome, *A Puritan Theology: Doctrine for Life*, seeks to dispel the legalistic conception of the Puritans and extol them as valuable voices to follow today.⁵ Whilst this work does helpfully exhibit the positive aspects of Puritan theology, it largely evades the issue of the danger of introspective legalism within Puritanism. Theodore Dwight Bozeman considers that, although the Puritans admirably sought to uphold God's grace in salvation, nevertheless some ended up introducing conditions, threats, and penalties.⁶ Assurance of salvation came to rest not upon the atonement alone but upon people's own pious endeavors.⁷ Bozeman describes this Puritan thinking as "bifocal": "On one side believers must look to the objectivity of election and Atonement; on the other they must engage in moral struggle."⁸ Some Puritans thereby commanded a "two-pronged strategy": people were directed not only to repose in God's promises but also to the necessity of obeying his commands.⁹ Whilst the Puritans's zeal was venerable, it unfortunately became misdirected. Bozeman reflects, "Increasingly, assurance was proportioned to achievement, to the experience and exercise of transforming graces as much as or more than to passive justification."¹⁰ This danger is unwittingly perpetuated by some

---

3. Deddo, "The Christian Life," 138.

4. See also J. I. Packer, *Puritan Portraits*; Ferguson, "The Puritans"; Kapic and Gleason, ed. *The Devoted Life*; Packer, *Rediscovering Holiness*; Packer, *A Quest for Godliness*; Ryken, *Wordly Saints;* Lloyd-Jones, *The Puritans*.

5. Beeke and Jones, *A Puritan Theology*.

6. Bozeman, *The Precisianist Strain*, 190. J. B. perhaps would consider this indicative of "the tendency of the human heart in all ages [which] is to *turn God's covenant of grace into a contract.*" J. B. T., "Covenant Concept," 230.

7. Ibid., 124. See also Beeke and Jones, *A Puritan Theology*, 592.

8. Ibid., 125.

9. Ibid., 139. Bozeman refers to George Gifford, Arthur Dent and Henry Scudder (125, 139).

10. Ibid., 139. See also Frost, *Richard Sibbes*. Frost explores Perkins's "anthropo-

well-intentioned conservative evangelicals who seek the contemporary recovery of Puritan teaching on sanctification, as will be seen in the course of part 2.

The Absence of Emphasis on the Subjective Nature of Sanctification

The subjective nature of sanctification has not typically been a Protestant emphasis.[11] Stanley Hauerwas suggests that this is because the Protestant condemnation of works-righteousness led to a focus on the objective work of God.[12] Discussion of the subjective nature of sanctification has even tended towards having a negative association. Thomas Noble observes that the notion of the possibility of living a holy life often provokes a negative reaction, particularly in the Reformed tradition, which he attributes to the historical Protestant reaction to the hypocrisy of claims to holiness amidst corruption in the church.[13] However, Noble was a student of T. F. and reflects that, whilst it might be expected that a Reformed theologian would not be positive about the language of "perfection," T. F. was remarkably encouraging of Noble's interest. Noble attributes this to T. F.'s deep knowledge of the Fathers, especially Athanasius and Cyril, in whom can be found a very positive discussion of sanctification.[14]

Although T. F. was remarkably encouraging about the exploration of the subjective nature of sanctification, both he and J. B. are characteristic of their Reformed tradition in largely avoiding the subject. J. B. explores the subjective implications of salvation most notably with regard to worship, and T. F. with regard to faith, conversion, worship, the sacraments, and evangelism.[15] Yet there is little exploration of the liberating implications

---

centric spirituality" (144) and "the modified synergism of his federalism" (90), whereby assurance of salvation was thought to be found through introspective examining of one's behavior (92). Frost observes how "self-concerned introspection tended to displace a Christological focus in both sanctification and assurance" (161).

11. The most notable exception within the tradition is John Wesley's concept of "perfection in love," although Thomas Noble regrets that this has been rejected by many Protestants on account of a misunderstanding of this as "sinless perfection" due its distortion by later Wesleyans. See Noble, *Holy Trinity*, 3.

12. Hauerwas, *A Community of Character*, 132; Hauerwas, *Vision and Virtue*, 50; Hauerwas, *Character and the Christian Life*, 129–30.

13. Noble, *Holy Trinity*, 45, 67.

14. Ibid., xii. See Radcliff, *Thomas F. Torrance and the Church Fathers*.

15. J. B. T., *Worship*; T. F. T, *Mediation*, 81–98.

of *sanctification* as we participate by the Spirit in what has been decisively accomplished through the vicarious humanity of Christ.

This lack of exploration could perhaps be attributable to their following the concern of their Reformed tradition to avoid works-righteousness. The Torrances were intensely troubled by preaching and teaching that, to use their recurring phrase, "throws people back upon themselves" to try and achieve their own salvation.[16] J. B. perceives that this problem stems from a distorted conception of God relating to us in contractual terms. Therefore, he repeatedly insists, "The God of the Bible, the God and Father of our Lord Jesus Christ is a covenant-God, and not a contract-God."[17] One of T. F.'s particular concerns is that people are turned back upon their own endeavors by an external conception of the atonement. An external scheme presents Christ merely as an example that we must follow rather than as our Head in whom humanity died and was resurrected. It fails to offer a convincing account of the transformation of humanity and therefore demands our own impossible efforts. T. F. feels strongly that a merely exemplar Christ leaves humanity "in utter darkness and despair."[18] He champions the objective nature of the atonement through the vicarious humanity of Christ.

This is an important contribution but, in order to counteract the problem of people being turned back upon themselves to works-righteousness, the necessity of following Christ as our example is minimized. Hauerwas argues that the dialectical tension between what God has done and our subjective human involvement must be kept in balance. In sympathy with the concern to uphold God's objective activity, Hauerwas recognizes that if the balance is tipped too far towards our subjective activity, sanctification is detached from the reality that upholds it. However, he argues that when the balance is tipped too far towards God's objective work, this makes our human response insignificant.[19] For this reason Hauerwas commends John Wesley in taking seriously the demand for the Christian's transformation into the likeness of Christ.[20] Whilst this demand carries with it the danger of being distorted into a works-righteousness, Hauerwas argues that the subjective nature of sanctification must not be overlooked because it is essential to the Christian life.[21]

---

16. T. F. T., "Preaching Jesus Christ," 28.
17. J. B. T., "Introduction," 6.
18. T. F. T., "Introduction," *The Incarnation*, xiv–xv.
19. Hauerwas, *Character and the Christian Life*, 130. Hauerwas associates this problem with both Rudolf Bultmann and Karl Barth.
20. Hauerwas, *Sanctify Them in the Truth: Holiness Exemplified*, 124.
21. Ibid. Hauerwas explores this in terms of an "ethics of character." See Hauerwas,

The Torrances certainly appreciate the "obligations of grace." T. F. argues that the "logic of grace" is that "all of grace" does not mean nothing of man but rather "all of man."[22] Likewise, J. B. believes that although God makes the covenant for us, it demands a response from us.[23] However, there is little exploration of the obligations of grace with regard to sanctification. Andrew Murray believes that the neglect of Christ as our example and of the imperative to live a holy life is symptomatic of Protestant Christianity as a whole:

> The doctrine that Christ lived on earth, not only to die for our redemption, but to show us how we were to live, did not receive sufficient prominence. While no orthodox church will deny that Christ is our Example, *the absolute necessity* of following the example of His life is not preached with the same distinctness as that of trusting the atonement of His death . . . In this respect, the Protestant Churches still need to go on to perfection. Only then will the Church put on her beautiful garments, and truly shine in the light of God's glory—when these two truths are held in that wondrous unity in which they appear in the life of Christ Himself.[24]

Murray perceives that people are content with salvation's pardon and feeling of peace but he argues that God desires more than that; he desires conformity to his Son.[25] Therefore, Christ as our *substitute*, on account of his vicarious humanity, must be affirmed together with Christ as our *example*, on account of the biblical imperative to grow into our likeness to Christ.

Character and the Christian Life, 129–30.

22. T. F. T., "The Atonement, the Singularity of Christ and the Finality of the Cross," 230.

23. J. B. T., "Covenant or Contract?," 23, 55.

24. Murray, *Like Christ*, 227–28. See also: "the Church indeed needs a second reformation. In the great Reformation three centuries ago, the power of Christ's atoning death and righteousness were brought to light—to the great comfort and joy of anxious souls. But, we need a second reformation to lift on high the banner of Christ's example as our law, and to restore the truth of the power of Christ's resurrection as it makes us partakers of the life and the likeness of our Lord. Christians must not only believe in the full union with their Surety for their reconciliation, but with their Head as their example and their life." Ibid., 62.

25. Ibid., 227. Murray asserts, "Christ lived on earth that He might show forth *the image of God in His life*. He lives in heaven that we may show forth *the image of God in our lives*." Ibid., 226. "He lives like us, so that we may live like Him." Murray, *The Secret of God's Presence*, 51. J. B. only later in life discovered and enjoyed Andrew Murray's devotional writing.

The Indicatives of Grace as Prior to the Imperatives of Law

John Webster argues that T. F.'s absence of attention to the subjective nature of sanctification is indicative of the problem that the objectivity of Christ's vicarious humanity diminishes our own human response: "The puzzling slightness of Torrance's attention to moral theology in his published work betokens the way in which a theology of Christ's vicarious humanity may dissolve the human action in incarnational grace."[26] However, this is to misunderstand T. F.'s conception of human action. Christ's vicarious humanity rightly diminishes any human response that is merit-based and therefore burdensome, and affirms human action in its proper place, that is, as a free and joyful response by the Spirit to what God has already accomplished in Christ.

What is perhaps more puzzling about T. F.'s absence of attention to moral theology is that he does not take more fully the opportunity to articulate the proper place of human activity in the outworking of sanctification. Whilst T. F.'s concern to challenge works-righteousness might have held him back from this task, he could have both challenged works-righteousness and upheld the obligations of grace by highlighting the proper place of subjective sanctification as rooted in the objective accomplishment of Christ.

The grounding of the subjective outworking of sanctification in the objective accomplishment of Christ is another instance whereby "the indicatives of grace are always prior to the obligations of law and human obedience."[27] Evident by his repeated affirmations, this is a crucial maxim for J. B., and although not explored in detail by the Torrances, it is true with regards to sanctification.[28] If the imperative to be holy is preached

---

26. Webster, "T. F. Torrance 1913–2007," 371.

27. J. B. T., "The Covenant Concept," 230. Purves's use of the language of "grace" in both the "indicative of grace" and the "imperative of grace" (rather than the "imperative of law") is helpful in reflecting that the imperative is rooted in the indicative and that godly living flows from the indicative of God's grace. Purves, *Reconstructing Pastoral Theology*, 176, 183.

28. Noble seeks a reappraisal of Wesley's doctrine of sanctification by doing what he perceives Wesley failed to do: the rooting of subjective sanctification in the objective Person and Work of Christ. See Noble, *Holy Trinity*. He suggests that Wesley failed to do this because he was influenced by scholastic seventeenth century federal categories (100). Noble writes, "The point is, of course, that the shape of what is sometimes called 'subjective soteriology' is determined by 'objective soteriology.' What is possible for us now in our Christian lives was determined by what Christ did for us then on the cross. In other words, what Christ does now, by his Spirit *in us,* is the outworking of what he did once and for all on the cross *for us.*" 136–37.

prior to, or in detachment from, the indicative truth that we are sanctified in Christ, we are thrown back upon ourselves to attempt to accomplish it for ourselves. However, the imperative to be holy is preceded by God's indicative act of grace in Christ's vicarious humanity whereby we have been made holy. Therefore, we are liberated to follow the imperative, not by relying upon our own resources, but by relying upon the vicarious humanity of Christ, in whom we may participate by the Spirit.

Herman Bavinck's distinction between "legal sanctification" and "evangelical sanctification" is valuable in this regard. Legal sanctification is the process whereby believers attempt to work out their own sanctification: "believers proceed to sanctify themselves by means of a holiness which they themselves newly and for the first time bring into being, or of one which exists already but which they by means of their exertion and good works must appropriate."[29] Evangelical sanctification, on the other hand, is rooted in God's act of grace in Christ.[30] The imperative call to be holy does not turn us back upon our own efforts because it is rooted in the indicative reality that we are sanctified in Christ.[31]

David Peterson has lamented that the indicative reality of our sanctification in Christ has not been given the primacy that it holds in Scripture as the basis for living holy lives.[32] As Paul wrote, we have been set free from sin (Rom 6:7); therefore we must not let sin reign (Rom 6:12). In Paul's writing, Hays observes that "the human moral action is given a distinct place in the syntax of the divine–human relationship; obedience is a consequence of salvation, not its condition."[33] This can be seen especially in Hebrews,

---

29. Bavinck, *Our Reasonable Faith*, 479.

30. Ibid., 480–81.

31. Ibid., 481–82. Barth rooted the imperative to live a holy life in the indicative sanctification which has already been achieved through Christ's vicarious "no" to sin and "yes" to a new life: "Your sanctification is such that it has happened independently of your good or bad will, because the 'no' to sin and the 'yes' to a new life that has no more interest in sin, that has turned to God, is fixed for ever and is therefore valid already here and now. You must, you shall therefore no longer live the old life but move in the new life. For you have no other! You only have the life in fellowship with him who has taken sin, your sin, unto himself and who has done away with it, and who now has only the life with God before him. This is the power of the imperative of your sanctification." Barth, *A Shorter Commentary on Romans*, 71.

32. Peterson, *Possessed by God*, 14. Although Peterson understands justification in primarily forensic and declaratory terms, he stresses the definitive act of sanctification in Christ, recognizing that if the imperative does not flow from the indicative, the outworking of sanctification "can so easily degenerate into a moralistic and perfectionist programme for believers to pursue." Ibid., 137.

33. Richard Hays, *The Moral Vision of the New Testament: A Contemporary*

where subjective sanctification is rooted definitively in Christ's once-for-all sacrifice.[34] Seifrid considers that sanctification is presented in Hebrews in equivalent terms to justification in Paul's letters: it is an accomplished reality in which we can share through Christ's continuing high priesthood. Seifrid observes, "As in Paul, the imperative paradoxically flows out of the indicative."[35]

The implications of the Torrances' objective soteriology for the outworking of sanctification are exemplified by Andrew Murray. In his devotional writings, he upholds both the imperative and indicative in their proper relationship. He stresses the imperative call to live a sanctified life but his exhortations are rooted in the indicative vicarious humanity of Christ.[36] Murray perceives that, as both God and man, Jesus was able to fulfill both sides of the covenant.[37] He also perceives that the atonement is not a mere external transaction that effects a retrospective forgiveness of sins but involves our intimate inclusion in Christ's death so that we are prospectively liberated to share in Christ's holiness:

> We know what the death of Christ means as an atonement, and we never can emphasize too much that blessed substitution and bloodshedding, by which redemption was won for us. But let us remember, that is only half the meaning of His death. The other half is this: just as much as Christ was my substitute, who died for me, just so much He is my head, in whom, and with whom, I die; and just as He lives for me, to intercede, He lives in me, to carry out and to perfect His life.[38]

Murray is conscious that Christ, although ascended, nevertheless remains in human flesh and continues to act as our vicarious High Priest and King: "As Priest He effected the cleansing of sins here below; as Priest-King He sits on the right hand of the throne to apply His work, in heavenly power to dispense its blessings, and maintain within us the heavenly life."[39] We share in Christ's sanctification by the Holy Spirit: "Christ is our sanctification, and the Holy Ghost comes to communicate Him to us, to work out all that is in

---

Introduction to New Testament Ethics, 45.

34. Noble, *Holy Trinity*, 41.
35. Seifrid, *Christ, Our Righteousness*, 178.
36. Murray, *The Master's Indwelling*, 79.
37. Murray, *Abide in Christ*, 238; See also Murray, *Absolute Surrender*, 94.
38. Murray, *The Master's Indwelling*, 48.
39. Murray, *The Holiest of All*, 48.

Christ and to reproduce it in us."[40] Murray stresses that "There is no other way of our becoming holy but by becoming partakers of the holiness of Christ."[41]

The indicative reality of the vicarious humanity of Christ gives Murray the confidence to stress the imperative call to be holy: "There is not, as so many think, one standard for Christ and another for His people. No, as branches of the vine, as members of the body, as partakers of the same Spirit, we may and therefore must bear the image of the Elder Brother."[42] Although Murray presents a high calling, he does not place a burden upon the believer because it is rooted in the indicative reality of our sanctification in Christ:

> Christ is not only our Surety who lived and died for us, our Example who showed us how to live and die, but also our Head, with whom we are one, in whose death we have died, in whose life we now live. This gives us the power to follow our Surety as our Example: Christ being our Head is the bond that makes the believing in the Surety and the following of the Example inseparably one.[43]

The Inseparability of Justification and Sanctification in Christ

Noble suggests that the lack of emphasis on the subjective nature of sanctification particularly notable in Protestant theology is due to the atonement being connected strongly to justification but not to sanctification.[44] He argues, "The Christian tradition (perhaps particularly Protestant tradition) has worked with an over-tidy separation of justification from sanctification in a way that is not truly biblical. And it does not seem to have given the same thought to how the cross effected our *sanctification*."[45] When our sanctification is not rooted definitively with justification in Christ, Noble considers, "we fit ourselves for heaven by the effort of our own sanctifying self-discipline."[46] Similarly, Campbell has criticized attempts to explain the

40. Murray, *The Master's Indwelling*, 82.
41. Murray, *Abide*, 75.
42. Murray, *Like Christ*, 232–33.
43. Ibid., 32.
44. Noble, *Holy Trinity*, 100.
45. Ibid., 135.
46. Ibid., 136.

dialectical tension between divine and human agency by separating sanctification from justification. He argues that, in Paul, justification and sanctification are in parallel, not sequence. When sanctification is sequential to justification, this makes sanctification conditional upon our own endeavors.[47] This is strongly condemned by G. C. Berkouwer as "a violation of the grace of God" for "it posits a substitute for the grace of God or tries to complete it with human works."[48]

For this reason the Torrances are concerned by Federal Calvinism's notion of a "second work" of sanctification. They perceive this to be a serious distortion of Calvin's teaching that justification and sanctification are inseparable in Christ.[49] There is a notable difference between the older Reformation Catechisms and the Westminster Catechism in this regard. In the later Westminster Catechism, sanctification is presented as a subsequent stage to justification in the *ordo salutis*.[50] Scholastic Protestant theology had separated sanctification from justification.[51] This led to a change in preaching whereby, instead of being directed to Christ, congregations were urged to work out their own sanctification.[52] J. B. observes that the discussion of sanctification in the Westminster Confession places its focus on the believer rather than on Christ who is sanctified for us or the believer's participation in him: "The emphasis is on what has to happen to us and in us, rather than on the One Baptism of Christ, in which we are given to participate."[53] T. F. considers,

> In the Westminster theology the main focus of attention is upon man's appropriation of salvation through justifying faith and the working out of sanctification. Ultimately the main content of these Catechisms is concerned with man's action, man's obedience, man's duty toward God, man's duty to his neighbour, and man's religion[54]

People are also turned back upon their own endeavors when sanctification is conceived of as a "second blessing" in some streams of Pentecostalism. Holiness teaching, influenced by a form of John Wesley's notion of

---

47. Campbell, *Deliverance of God*, 185–87.
48. Berkouwer, *Faith and Sanctification*, 129. See also 20–21.
49. T. F. T., *Theology in Reconstruction*, 158. See Calvin, *Institutes*, III.16.i.
50. T. F. T., "Introduction," *The School of Faith,* xvii–xviii.
51. T. F. T., *Reconstruction*, 157.
52. T. F. T., "Introduction," *The School of Faith*, xlviii.
53. J. B. T., "Strengths and Weaknesses," 44–45.
54. T. F. T., "Introduction," *The School of Faith*, xvii–xviii.

perfection, has been adopted into Pentecostal denominations such as the Church of God, the Pentecostal Holiness Church and the Church of God in Christ. According to Holiness teaching, there is a second blessing subsequent to conversion whereby the believer receives entire sanctification.[55] The separation of sanctification from justification can lead to the problem, as Smail observes, of people trying to accomplish their own sanctification:

> All second blessing teaching whether of a Pentecostal or 'holiness' type, is in danger of dividing the Christian life into a salvation which is gift to the sinner, and the fullness of the Spirit which is reward of the saint, and thus maligning the central gospel principle that from beginning to end it is all of grace.[56]

As with the notion of a "second work," sanctification as a "second blessing" is presented as a subsequent stage to justification in the *ordo salutis*.[57] Sanctification is separated from its definitive ground with justification in Christ which means that people then feel the burden to attempt to achieve it themselves.

Hauerwas considers that the rooting of sanctification with justification takes seriously the implications of our sanctification whilst also defying a moralistic interpretation:

> The dialectical interdependence of justification and sanctification is a way of indicating the real effect of Christ's work upon the believer without separating that effect from its source. Justification is a necessary aspect of sanctification in order that "Christ for us" is kept at the center of the Christian life. This emphasis always erects a permanent barrier to any attempt to interpret the Christian life in a moralistic fashion. Sanctification must be equally emphasized, however, to prevent understanding Christ's work in a way that separates it from the effect it has on the believer.[58]

---

55. Synan, "Sanctification" 422–24. See also Kagarise, "Theology of Experience," 192.

56. Smail, *Reflected Glory*, 48–49.

57. Pointing to the perfect passive participle "*hegiasmesnois*" in Acts 26:18 and 20:32, Peterson argues that sanctification is not an event subsequent to forgiveness in the *ordo salutis*. This means that it cannot be deemed a "second work" or "second blessing." He argues that, in the New Testament, when the verb "*hagiazein*" (to sanctify) and noun "*hagiasmos*" (sanctification) are used, they emphasize the once-for-all saving work of God in Christ. Peterson, *Possessed by God*, 55, 27.

58. Hauerwas, *Character and the Christian Life*, 188. He goes on to assert, "This is what prevents the Christian life from being reduced to an intellectual adherence to certain beliefs."

This rooting of sanctification with justification is a significant aspect of the Torrances' soteriology. What holds the two together is the vicarious humanity of Christ. For the Torrances, the vicarious humanity of Christ means that "Christ takes our place and represents us, so that what is true of him is true of us, and what he did in his (our) humanity is ours."[59] This is what they believe is expressed by Jesus's assertion, "And for their sakes I sanctify myself, so that they also may be sanctified" (John 17:19).[60] They also believe it to be indicative in Paul's claim that Christ "became for us wisdom from God, and righteousness and sanctification and redemption" (1 Cor 1:30).[61]

Following Athanasius, T. F. describes the very act of the Word assuming human flesh as sanctifying our human nature.[62] He writes,

> God has joined himself to us in our estranged human life in order to sanctify it, to gather it into union with his own holy life and so lift it up above and beyond all the downward drag of sin and decay, and that he already does simply by being one with man in all things. Thus the act of becoming incarnate is itself the *sanctification* of our human life in Jesus Christ.[63]

Yet the incarnation was only the beginning of the sanctification of humanity, for it was also wrought out for and in us throughout Christ's earthly life.[64] The Holy Spirit's descent upon Jesus at his baptism was "for our sanctification."[65] Jesus then lived a life by the Spirit of perfect faithfulness to the Father for our sanctification. As J. B. asserts, "In our name, on our behalf, in a human body, Jesus lived a life of prayer, a life in the Spirit in communion with the Father, to sanctify our humanity."[66] Jesus's faithfulness to the Father even led him to submit to death on the cross, whereby the old

---

59. T. F. T., *Incarnation*, 205.

60. J. B. T., "Christ in our Place," 45; T. F. T., *The Trinitarian Faith*, 167; T. F. T., *Theology in Reconciliation*, 141.

61. T. F. T., *Atonement*, 129.

62. T. F. T., *Reconciliation*, 53. "In his holy assumption of our unholy humanity, his purity wipes away our impurity, his holiness covers our corruption, his nature heals our nature." T. F. T., *Theology in Reconstruction*, 155–56.

63. T. F. T., *Incarnation*, 66.

64. T. F. T., *Trinitarian Faith*, 167.

65. Ibid., 190.

66. J. B. T., *Passion*, 47. See also T. F. T., *Mediation*, 81. For further elaboration of the role of the Spirit in the sanctifying events of Jesus's vicarious life, see Noble, *Holy Trinity*, 184–91.

fallen nature of humanity was crucified and buried. Humanity is therefore sanctified both by Jesus's active and passive obedience.[67] J. B. writes,

> The Son of God takes our humanity, sanctifies it by his vicarious life in the Spirit (John 17:17–18), carries it to the grave to be crucified and buried in him, and in his resurrection and ascension carries it into the holy presence of God. 'And by that will, we have been made holy through the sacrifice of the body of Jesus Christ once for all' (Heb 10:10).[68]

This once-for-all rooting of sanctification with justification in the vicarious humanity of Christ is crucial in order to avoid people being made dependent upon their own efforts to try and achieve sanctification. T. F. perceives that when sanctification is rooted definitively with justification in the vicarious humanity of Christ, there is no need for the believer to try and achieve it for himself:

> Justification by grace alone remains the sole ground of the Christian life; we never advance beyond it, as if justification were only the beginning of a new self-righteousness, the beginning of a life of sanctification which is what we do in response to justification. Of course we are summoned to live out day by day what we already are in Christ through his self-consecration or sanctification, but sanctification is not what we do in addition to what God has done in justification.[69]

The Holy Spirit as the Means By Whom we Participate in Christ

The Torrances believe that the outworking of this sanctification found objectively with justification in Christ comes as we participate by the Holy Spirit in Christ.[70] The role of the Holy Spirit is to turn us out of ourselves to

---

67. T. F. T., *Theology in Reconstruction*, 155.
68. J. B. T., "Christ in our Place," 62.
69. T. F. T., *Theology in Reconstruction*, 161–62.
70. J. B. T., "Priesthood of Jesus," 165–66. See also J. B. T., "Christ in our Place," 48; T. F. T., *Atonement*, 387: "Because the church is the body of Christ in which he dwells, the temple of the Holy Spirit in which God is present, its members live the very life of Christ through the Holy Spirit, partaking of and living out the holy life of God." See also Barth, *Church Dogmatics* IV/2, 517: "As we are not asked to justify ourselves, we are not asked to sanctify ourselves. Our sanctification consists in our participation in His sanctification as grounded in the efficacy and revelation of the grace of Jesus

share in this sanctification found definitively in Christ. T. F. describes this as the Spirit "opening us up within our subjectivities for Christ in such a radical way that we find our life *not in ourselves but out of ourselves, objectively in him.*"[71]

This notion of participating by the Spirit in Christ's holiness is challenged by Webster.[72] His concern with the concept of "participation" is primarily with regards to his disbelief that it has a convincing scriptural basis, but also his apprehension that it does not take seriously the distinction between the Creator and creature.[73] Webster proposes conceiving of the relationship between the Creator and creature in terms of "fellowship" instead of participation.[74] He seeks to avoid the problem of people being turned back upon their own efforts by rooting sanctification in the Father's election:

> Our thinking about sanctification would be disorderly if we were to suggest that, although in the matter of reconciliation we have to talk of a divine determination, when we move to speak of human holiness we are required to shift to talk of our own agency, perhaps co-operating with God, perhaps rendering God his due for the gift of salvation. But, if we are elected to holiness, then we have been extracted from the sphere of human autonomy; the Christian's holiness does not stem from the Christian's decision.[75]

Daniel A. Keating has sought to address these concerns of Webster. Keating argues that Scripture does describe God's relationship with humanity in terms of participation. Both Paul and John write of a real indwelling and abiding of humanity in God. Keating also argues that the concept of

---

Christ."

71. T. F. T., *Theology in Reconstruction*, 238.

72. Webster writes, "The Church is holy; but it is holy, not by virtue of some ontological participation in the divine holiness, but by virtue of its calling by God, its reception of the divine benefits, and its obedience of faith." Webster, *Holiness*, 57.

73. Webster, "Perfection and Participation," 380. However, Webster does recognize that T. F. is very cautious with regard to blurring the Creator–creature distinction. Webster, "T. F. Torrance 1913–2007," 370. See chapter 3 for a discussion of how T. F. maintains the Creator–creature distinction.

74. Webster, *Holiness*, 57, 62. Webster believes that the Scriptural references to "in the Lord" and "in the Spirit" refer to fellowship, not participation. Ibid., 62. Similarly, Allen prefers a concept of "covenant fellowship" over the Torrances' notion of participation which he believes weakens the distinction between Creator and creature. Allen, *Justification and the Gospel*, 15, 46–47.

75. Webster, *Holiness*, 79–80, 60.

participation does not necessarily entail denial of the distinction between Creator and creature. He points to how the Christian tradition has upheld the distinction between Creator and creature by understanding participation as a sharing in the divine life not by nature but by grace. He upholds eminent figures such as Athanasius (*Contra Arianos* 1.9) and Augustine (*Enarrationes in Psalmos* 49.2) in this regard.[76] Julie Canlis has also sought to defend the concept of participation from Webster's criticism. She points to Calvin's discussion of the insufficiency of "fellowship" as a concept and argues that participation, expressed by the word *koinonia* in the New Testament, is considerably different from a Platonic notion of consubstantiality.[77]

Webster's rooting of sanctification in election affirms the objectivity of sanctification yet this objectivity seems to be undermined by his notion of fellowship. Without a concept of participation by the Spirit in Christ, there is nevertheless the danger that we are turned back upon our own endeavors to *apply* to our lives the sanctification that Christ has definitively achieved for us. Rather than a free sharing by the Spirit in Christ's sanctification, our actions can be conceived of as an external, autonomous, logico-causal response, aided by the Spirit, to apply what Christ has accomplished.[78] According to this perspective, God did his part in Christ; now we must do our part to apply the benefits of Christ with the help of the Holy Spirit.[79]

This risk can be seen in some Puritan teaching and is being advanced today by some well-intentioned conservative evangelicals.[80] Seeking to

---

76. Keating, "Trinity and Salvation," 450–52. See T. F. T., *Atonement*, 294: "The staggering thing about this is that the exaltation of the human nature into the life of God does not mean the disappearance of man or the swallowing up of human and creaturely being in the infinite ocean of the divine being, but rather that human nature, while remaining creaturely and human, is yet exalted in Christ to share in God's life and glory."

77. Canlis, *Calvin's Ladder*, 13. On the insufficiency of the concept of fellowship, see also Letham, *The Holy Trinity*, 469; and Dulles, "The Trinity and Christian Unity," 74.

78. See, for example, Sinclair B. Ferguson: "All that is true *for me* in Christ has not yet been accomplished *in me* by the Spirit." Ferguson, "The Reformed View," 62–3.

79. Smail also recognizes the problem of perceiving the Holy Spirit as our aid to our own autonomous endeavors: "It is not surprising that when the Christian life is understood as having its origin in a human choice of faith, it should also be seen to continue through human efforts after faithfulness, obedience, sanctification, where no doubt the Spirit appears as subsidiary helper at each stage, but where the initiative is seen to rest upon us, so that we are urged to a series of decisive steps towards our own consecration, and promised his help only when we have taken them." Smail, *Reflected Glory*, 84.

80. Although the Puritans sought to affirm God's working in our lives, and were driven by a well-intentioned zeal for holiness, there can nevertheless be seen

recover Puritan teaching, J. I. Packer's instructions for the outworking of sanctification tend towards an external, anthropocentric endeavor:

> Puritan teaching on mortifying the lusts that tempt us is businesslike and thorough. It includes the disciplines of self-humbling, self-examination, setting oneself against all sins in one's spiritual system as a preliminary to muscling in on any one of them, avoiding situations that stoke sin's boiler, watching lest you become sin's victim before you are aware of its approval, and praying to the Lord Jesus Christ specifically to apply the killing power of his cross to the particular, vicious craving on which one is making one's counterattack.[81]

Packer believes that the outworking of our sanctification is dependent upon Christ and the Holy Spirit.[82] Yet he presents an external, imitative concept of holiness that depends upon our own autonomous endeavors: "Carefully and prayerfully modelling our attitudes and responses to pressure after those of Jesus is what holiness means."[83] Packer believes that we endure in the battle for sanctification by fixing our eyes on Jesus as the "model and standard of godliness."[84] Jesus appears more as an example to strive to emulate than the ground of our sanctification in whom we freely participate by the Spirit. Packer's work is reflective of a popular conservative evangelical understanding of sanctification in the contemporary church.

Although we are called to live out our sanctification, the Holy Spirit does not aid us in the external, logico-causal application of Christ's definitive sanctification. This would be to detach the outworking of sanctification from the vicarious humanity of Christ, thereby making the reality of our sanctification only a potentiality that demands our efforts for its actualization. This then places a burden upon humanity so that the outworking of sanctification becomes the impossible task of an autonomous believer. According to the Torrances, sanctification is a reality in which we participate, rather than a potentiality to be actualized. As Gary Deddo writes,

---

a recourse to our anthropocentric efforts in the outworking of sanctification. "The Puritans stressed that you cannot expect God's Holy Spirit to give you strong, joyful assurance unless you strive on a daily basis to live a holy life." Beeke and Jones, *A Puritan Theology*, 529. Thomas Boston, for example, seems to reflect this understanding of God simply aiding our autonomous, anthropocentric endeavors in sanctification. Ibid., 530.

81. Packer, *Rediscovering Holiness*, 108. See also Beeke and Jones, *A Puritan Theology*, 531.

82. Ibid., 193.

83. Ibid., 93.

84. Ibid., 243. See also Hoekema, "The Reformed Pespective," 66–85.

> What is complete and actual in Christ is truly and really ours even if it does not yet appear to be so. Our lives *are* hidden in Christ (Col 3:3). Our life *in him* is being worked out *in us* by the Spirit. But this new being wrought in us comes through the sheer gift of our union with Christ. It does not come through our working out a potential that might be true if we properly apply ourselves. Rather the Christian life is living out and manifesting the present reality of our union with Christ.[85]

The Holy Spirit does not enable the autonomous believer to work out his own sanctification; the Holy Spirit enables the believer to participate in Christ's definitive sanctification. This liberates humanity from the burden of depending upon our own endeavors for the outworking of sanctification in our lives.

Conclusion

The Torrances appear to be somewhat characteristic of their Reformed tradition in their emphasis upon the objective work of God and lack of exploration of the subjective nature of sanctification. Although this may have been due to a concern to avoid moralism, the Torrances' soteriology actually offers the crucial foundation for challenging moralism whilst also appreciating the obligations of grace. Therefore, this chapter has sought to explore more fully the liberating implications of the Torrances' soteriology for the outworking of sanctification.

The Torrances root sanctification objectively with justification in Christ. We have been sanctified once-for-all through Christ's vicarious humanity. This is significant because when sanctification is made subsequent to justification, as in the Federal notion of a "second work" or Pentecostal "second blessing," it is separated from its definitive ground with justification in Christ and the danger is that people find themselves dependent upon their own resources to attempt to achieve it themselves. When sanctification is rooted definitively with justification in the vicarious humanity of Christ, there is no burden upon us to achieve it ourselves.

The Torrances conceive of the subjective outworking of this definitive sanctification in terms of participating by the Holy Spirit in Christ. If the subjective outworking of sanctification is an external, logico-causal response by the Christian, aided by the Spirit but detached from the vicarious humanity of Christ, it becomes an autonomous, burdensome endeavor. This can be unwittingly perpetuated by the current movement to recover

---

85. Deddo, "The Christian Life," 142.

Puritan theology. However, the Holy Spirit does not enable the autonomous Christian to work out his own sanctification; the Spirit enables him to participate in Christ's definitive sanctification. This liberates humanity from the burden of depending upon our own efforts for the subjective outworking of sanctification.

It must be stressed that, for the Torrances, participation in the divine life does not entail a loss of creaturely being, nor does the objectivity of our sanctification diminish any possibility of our own human response. According to the Torrances, it rightly diminishes any human response that is merit-based and therefore burdensome, but it also affirms human action in its proper place as a free and joyful participation by the Spirit in what God has already accomplished in Christ.

When the imperative to be holy is made prior to, or detached from, the indicative truth that we are sanctified in Christ, we are thrown back upon ourselves to attempt to accomplish it. In the Torrances' scheme of salvation, the imperative to be holy is preceded by God's indicative act of grace in Christ. Therefore, we are set free to follow the imperative, not by relying upon our own resources, but by relying upon the vicarious humanity of Christ, in whom we may participate by the Spirit. Liberated from any burdensome, moralistic notion of sanctification, we are free, motivated, and inspired to grow into the reality of our holiness in Christ, the nature of which shall be explored in the following chapter.

5

Growing Up into Christ
Ontological over External

THE OBJECTIVE ROOTING OF SANCTIFICATION WITH JUSTIFICATION IN THE vicarious humanity of Christ liberates us to grow into the reality of our holiness as we participate by the Spirit in Christ. It is the purpose of this chapter to explore more fully the nature of our holiness and our growth into Christ by taking into account both the eschatological reserve created by Christ's ascension and our new eschatological orientation in the risen humanity of Christ. This chapter seeks to argue that the Torrances' scheme of salvation corrects a poor perspective of humanity and the outworking of sanctification, instead offering the confidence to grow up into our ontological reality in Christ.

For the Torrances, the eschatological reserve created by Jesus's ascension means that sinfulness is a continuing presence as we await the full manifestation of our sanctification at the *Parousia*. Nevertheless, although hidden, our holiness is a definitive reality, which means that we do not depend upon our own endeavors in an external process of becoming progressively more holy. The outworking of our sanctification comes from a place of rest in what Christ has already accomplished and is a process of the unveiling of that reality.

Constructively extending the implications of the Torrances' scheme of salvation, this chapter explores our new eschatological orientation in the risen humanity of Christ, whereby we are able to share by the Spirit in Christ's risen and ascended humanity here and now. This is our primary ontological reality and it challenges a poor view of humanity defined primarily in terms of sinfulness, which is fuelled by an external understanding of the atonement that fails to offer an adequate account of the transformation of humanity. The ontological transformation of our humanity through the vicarious humanity of Christ means that humanity is truly holy and it is important to affirm this reality. Our boast is not in ourselves but in Christ and arguably it most honors God to accept our new nature and clothe ourselves with Christ.

Taking the implications of the Torrances' soteriology further, the eschatological orientation of the risen humanity of Christ means that we do not have to endure a life-long struggle with sin, a perspective perpetuated by the current movement to reclaim Puritan theology. Although in one sense the ascension means the removal of Christ from the world, in another sense it means that humanity is raised up and seated in heavenly places in Christ. As we participate by the Spirit in Christ, from this place of victory and rest, the outworking of sanctification does not have to be a struggle. Grounded in the realism of the eschatological tension, this does not lead to triumphalism, but it reflects the confidence of the biblical witness that although humanity lives in the eschatological reserve, in a world of continuing sin and evil, it is neither defined nor ruled by it. We are liberated to grow into the reality of who we are in Christ.

The Eschatological Reserve Created by Christ's Ascension

According to the Torrances, through God's objective sanctifying work in the vicarious humanity of Christ, humanity has been made definitively holy. Yet after the old Adamic flesh was crucified and buried and humanity had been resurrected to new life, Christ ascended to heaven. On account of Christ's continuing ascended humanity, the church is united to Christ by the Spirit. This means that in one sense he is present to us, yet in another sense his ascension means a withdrawal from us; Christ is at one and the same time both present and absent. For T. F., the absence of Christ after the ascension establishes an "eschatological reserve."[1]

> On the one hand, then, the Church through the Spirit is joined to the Body of the risen Christ and is One Body with Him; but on the other hand, Christ has removed His Body from us so that we have to think of the relation of the Church to the risen Body of Christ in terms of the distance of the ascension and the nearness of His *parousia* in Glory. There is an eschatological reserve in the relation of our union with Christ, an eschatological lag waiting for the last Word or the final Act of God. There is an element of pure immediacy in the Church's relation to the risen

1. T. F. T., *Royal Priesthood*, 45–46. See also T. F. T., *Atonement*, 33, 313.

> Body of Christ so that His *parousia* is a presence here and now through the Spirit. But there is also an element in the Church's relation to the risen Body of Christ which from our experience and our understanding is still in arrears and awaits the divine fulfilment. Christ has distanced His Body from us and yet through His Spirit He has come and filled the Church with His own Self. In one sense, then, the Church is already One Body with Christ—that has once for all taken place in the crucifixion, resurrection, and in Pentecost—and yet the Church is still to become One Body.[2]

This eschatological reserve means that there is an eschatological tension between the hidden and the manifest. Although the church is already One Body with Christ, this truth is partly hidden and not fully manifest.[3] The Kingdom of God is a present but veiled reality.[4] We are conscious of the end because it has broken into the present through Christ's vicarious life but it remains beyond our grasp because of his ascension and awaited *Parousia*.[5]

T. F.'s understanding of the eschatological reserve has significant implications for the nature of the outworking of our sanctification. First, it means that the outworking of sanctification is not an external process of becoming progressively more holy, which throws us back upon our own efforts.[6] This would be to rely upon a linear conception of time. We do not become any more holy through the progression of time; we have already been made completely holy in Christ. The progression of time only serves the unveiling of this definitive reality. The eschatological tension is not between humanity being partially holy and partially unholy, but between the hidden reality of our holiness and its full manifestation. The definitive, ontological reality of our sanctification in Christ means that there is nothing that we can do to make ourselves any more holy. The outworking of sanctification is the process of the unveiling of the reality of our sanctification in Christ.

Second, as a process of unveiling the definitive reality of our sanctification, the outworking of sanctification does not depend upon our own endeavors. The eschatological reserve does not mean that holiness is a

---

2. Ibid.
3. T. F. T., "Eschatology," 7.
4. Ibid., 16.
5. Ibid., 5.
6. Hauerwas considers that the language of "growth" in holiness can lend itself to a moralistic distortion whereby our own efforts make us more holy. Hauerwas, *Character and the Christian Life*, 218.

potentiality that we must work to attain, but rather an ontological reality that we can look forward to being revealed.[7] T. F. writes, "The final *parousia* of Christ will be more the apocalypse or unveiling of the perfected reality of what Christ has done than the consummating of what till then is an incomplete reality."[8] T. F.'s eschatology is criticized by Stanley MacLean for reducing the eschatological nature of the church to an unveiling of what it already is.[9] Yet this is an essential truth if humanity is not to be thrown back upon its own resources.

Third, although the unveiling of our sanctification does not depend upon our own endeavors, this does not deny our subjective human activity but rather puts it in its proper place. In stressing the objective and definitive activity of Christ, T. F. is often misunderstood as disregarding our subjective human activity. MacLean is critical of T. F.'s eschatology for being "christologically over-determined"; in laying emphasis on Christological objectivity, MacLean perceives T. F. as diminishing human subjectivity.[10] Yet the only subjective human activity that T. F. diminishes is that which is enslaved by a contractual conception of our relationship with God. T. F. stresses Christ's vicarious humanity in our place because it is only by wholly sanctifying us in himself that our subjective human activity is liberated from its own endeavors. We are set free from the burden of trying to accomplish our own sanctification and enabled to participate by the Spirit in Christ's holiness.

---

7. T. F. T., "Eschatology," 10. He writes, "The New Testament constantly thinks of the Parousia in terms of Epiphany, for the relation between the today (*semeron*) and the eschaton is much more a tension between the hidden and the manifest, the veiled and the unveiled, than between dates in calendar time. What is still in the future is the full unveiling of a reality, but the reality itself is fully present here and now." T. F. T., "Eschatology," 7.

8. T. F. T., *Space, Time and Resurrection*, 152.

9. MacLean, *Resurrection, Apocalypse and the Kingdom of Christ*, 197. MacLean's book engages with what he perceives to be a neglected aspect of T. F.'s theology: his eschatology (xii). It offers a historical account of the development of T. F.'s thought using unpublished material from the Thomas F. Torrance Manuscript Collection at Princeton Theological Seminary.

10. MacLean, *Resurrection, Apocalypse and the Kingdom*, 198–99. The Torrances would perhaps also be included in Hauerwas's criticism of those who emphasize God's objective work in order to counteract anthropocentrism in sanctification, which Hauerwas believes to be at the expense of our subjective response. Hauerwas, *Character and the Christian Life*, 130–41, 157, 170–75. To redress the balance in the dialectical tension between what God has done (indicative) and our human subjective response (imperative), Hauerwas calls for an "ethics of character," mindful that God's objective work demands a response from humanity of growth in sanctification. Yet without the concept of participation in Christ there is the risk of throwing us back upon our own endeavors.

This means at one and the same time that we can rest in what has been decisively accomplished in Christ but also that we can be active in leading holy lives. We typically think in external, logico-causal categories so that rest is an activity that follows work; we work "nine to five" and then we rest from work in the evening. This perspective can be seen in the Puritans. As Beeke and Jones write, "The Puritans recognized that holiness takes planning, hard work, and prayer . . . In this life, work is our lot, but rest is waiting for us in eternal glory."[11] Yet the Torrances' understanding of salvation presents our work as coming out of a contemporaneous place of rest and satisfaction in what has been definitively accomplished in Christ. This satisfaction in Christ seems to be overlooked by Packer when he conceives of the Christian who grows in holiness becoming increasingly discontented: "Increase of real holiness always brings increase of real discontent, because of what has not yet been achieved."[12] Arguably it is dependency upon our own inadequate resources that breeds discontent. The biblical witness exhorts the Christian to put his "effort" into entering God's "rest" (Heb 4:11), which is perhaps indicative of the impossibility of fitting divine and human agency into logico-causal categories. Both an external, logico-causal paradigm and a participatory paradigm lead to exertion on the part of the Christian. The crucial difference is that an external, logico-causal perspective makes this exertion a burden, whereas participation by the Spirit in Christ is radically freeing because it is rooted in a place of rest in what Christ has already accomplished.

Fourth, the eschatological reserve means that our sanctification will not be fully manifest until the *Parousia*.[13] Sinfulness is a continuing real-

11. Beeke and Jones, *A Puritan Theology*, 533.

12. Packer, *Rediscovering Holiness*, 222.

13. T. F. T., *Atonement*, 33, 313. J. B. writes, "What has been realized for us intensively in Christ will one day be revealed extensively in a new heaven and a new earth." J. B. T., "The Priesthood of Jesus," 166. See also: "Jesus Christ is present in the power of the Spirit, but the same Spirit keeps us in suspense (*suspension*). The end is not yet. Now we are the children of God, enjoying real communion with Jesus Christ, the whole Christ. It does not yet appear what we shall be, but when he appears we shall be like him, and enjoy endless communion with him." J. B. T., *Worship*, 82. Possible scriptural support for this includes: Paul writes of his expectation of the return of Jesus, when the Philippians will see themselves conformed to his likeness: "But our citizenship is in heaven, and it is from there that we are expecting a Saviour, the Lord Jesus Christ. He will transform the body of our humiliation that it may be conformed to the body of his glory, by the power that also enables him to make all things subject to himself" (Phil 3:20). Similarly, the first letter to John asserts, "Beloved, we are God's children now, and what we will be has not yet appeared; but we know that when he appears we shall be like him, because we shall see him as he is" (1 John 3:2). Paul describes to the Corinthians a process of transformation into the likeness of Christ:

ity manifest in the present, which Paul argued was evident in the lives of the early Christians. Paul describes the Romans as "full of goodness" yet he continues, "Nevertheless, on some points I have written to you rather boldly by way of reminder, because of the grace given me by God to be a minister of Christ to the Gentiles in the priestly service of the gospel of God, so that the offering of the Gentiles may be acceptable, sanctified by the Holy Spirit" (Rom 15:14–16). In the preceding chapters (Rom 12–14), Paul sets out ways in which the Romans could lead holy lives which indicates that they had not been living up to these standards. Paul acknowledges the Corinthians's quarrelling (1 Cor 1:11; 3:3; 11:18), sexual immorality (5:1) and boasting (4:19; 5:6), and explicitly admonishes their immoral behavior (1 Cor 4:14). He admonishes the Galatians for beginning in the Spirit but returning to the flesh (Gal 3:3; 4:9–10). He also exhorts the Ephesians and Colossians to put off the old man (Eph 4:22; Col. 3:8–9).[14] Sinfulness is a continuing presence in the lives of Christians as we await the full manifestation of our sanctification, and so T. F. would assert, "This Tom Torrance you see is full of corruption, but the real Tom Torrance is hid with Christ in God and will be revealed only when Jesus Christ comes again."[15]

The eschatological tension between the hidden and the manifest leads T. F. to criticize two eschatologies that deny an eschatological reserve. The first, "realized eschatology," asserts the complete fulfillment of the Kingdom of God.[16] The second, "realized teleology," identifies the Kingdom with the church and perceives the church to be an extension of the incarnation.[17] Essentially, they affirm that either the teleological or the eschatological end

---

"And all of us, with unveiled faces, seeing the glory of the Lord as though reflected in a mirror, are being transformed into the same image from one degree of glory to another" (2 Cor 3:18). In his letter to the Romans, Paul looks forward to the "glory that will be revealed in us: (Rom 8:18). He writes, "For the creation waits in eager expectation for the children of God to be revealed" (Rom 8:19). Similarly, the first letter of Peter speaks of "a salvation ready to be revealed in the last time" (1 Pet 1:3–5). This all seems to suggest that our true identity in Christ will not be wholly revealed until his return and so our sanctification awaits full manifestation.

14. Cf. Saucy, "'Sinners' Who are Forgiven or 'Saints' Who Sin?," 403–4. Saucy cites the following biblical passages as evidence that Christians still sin: they are described as behaving carnally (1 Cor 3:1–3); there is promise of the cleansing of their sin (1 John 1:7); confession of sins is written of in the present tense (1 John 1:9); John wrote that those who claim to be without sin deceive themselves (1 John 1:8); and Paul exhorted the Ephesians and Colossians to put off the old man (Eph 4:22; Col 3:8–9).

15. T. F. T., *Mediation*, 95. Cf., T. F. T, *Atonement*, 371.

16. T. F. T., "Eschatology," 11.

17. Ibid., 18–19.

is fully realized in the present.[18] T. F. contends that the Kingdom awaits full manifestation in order to give humanity time to hear the gospel and respond to God.[19] Eschatology cannot be thought of in purely linear terms because the Kingdom of God is present whilst also being hidden.[20] Moreover, to deny the eschatological reserve is to contradict the sacraments of baptism and the eucharist:[21]

> While on the one hand we are given the real presence of the whole Christ, yet on the other hand that is to be realised in sacramental obedience enacted into our daily life. It is a reconciliation, as we have seen, thrust into a world that continues in its estrangement from and contradiction to God, and that is why in addition to the sacrament of baptism we have the eucharist. We are taught thereby that while in new time we are complete in Christ Jesus, yet in the conflicts and abstractions of fallen time we are unable to realise that wholeness, but must nevertheless reckon that we are dead to the old life and created again in the new. That means that while in faith we are a new creation yet we are unable as yet to join body and soul, the invisible and the visible, the material and the spiritual, etc., in any closer union than is given to us in the tensions of the Cross through holy communion.[22]

According to T. F., baptism and the eucharist are indicative of the eschatological tension because they remind us of both Christ's presence and our estrangement from him at one and the same time.[23] As the church lives in the eschatological reserve between Christ's ascension and *Parousia*, "It is still characterised by sin and evil and partakes of the decay and corruption of the world of which it is a part," T. F. writes, "so that it is not yet what it shall be, and not yet wholly in itself what it is already in Christ."[24]

---

18. Ibid., 33. This criticism applies to Pentecostal Perfectionism, which affirms full manifestation of our sanctification.

19. Ibid., 15. Cf. *Space, Time and Resurrection*, 146–7.

20. Ibid., 29–30.

21. Ibid., 20.

22. Ibid., 37.

23. For more of T. F.'s view of the sacraments, see T. F. T., *Atonement*, 413–24. He considers that the New Testament expresses the union and distance between Christ and the church through two images: (1) the church as the body of Christ and; (2) the church as the bride of Christ.

24. T. F. T., *Atonement*, 312.

The Eschatological Orientation of the Risen Humanity of Christ

Although the church lives in the eschatological reserve between the ascension and *Parousia,* partaking of the corruption of the world, T. F. believes that it has been given a new eschatological orientation whereby it "lives a life from beyond itself, and therefore looks beyond the historical forms of its orders to find its true being and form in the risen Humanity of Christ."[25] T. F. writes of the members of the church, "Their true being is hid with Christ in God. The whole focus of their vision and the whole perspective of their life in Christ's name will be directed to the final unveiling of that reality of their new being at the *parousia.*"[26] The church is turned out of itself to find its true identity in Christ's risen humanity. It is "caught up in the onward and outward thrust of the resurrection of Christ toward the new creation."[27] MacLean writes, "The church of course cannot simply extricate itself from the power of *nomos*. It is still involved in the structural forms of this fallen world, and it has its mission within this world. But these forms must be "relativized," since the church is given a "new orientation within" them."[28] As Smail asserts:

> Thus if we wish to measure the possibilities of our humanity, whether in the realm of its sanctification or its empowering, we are not to look at ourselves and scale Christ down to us, or worship the goodness and greatness of a divinity that is in principle inaccessible to us, but we are to look at him, to behold the Man that he is, and therefore the men that we shall be in him.[29]

The eschatological reserve does not discourage T. F. from remaining positive that the end has already come with the incarnation of Christ. In one sense, there is no delay of the *Parousia* because Christ's life, death, resurrection, ascension, and second advent are one redemptive event.[30] Our salvation is definitive; there is nothing left to be achieved. What the future awaits

---

25. T. F. T., *Royal Priesthood,* 56. T. F. laments that the eschatological orientation as evident in the New Testament is not appreciated by the church and theologians. T. F. T, *Atonement,* 402. See also T. F. T., *Incarnation,* 298–304.

26. T. F. T., *Atonement,* 314.

27. T. F. T., *Space, Time and Resurrection,* 105.

28. MacLean, *Resurrection, Apocalypse and the Kingdom,* 177.

29. Smail, *Reflected Glory,* 70–71.

30. MacLean, *Resurrection, Apocalypse and the Kingdom,* xvi. For T. F.'s discussion of one *Parousia,* see T. F. T., *Atonement,* 302–3. There is one *Parousia,* with an "eschatological pause" created by the ascension.

is a full manifestation of that reality. Whilst the word "apocalypse" tends towards a negative connotation today, in T. F.'s theology it is positively associated with the final unveiling of God's redemptive purposes.[31] He asserts, "Apocalypse is the unveiling to faith of the new creation as yet hidden from our eyes behind the ugly shapes of sinful history, but a new creation already consummated and waiting for eschatological unfolding or fulfilment in the advent presence of Christ."[32] This means that T. F. is less concerned with the last things, as is typical in eschatology, and more concerned with the significance of Christ's resurrection power in the present.[33] MacLean comments that T. F.'s eschatology is more about the *Eschatos* (Last One), than the *eschata* (last things).[34]

The church is able to share by the Spirit in the new risen humanity of Christ in the present.[35] T. F. describes the church as "the new humanity within the world, the provisional manifestation of the new creation within the old."[36] Here T. F. aligns himself more with Calvin than Luther. Calvin believes that, as the church participates in Christ, the glory of the new creation can to an extent be manifest; for Luther, the new humanity, whilst a reality, remains wholly concealed.[37] Like T. F., Calvin perceives the eschatological tension arising between what has been accomplished and what is visibly manifest; for Luther, the eschatological tension arises between a "having" and a "not having."[38] T. F. ascribes the greater optimism in Calvin's eschatology to the influence of the Greek Fathers, as opposed to the somewhat more pessimistic Latin tradition that had a larger influence on Luther.[39]

---

31. MacLean, *Resurrection, Apocalypse and the Kingdom*, 93. See T. F. T., *The Apocalypse Today*, 180.

32. T. F. T., *Atonement*, 412.

33. MacLean, *Resurrection, Apocalypse and the Kingdom*, 9, 23, 195. MacLean gives an example from T. F.'s sermon on 2 Peter 3 where he is not interested in the apocalyptic return of Christ; "Instead, his message is about meeting the eternal God in the midst of time" (29).

34. Ibid., 19. T. F.'s eschatology is thoroughly Christocentric. MacLean describes his eschatology as a "component" of his Christology (xvi).

35. T. F. T., *Reconstruction*, 248. The Spirit is the Spirit of Holiness who "comes to us from the triumphant obedience and victory of Christ in his Cross and Resurrection, as the Spirit clothed with mighty, redemptive acts transmitting the energy of Christ's risen and glorified Humanity, and as the Spirit of him who has entered into the new life and inherited all the promises of God, and therefore he comes in all the transforming power of the Saviour and Redeemer of men" (248).

36. T. F. T., *School of Faith*, cxxi.

37. T. F. T., *Kingdom and Church*, 149–50, 160.

38. Ibid., 142.

39. MacLean, *Resurrection, Apocalypse and the Kingdom*, 112. Cf. T. F. T, *Kingdom*

T. F. is critical of Luther for not appreciating more fully the significance of Christ's resurrected humanity for the present:

> It was not that Luther had no sense of the new creation either as regards the Church or as regards the individual believer, but that his weak stress on the renewal of the whole creation tended to rob it of temporal relevance and force . . . [and] means that the believer does not really learn to live on the resurrection side of the Cross.[40]

T. F. associates this problem in part to a negative emphasis on *peccator* over *justus*: " . . . the realisation, inherent in the *justus et peccator* dialectic, that before God the believer is always in the wrong, helped him at times to lose sight of the new creation in Christ as already accomplished fact, as a '*perfectum praesens*.'"[41] T. F. follows his Reformed tradition in holding to Luther's conviction that the believer is *simul justus et peccator*.[42] Yet it is *justus* that is our primary reality in Christ and which describes the eschatological orientation of humanity. Although the *simul justus et peccator* dialectic expresses well the continuing reality of sin, Hays considers that there is a danger that it may "underestimate the transformative power of God's grace."[43] As Matt Jenson argues, although humanity is still *peccator* until the *Parousia*, it is only a "secondary reality" or "non-ontological status."[44] To make it a primary or an ontological reality is to dispense with Christ:

> To speak of persons in the first light of sin, even to speak of them as that which sin is not, is to circumscribe humanity within boundaries inappropriate to creatures of God. What's more, if Christ is (among so many other things) the most exemplary, but even more the most real, the most true person, and if we confess his sinless obedience to the Father as axiomatic, then to

---

and *Church*, 149–50. T. F. argues that later Calvinists distorted Calvin's theology by presenting him as having a "thoroughly pessimistic" view of humanity. They made the doctrine of the fall of man and human depravity prior to grace, whereas Calvin considered fallen humanity and sin within the context of God's covenant of grace. T. F. T., *Calvin's Doctrine of Man*, 20.

40. T. F. T., *Kingdom and Church*, 72.

41. Ibid.

42. Much debate as to how to understand *simul justus et peccator* has been raised by the New Finnish Interpretation of Luther which interprets his doctrine of justification in participatory rather than external terms. See Mannermaa, *Christ Present in Faith*.

43. Hays, *Moral Vision*, 44.

44. Jenson, *The Gravity of Sin* 189.

take sin as the primary locus for understanding personhood is to disqualify Christology (and, therefore, anthropology) from the discussion from the start.[45]

The significance of Christ's resurrected humanity is also maligned when Paul's description of struggling with sin in Romans 7:14–25 is interpreted as normative Christian experience. Hays considers that the notion of *simul justus et peccator* can perpetuate this misunderstanding of Romans 7 because it does not adequately reflect Christ's transformative power.[46] Donald Alexander has observed that many Christians identify with Paul's description of struggling with sin and interpret it to be normative.[47] Paul writes:

> For we know that the law is spiritual; but I am of the flesh, sold into slavery under sin. I do not understand my own actions. For I do not do what I want, but I do the very thing I hate. Now if I do what I do not want, I agree that the law is good. But in fact it is no longer I that do it, but sin that dwells within me. For I know that nothing good dwells within me, that is, in my flesh. I can will what is right, but I cannot do it. For I do not do the good I want, but the evil I do not want is what I do. Now if I do what I do not want, it is no longer I that do it, but sin that dwells within me. So I find it to be a law that when I want to do what is good, evil lies close at hand. For I delight in the law of God in my inmost self, but I see in my members another law at war with the law of my mind, making me captive to the law of sin that dwells in my members. Wretched man that I am! Who will rescue me from this body of death? Thanks be to God through Jesus Christ our Lord! So then, with my mind I am a slave to the law of God, but with my flesh I am a slave to the law of sin. (Rom 7:14–25)

"[This speech] is so compelling and so poignant," Francis Watson considers, "that generations of readers have assumed that Paul must be articulating his present experience as a Christian."[48] This is the typical Reformed

---

45. Ibid.

46. Hays, *Moral Vision*, 44.

47. Alexander, "The Riddle of Sanctification," 7. Hauerwas observes, "We are happier thinking of ourselves at best as troubled sinners and certainly not as righteous saints." Hauerwas, *Sanctify Them*, 125.

48. Watson, *Paul, Judaism and the Gentiles*, 290. For an interpretation of Rom 7:14–25 as normative Christian experience, see Dunn "Romans 7:14–25 in the Theology of Paul," 257–73.

perspective.[49] However, this understanding of Romans 7 is disputed by those who believe that Paul is actually recounting his pre-Christian experience and by others who believe that it is not autobiographical but rather a description of life under the law.[50]

The crucial question is whether Paul's description of struggling with sin is supposed to be normative for the Christian. Packer believes that Paul's speech is "the word of the dynamic, spiritually healthy man."[51] Advocating the Puritan doctrine of sanctification for the contemporary church, Packer follows their description of the Christian life as a long and hard-fought war.[52] He describes the battle against sin as "a long-drawn-out, bruising struggle."[53] Yet the wider context of Romans chapters 6–8 suggests that, although a struggle with sin may be the experience of a Christian, it is not how a Christian is intended to live. Francis Watson proposes that Romans 7 must be interpreted together with Romans 6 as an "antithetically constructed diptych" which contrasts Christ and law, righteousness and sin.[54] Romans 7 must also be understood together with Romans 8, which shows that the alternative to a life under the law in Romans 7 is a life in the Spirit. Watson argues that this means that Paul is not resigned to a life of struggle; he is showing that "the nightmare of self-incomprehension and despair" can come to an end.[55] Similarly, Hays contends that Romans 6 and 8 testify to humanity's liberation from the powers of sin. Whilst Rom 8:17–30 acknowledges the eschatological reserve, Paul's emphasis is upon God's present power in the church. Paul's exclamation of praise in Rom 7:25a is not merely a celebration of God's forgiveness but of God's liberation from bondage to

---

49. Allen, *Reformed Theology*, 87. For examples of this perspective, see Bavinck, *Our Reasonable Faith*, 492–93; Packer, *Rediscovering Holiness*, 151; Horton, *Pilgrim Theology*, Kindle ed., Loc 6432.

50. For an example of the interpretation of Rom 7:14–25 as pre-Christian experience, see C. H. Dodd, *The Epistle of Paul to the Romans*. Dodd argues that the use of "I" refers to Paul himself and the use of the present tense indicates that he is recalling a previous experience. For an example of the interpretation of Rom 7:14–25 as life under the law, see Kümmel, *Romer 7 und die Bekenhrung des Paulus*. Kümmel argues that the "I" is not autobiographical and points to its rhetorical use elsewhere in Romans and the wider New Testament.

51. Packer, *Rediscovering Holiness*, 221.

52. Packer, "What is Sanctification?"

53. Packer, *Rediscovering Holiness*, 175.

54. Watson, *Paul, Judaism and the Gentiles*, 277–78.

55. Ibid., 291–92.

sin.⁵⁶ Therefore Hays asserts, "The agonized struggle of Romans 7 is hardly offered by Paul as a normative account of Christian experience."⁵⁷

Paul decisively proclaims the end of our enslavement to sin. As Barth argues, the heart of Paul's argument in Romans is that we have been liberated from sin. Romans 7:14–25 is useful only insofar as it shows what we have been liberated from. Barth writes,

> Paul describes the meaning and the action of that law from which by our faith we have in fact been liberated—or rather for which in our faith we ourselves are no longer able. These verses therefore picture a situation which can only interest us as our past situation which is outdated in the faith, a situation in which we did not have the right attitude to sin or to the Law. And Paul's words about it certainly do not invite us to remain in that situation or to take it seriously. He does not desire to draw our attention to what *prevails and happens* in the situation from which we have been called away in the faith, but to the fact that we have been *called away* from it.⁵⁸

Struggling with sin as normative experience can be fuelled by an external, forensic understanding of the atonement whereby the believer is declared to be covered by Christ's righteousness but is "actually unrighteous in himself/herself."⁵⁹ Allen argues that an external scheme of imputation is the liberating impetus for living a holy life: "Being declared just before God's judgment frees and empowers obedience, inasmuch as it renders moot and futile the accusations of sin."⁶⁰ Yet an external scheme fails to offer an adequate account of the transformation of humanity. Noble argues, "It offers no explanation of what Paul meant when he wrote of the cross as a 'dying to sin.'"⁶¹ Put in extreme terms, we are only forgiven sinners who have a positional righteousness and a second chance to attempt to be good. Noble asserts that Christ's death was the death of sinful Adamic humanity; only by recognizing this can humanity truly be sanctified.⁶² Otherwise the outworking of sanctification places an "enormous weight" on the individual

---

56. Hays, *Moral Vision*, 44.
57. Ibid., 38, 44–45.
58. Barth, *Romans*, 75.
59. Horton, *Pilgrim Theology*, Kindle ed., Loc 5640.
60. Allen, *Justification and the Gospel*, 140. He writes, "forensic declaration before God fuels lives of service and good works" (131). See also Horton, *Pilgrim Theology*, Loc 6182.
61. Noble, *Holy Trinity*, 145–53.
62. Ibid., 148.

Christian.[63] We are turned back upon our own impossible efforts to struggle with sin. Smail argues that the "sober estimate" of the church as a company of "justified sinners" makes Christ remote, sanctification incomplete, and throws people back upon themselves to strive to achieve it.[64] According to the Torrances' understanding of salvation, humanity is ontologically transformed through the vicarious humanity of Christ. Christ became incarnate to be an example *of* us, not just *for* us. This means that humanity is truly holy and we are liberated to grow into that reality as we participate in Christ by the Spirit.

Robert Saucy suggests that it is better to describe the Christian as "a saint who sins" rather than as "a sinner who is forgiven."[65] Addressing the language of "miserable sinner" Christianity, Saucy recognizes that it is not intended as an end in itself, for as the "miserable sinner" seeks refuge in the grace of God he finds true joy and forgiveness. However, Saucy is concerned that many Christians perceive this to be their fundamental identity.[66] He argues that, although the New Testament witness records the early Christians sinning, it does not describe the early Christians as "sinners." Christians are defined by their identity as "saints" in Christ.[67] Christians are depicted as having a new orientation towards righteousness (1 John 2:29–3:2; Eph 5:8; 1 Thess 5:5; 2 Cor 5:17; Col 3:9–10).[68] He also refers to Paul's exhortation to moral behavior on the basis of a new identity in Christ; Saucy argues that this moral behavior only has a basis if they truly have a new nature.[69]

---

63. Ibid., 152–53.

64. Smail, *Reflected Glory*, 124–27.

65. Saucy, "Sinners," 403. Peterson laments that the veneration of only particular individuals as saints fuels the misunderstanding that sainthood is something that we must achieve by our own efforts rather than a definitive gift for all in Christ. Peterson, *Possessed*, 41.

66. Saucy, "Sinners," 400–401. Saucy points to Luther's Short Catechism, Anglican liturgy, and the theology of B. B. Warfield.

67. Ibid., 402. See Rom 1:7; 12:13; 15:25–26, 31; 16:2, 15; 1 Cor 1:2; 6:1; 14:33; 16:1, 15; 2 Cor 1:1; 8:4; 9:1, 12; 13:13; Eph 1:1, 15, 18; 3:8, 18; 4:12; 5:3; 6:18; Phil 1:1; 4:22; Col 1:2, 4, 12, 26; 1 Thess 3:13; 2 Thess 1:10; 1 Tim 5:10; Phlm 1:5, 7; Heb 6:10; 13–24; Jude 1:1. See also Noble, *Holy Trinity*, 22. Saucy addresses the contention that Paul described himself as "the foremost of sinners" (1 Tim 1:15–16) by arguing that this was not a definition of his true identity (404–5). This seems correct because Paul is speaking in relation to Jesus's salvation of sinners, which granted for us a new identity in him as saints. Saucy also addresses Paul's description of struggling with sin (Rom 7:14–25) which he argues actually points to the positive identity of the Christian. He argues that the "I" is good but has been overcome by the power of sin (410–11).

68. Saucy, "Sinners," 402.

69. Ibid., 403

Furthermore, this new nature is greater than the old nature because Paul is confident that they will cultivate a holy life. Saucy writes, "The very assumption that Christians should grow demonstrates a belief that the positive dominates over the negative in their being. For a Christian to grow, there must be a stronger inclination toward God than toward sin."[70] Thus he argues that it is better to affirm our identity as "saints" rather than "sinners."[71]

In his preaching, T. F. affirmed his congregation's identity as saints in Christ:

> Don't you see, in God's sight, you are already secluded in the heart of Jesus Christ, you are already a new creature though to all outward appearances you may be far from it, you are already a saint though you know yourself to be a sinner. That is the glorious paradox of the Gospel.[72]

Similarly, for Barth, although it is not yet fully revealed, sainthood is our new form of existence.[73] He upholds the Reformed language of *simul iustus et peccator* yet believes that it is important to affirm and celebrate our identity as saints:

> We who were once "children of wrath," "dead in trespasses and sins," are saints. We are holy . . . This is no time for false modesty . . . Hold your head high! You have dignity. You have worth. Not only have you been created by the gracious and omnipotent hand of God, you have been redeemed in the blood of His Son and sanctified by the power of His Spirit through Word and Sacrament.[74]

Barth cites Martin Luther as having the same attitude:

> All of us are saints, and accursed be he who does not call himself a saint and glory in it. If you believe the words of Christ, you are a saint as well as St. Peter and all the other saints; for, depend on it, Christ will not lie to you. Therefore if you do not say: I have as much as St. Peter and am as saintly as St. Peter, then you are ungrateful to your Lord Christ . . . Nor is such glorying in our sainthood arrogance but modesty and thankfulness. In fact, he who does not do it is slandering Christ and Baptism.[75]

---

70. Ibid., 412.
71. Ibid., 403.
72. T. F. T., "Philippians 2:12."
73. Barth, *Church Dogmatics* IV/2, 511, 516–17 523, 674–75.
74. Barth, "Simultaneous Saints and Sinners," 215.
75. Ibid.

Barth and Luther both acknowledge the contention that affirming our identity as saints is perceived as immodesty or arrogance. However, as Paul wrote, our boast is not in ourselves but in Christ (Rom 15:17; Gal 6:14). Our confidence is not in our own creaturely capacity or possibilities but in Christ.[76] Inherent in the affirmation that God has made us holy in Christ is the recognition of our weakness and sinfulness for it is an acceptance that we cannot achieve sanctification ourselves. T. F. asserts,

> It is the very fact of the church's holiness in Christ, the reality that in Christ the church is already justified and sanctified for ever, that reminds the church that so long as it lives in this world that passes away, and partakes of its sinful patterns and forms, it is involved in error and wrong. Therefore it lives in such a way that its participation in divine holiness is the condemnation of sin in its flesh; it lives bearing about in its body the dying of the Lord Jesus Christ that the life of Jesus may be manifest even in its mortal flesh; and therefore from day to day and from age to age, until Christ comes again, it must live by putting off the old nature with its corruption and sin, and putting on the new nature with which it is clothed through the baptism of the Spirit uniting it to the risen and glorious body of Jesus Christ.[77]

It is a false humility to make sinfulness our primary identity because it is a rejection of what God has done for us in Christ. It most honors God to accept our new nature and clothe ourselves with Christ.[78] Unfortunately this

---

76. Barth believes that affirmation of our sainthood does not give rise to boasting in ourselves: "We are not saints because we make ourselves such. We are saints and sanctified because we are already sanctified, already saints, in this One." Barth, *Church Dogmatics*, IV/2, 516–17.

77. T. F. T., *Atonement*, 388. He writes, "The church is not holy because its members are holy or live virtuous lives, but because through his presence in the Holy Spirit Christ continues to hallow himself in the midst of the church, hallowing the church as his body and the body as his church. Thus the true holiness of the members is not different from this but a participation in it, a participation in the holiness of Christ the head of the church and in the holiness of the church as the body hallowed by Christ" (387).

78. Murray suggests that it is God's grace, not our sin, which is the truest basis of our humility: "Christ's example teaches us that it is not sin that must humble us. This is what many Christians think. They consider daily falls to be necessary in order to remain humble. This is not so. There is indeed a humility that is very lovely, and of such great value as the beginning of something more, which consists in the acknowledgement of transgressions and shortcomings. But, there is a humility which is more heavenly still, and which consists, even when grace keeps us from sinning, in the self-abasement that can only wonder that God should bless us . . . It is grace we need, and not sin, to make and keep us humble. The heaviest laden branches always bow the

identity is often not claimed on account of the misunderstanding that we have to abase ourselves to glorify God. Packer emphasizes the importance of awareness of our sinfulness and calls for "a progress into personal smallness that allows the greatness of Christ's grace to appear."[79] Packer does not seem to have a concept of humility and dependence upon God's grace that does not involve shame and debasement. T. F. believes that we are brought to our "fullest reality" in Christ, the "personalising Person" and "humanising Man."[80] The Torrances affirm both the reality of our new ontological identity in Christ's risen humanity and our dependence upon God's grace.

Confidence in Christ

The eschatological orientation of our humanity in Christ offers us a confidence for the "now" which is a necessary corrective to a poor view that is focused on the "not yet." Although humanity lives in the eschatological reserve, in a world of continuing sin and evil, it is neither defined nor ruled by it; we are determined by the risen humanity of Christ. As T. F. asserts,

> The Church of the risen Lord has no right to be a prophet of gloom or despair, for this world has been redeemed and sanctified by Christ, and he will not let it go. The corruptible clay of our poor earth has been taken up in Jesus, is consecrated through his sacrifice and resurrection, and he will not allow it to sink back into corruption . . . The Church must learn to take into its mouth the Good News of the resurrection and new creation, for that must be its primary note, one of limitless joy and thanksgiving.[81]

A fuller appreciation of the significance of this present reality challenges the tendency to conceive of humanity primarily in terms of sinfulness and the resulting understanding of sin as a life-long struggle.[82] It gives us confidence to grow into the reality of who we are in Christ.

---

lowest." Murray, *Like Christ*, 149–50.

79. Packer, *Rediscovering Holiness*, 121. Packer conceives this in terms of "realism about our sinfulness and our sins" (109) yet it is profoundly distortive because it fails to adequately appreciate our new ontological identity in Christ's risen humanity.

80. T. F. T. *Mediation of Christ*, 78–79.

81. T. F. T., *Space, Time and Resurrection*, 105.

82. A significant contribution of the Wesleyan tradition and the Pentecostal-Charismatic movement has been their optimism regarding holiness. For a discussion of the Wesleyan tradition, see Noble, *Holy Trinity*, 193. For the Pentecostal-Charismatic movement, see Tugwell, *Did You Receive the Spirit?*, 83: "While we may agree with

Whilst grounded in a realism regarding the eschatological reserve, T. F. displays an intense confidence on account of our new eschatological orientation in Christ. He writes,

> The church that is launched into this situation in history is the suffering servant, the church under the cross, and to all outward appearances the weak and helpless, the despised and downtrodden church, but it is also the church of the victorious king. The shout of a king is in its midst! A new song is in its mouth, the song of final and complete triumph, a song of indescribable joy and confidence in Jesus Christ.[83]

For T. F., it is the present reality of the new creation in Christ that should consume us: "Throughout this the accent must undoubtedly fall upon the triumphant certainty of the finished work of Christ, for Christ is already the new man in whom all things are become new and in whom we have proleptically even now the consummation of the divine purpose of creation."[84]

However, there is a general lack of discussion of this confidence by the Torrances in relation to the subjective outworking of sanctification. Whilst this is perhaps characteristic of their Reformed tradition, more particularly this may be on account of their focus on Christ's priesthood as opposed to the other offices of Christ as prophet and king.[85] J. B. perceived a focus

---

Bruner that Christianity plus is no longer Christianity, Pentecostalism has come in protest against Christianity minus." Pentecostalism has been commended for not being satisfied with lack and for believing that there can be greater actualization of the promises given in the Gospel. See Pinnock, *Flame of Love,* 170; Smail, *Forgotten Father,* 138–42. Some current voices within the Pentecostal-Charismatic movement are appreciative of the Torrances but wish to see in their work a greater confidence in the outworking of our sanctification. See John Crowder, "The Inner Sanctum," Accessed 05.22.12. http://thenewmystics.payperlive.com/archive/view/191483266/May%20 22%20-%20Part%201.

83. T. F. T., *Atonement,* 436. He writes, "The new creation is as yet a hidden creation, hidden with Christ in God, but always on the point of becoming manifest. Until then the church lives in the eschatological tension between the first coming of the kingdom and the final coming, and carries out her task as the crucified body in the realm where sin and the flesh are still found and where the subordinate powers still try to break free from the lordship of Christ. Nevertheless the church lives in the Spirit on the day of the Lord, that is to say, on the victory side of the kingdom, and the song in her mouth is the triumphant chant of Psalm 3, 'Why do the nations conspire, and the peoples plot in vain? . . . I have set my king on Zion, my holy hill . . . Ask of me, and I will make the nations your heritage, and the ends of the earth your possession." T. F. T., *Atonement,* 409. "In spite of being in the likeness of sinful flesh the new community is indeed the body of Christ." T. F. T., *Atonement,* 405.

84. T. F. T., *Atonement,* 406–7.

85. See J. B. T., *Worship,* 59–60. For further discussion upon this, see chapter 4. J.

in the church upon Christ's prophetic office that presented Jesus only in terms of bearing God's word to humankind and neglected his vicarious human response, thereby placing the burden upon humanity. J. B. believed that Christ's prophetic office needed to be balanced with an understanding of his priestly office, whereby he offers the human response to God on our behalf.[86] J. B. was particularly concerned with the problem of a "unitarian" attitude to worship, which has no concept of Christ's priestly role as mediator, in whose worthy worship we participate by the Spirit. A unitarian approach places a burden upon the worshipper to offer this worthy worship himself.[87] The Torrances sought to emphasize Christ's priestly office in order to counteract attitudes that bypassed his vicarious and mediatorial role and therefore throw people back upon themselves.[88]

Christ's priestly office is indispensable for understanding the subjective outworking of sanctification. Jesus's sanctification of humanity by offering the perfect human response to God in our place liberates us from endeavoring to attain sanctification ourselves. However, Christ's kingly office is also necessary for understanding the subjective outworking of sanctification. Furthermore, it would contribute to the Torrances' determination to counteract attitudes that throw people back upon themselves. Noble argues that Christ's kingly office expresses his victory over evil and the death of old sinful Adamic humanity and therefore must not be overlooked when considering sanctification.[89] Whilst T. F. recognizes Christ's kingly office,

---

B. considered that, if the Holy Spirit inspired Jesus's actions, and we now have the same Holy Spirit, we can have confidence in being like Christ. See J. B. T., "The Priesthood of Jesus," 163. Davidson and Habets criticize T. F. for not offering a more comprehensive pneumatology (see chapter 3). Perhaps further exploration of the Spirit would also have yielded a greater confidence in the subjective outworking of our sanctification.

86. J. B. T., "The Priesthood of Jesus," 163.

87. J. B. T., *Worship*, 7–18.

88. MacLean observes that T. F. refers to Christ's kingly office as his "Royal Priesthood," which is indicative of his emphasis on Christ's priestly office. MacLean, *Resurrection, Apocalypse and the Kingdom*, 18.

89. Noble, *Holy Trinity*, 149, 140. Noble points to Wesley and Irenaeus as examples of those who appreciate Christ's victory over the power of sin (139). Noble seeks to uphold each of Christ's offices: Christ's priestly office is indispensable for expressing that the atonement was not a mere external transaction, but effected an ontological transformation through Christ's vicarious humanity (143–48); Christ's kingly office expresses Christ's victory over evil and the death of old sinful Adamic humanity (149); Christ's prophetic office reveals the heart of God on the cross and calls for our response in the freedom of what has already been achieved (150–55).

there is rather little positive discussion of what this means for humanity in the outworking of sanctification.[90]

The death of sinful humanity and Christ's victory over evil offers us confidence in the nature of our new humanity and the outworking of our sanctification. Paul declares that our inclusion in Christ's death and resurrection has set us free from sin:

> How can we who died to sin go on living in it? Do you not know that all of us who have been baptised into Christ Jesus were baptised into his death? Therefore we have been buried with him by baptism into death, so that, just as Christ was raised from the dead by the glory of the Father, so we too might walk in newness of life. For if we have been united with him in a death like his, we will certainly be united with him in a resurrection like his. We know that our old self was crucified with him so that the body of sin might be destroyed, and we might no longer be enslaved to sin. For whoever has died is free from sin. But if we have died with Christ, we believe that we will also live with him. We know that Christ, being raised from the dead, will never die again; death no longer has dominion over him. The death he died, he died to sin, once for all, but the life he lives, he lives to God. So you also must consider yourselves dead to sin and alive to God in Christ Jesus. Therefore, do not let sin exercise dominion in your mortal bodies, to make you obey their passions. No longer present your members to sin as instruments of wickedness, but present yourselves to God as those who have been brought from death to life, and present your members to God as instruments of righteousness. For sin will have no dominion over you, since you are not under law but under grace. (Rom 6:2–14)[91]

---

90. T. F. T., *School of Faith,* civ. It is notable that in T. F.'s exploration here of the nature of Christ's ascension as Prophet, Priest and King, it is Christ as Prophet and Priest that receives a lengthy discussion including the implications for humanity. T. F.'s discussion of Christ as King focuses on Jesus without recourse to the implications for humanity sharing in his victory. When he writes that the ascension means the exaltation of the new man, he is more concerned to qualify this with the danger of vertigo. See T. F. T., *Atonement,* 270–95.

91. The first letter of John also points to the possibility of the Christian not sinning: "I am writing these things to you so that you may not sin" (1 John 2:1); "No one who abides in [Christ] keeps on sinning" (2:28); "Everyone born of God does not keep on sinning" (5:18). Paul writes of God's intention that we live holy lives: "For this is the will of God, your sanctification: that you abstain from sexual immorality; that each one of you know how to control his own body in holiness and honour . . . God has not called us for impurity, but in holiness" (1 Thess 4:3–4, 7). There is a clear biblical imperative to live holy lives. 1 Peter 1:15–16 exhorts, "But just as he who called you

Although in one sense the ascension means the removal of Christ from the world, in another sense it means that humanity is raised up and seated in heavenly places in Christ.[92] When Christ's ascension is only understood in terms of his withdrawal from humanity, we are thrown back upon ourselves in the task of sanctification. As Smail considers:

> The ascension of Christ can be seen as his withdrawal into heavenly glory, with all his work ended, so that the burden of his cause and mission falls upon the human shoulders of his people. The way is thus opened for the activity emphasis of so much Protestantism, the pressure of all that we have to do for him, of his dependence upon us, and of our responsibility to bring in his kingdom for him.[93]

Yet the ascension also means that we are raised up with Christ and share in his victory over sin (Eph 1:17–21).

Although a typically Reformed perspective tends to conceive of the outworking of sanctification as a life-long struggle, Christ's kingly office indicates that we are seated in a place of victory and rest.[94] He is now sat at the right hand of the Father (1:20) in Christ who has put all things under his feet (1:22).[95] The eschatological tension of Christ's awaited *Parousia* explains why it is still possible for a Christian to experience a struggle with sin, but it does not make this an inevitable experience. The tension that Paul describes between the Spirit and the flesh does not necessarily entail struggle (Gal 5:17). Paul contrasts sinful behavior (Gal 5:19–21) with the "fruit of the Spirit" (5:22–23). This suggests that holy behavior is something that the Spirit produces in us, rather than something that we can attain through our

---

in holy, so be holy in all you do; for it is written: "Be holy, because I am holy."'" Paul writes, "I urge you, brothers and sisters, in view of God's mercy, to offer your bodies as a living sacrifice, holy and pleasing to God—this is your true and proper worship" (Rom 12:1). The biblical witness thus seems to point to the possibility of the Christian living without sin.

92. This offers a theological basis for Pentecostal-Charismatic mystical experience of encountering God in the heavenly throne room. However, the ascension leads T. F. to be more reserved about Pentecostal-Charismatic experience, on account of his focus on the absence of Christ, rather than the presence of humanity in heaven. See Molnar, *Thomas F. Torrance*, 262. See T. F. T., *Space, Time and Resurrection*, 149.

93. Smail, *Reflected Glory*, 127.

94. Bavinck describes the life of the Christian as "a continuous struggle." Bavinck, *Our Reasonable Faith*, 492.

95. Jesus "has gone into heaven and is at the right hand of God, with angels, authorities, and powers having been subjected to him" (1 Pet 3:21–22).

own struggles.[96] Jesus proclaimed, "I am the vine; you are the branches. If a man remains in me and I in him, he will bear much fruit; apart from me you can do nothing" (John 15:5). Murray takes this metaphor further, arguing, "The vine has to do the work, and the branch enjoys the fruit of it."[97] The outworking of sanctification is not a struggle; it comes from a place of rest.[98] This metaphor of the vine and the branches and the language of abiding in Christ also expresses the intimate nature of humanity's relationship to Christ. When sanctification is conceived of in external, logico-causal categories of endeavoring to follow Jesus's example, it becomes a life-long struggle to battle with the sinful nature. This is an impossible task and the very reason for Christ's vicariously taking sin upon himself in order to destroy it. Such a perspective detracts from what has been accomplished for us in the vicarious humanity of Christ. When the outworking of sanctification is conceived of in terms of participating by the Spirit in Christ, and therefore from a place of rest in what Christ has already accomplished, the Christian life does not have to be a struggle. As T. F. writes,

> By the death of Christ, Christ comes to dwell in me. Instead therefore of living a life of incessant struggle (Rom 7) against an external law, the Living Christ takes up His abode in the heart and becomes the fountain of all actions, the prime motivation of all deeds and thoughts. The Righteousness of God results as a spontaneous outflow radiating from the indwelling Christ.[99]

This confidence in the nature of our new humanity and the outworking of sanctification may be deemed triumphalism.[100] Yet it must be emphasized

---

96. See T. F. T., *Atonement*, 387.

97. Murray, *Absolute Surrender*, 113.

98. Jesus proclaims, "Come to me, all you who are weary and burdened, and I will give you rest. Take my yoke upon you and learn from me, for I am gentle and humble in heart, and you will find rest for your souls. For my yoke is easy and my burden is light" (Matt 11:28–30). This rest is also echoed in Hebrews 4:1: "Therefore, since the promise of entering his rest still stands, let us be careful that none of you be found to have fallen short."

99. T. F. T., "The Death of Christ in St Paul," 23.

100. Triumphalism is a common charge against the Pentecostal-Charismatic movement. See Hudson, "Worship," 196. MacLean criticizes T. F.'s early eschatology, as expressed in his sermons, for being "somewhat triumphalistic." MacLean, *Resurrection, Apocalypse and the Kingdom*, 35. In T. F.'s sermon on John 14:19, he preaches about how Christ's resurrection life can be a "present power in the believer" and that it is not necessary "to wait for a great change at the end of life" (31–33). For MacLean, T. F.'s eschatology matures as it becomes more muted by recourse to the eschatological reserve (38–39). In contention with MacLean, first, it is difficult to assert that T. F.'s

again that this confidence is a boast in God, not our own human efforts, as Paul was proud to do (Gal 6:14; Rom 15:17; 2 Cor 12:9–10). It is confidence in God's victory rather than claiming powerlessness that surely most glorifies God. This confidence reflects the triumphal tone of the biblical witness (Rom 6:14; 8:31; 1 Cor 15:57; 2 Cor 4:8; Eph 6:10–13; Phil 4:13; Col 2:15; Jas 4:7; 1 Pet 2:9; 1 John 5:4). Christ's resurrection power is greater than the sin that held sway over our old human nature. As Paul proclaimed, although all die in Adam, so in Christ all are made alive (1 Cor 15:22). Christ's victory is greater than the powers of evil so that as co-heirs with Christ (Gal 4:7) we are described as "more than conquerors" (Rom 8:37) and God leads us in "triumphal procession in Christ" (2 Cor 2:14).

In seeking to do justice to the eschatological tension, Smail argues that the balance must not be so tipped towards the "now" that the eschatological reserve is disregarded.[101] It is the talent of T. F. that he remains realistic about the eschatological reserve. His confidence is not a denial of this eschatological tension and therefore cannot be deemed triumphalism. Yet, as Smail considers, if the balance is tipped towards the "not yet," Christ is made remote and we are thrown back upon our own efforts, instead of participating in Christ.[102] The Torrances' scheme of salvation corrects a poor perspective on humanity and of sanctification as a life-long struggle. Our new eschatological orientation in Christ gives us confidence in the nature of our humanity and the outworking of our sanctification. Although there is an eschatological reserve and our holiness will not be fully manifest until the *Parousia*, we can take pleasure in the process of becoming who we are.

Conclusion

For the Torrances, the eschatological reserve created by Jesus's ascension means that, although humanity has been made definitively holy, this truth is partly hidden and not fully manifest. This defies a realized eschatology or teleology; sinfulness is a continuing presence as we await the full manifestation of our sanctification at the *Parousia*. Nevertheless, although hidden, it is a definitive reality, which means that the outworking of sanctification is not an external process of becoming progressively more holy. It does not

---

eschatology has matured from the basis of his sermons. Sermons are not systematic theologies and entail emphases relevant to specific circumstances. Second, T. F.'s optimism should not be criticized as triumphalism; his attitude is arguably a faithful reflection of biblical confidence.

101. Smail, *Reflected Glory*, 124–25.

102. Ibid.

depend upon our own endeavors because there is nothing that we can do to make ourselves any more holy. The outworking of sanctification is the process of the unveiling of the reality of our sanctification in Christ. This is not a denial of our subjective human activity but rather puts it in its proper place, coming from a place of rest in what Christ has already accomplished.

Although we live in the eschatological reserve between the ascension and *Parousia,* partaking of the corruption of the world, we have been given a new eschatological orientation in the risen humanity of Christ. We are able to share by the Spirit in the new risen humanity of Christ here and now. T. F. follows his Reformed tradition in holding to Luther's conviction that the believer is *simul justus et peccator.* Yet it is *justus* that is our primary reality in Christ and which describes the eschatological orientation of humanity. To make *peccator* our primary, ontological reality is to diminish Christ. Although struggling with sin may be the experience of a Christian, it is not how a Christian is intended to live. Struggling with sin as normative experience can be fuelled by an external understanding of the atonement. This is because an external scheme does not truly transform humanity. Yet, according to the Torrances' understanding of salvation, humanity is ontologically transformed through the vicarious humanity of Christ. This means that humanity is truly holy and that we are liberated to grow into this reality as we participate in Christ by the Spirit. It is important to affirm the reality of our identity as saints in Christ. This is not immodesty or arrogance because inherent within this affirmation is the recognition of our weakness and the acceptance that we cannot sanctify ourselves. Our boast is not in ourselves but in Christ and it most honors God to accept our new nature and clothe ourselves with Christ.

A fuller appreciation of the significance of this present reality challenges the tendency to conceive of humanity primarily in terms of sinfulness and, consequently, of sanctification as a life-long struggle. Whilst T. F. displays an intense confidence on account of our new eschatological orientation in Christ, there is little positive discussion of what this means for humanity in the outworking of sanctification. This is perhaps due to the concern of the Torrances to emphasize Christ's priestly office in order to counteract attitudes that throw people back upon themselves. Yet a deeper exploration of Christ's kingly office would further this concern for it declares that we are seated in a place of victory and rest. Although in one sense the ascension means the removal of Christ from the world, in another sense it means that humanity is raised up and seated in heavenly places in Christ. Therefore, although humanity lives in the eschatological reserve, in a world of continuing sin and evil, it is neither defined nor ruled by it. We have confidence to grow into the reality of who we are in Christ. When the outworking of sanctification is conceived of in terms of participating in Christ, and therefore from a place of rest in what Christ has already accomplished, the Christian life does not have to be a struggle. This confidence cannot be deemed triumphalism for it is grounded in a realism regarding the eschatological tension, reflects the triumphal tone of the biblical witness and gives the glory to God. The final chapter will go on to explore the nature of sin as we live in the eschatological reserve and the liberating and transforming implications of finding our lives out of ourselves in relationship with the triune God of grace.

6

Fixing Our Eyes on Jesus
Filial over Federal

THE ESCHATOLOGICAL RESERVE CREATED BY CHRIST'S ASCENSION MEANS the abiding presence of sin in the world, and this chapter seeks to explore further the nature of sin as we await the *Parousia*. Yet the risen humanity of Christ also gives us a new eschatological orientation and this chapter explores further what this means for us as we seek to live holy lives today. For the Torrances, our new eschatological orientation in Christ means that we are given to share by the Spirit in Christ's communion with the Father. A holy life does not stem from an introspective concern with our sin or from attempting to follow moral rules and regulations, but from our free participation by the Spirit in Christ's intimate relationship with the Father.

According to the Torrances' theology, sin is essentially *homo incurvatus in se* (man turned in upon himself). It is the unfathomable rejection of God, seeking the place of God for oneself. It is driven by a misunderstanding of God and of our own human nature and, ultimately, arises from not knowing what has objectively been achieved for us in Christ. Thus it expresses itself in the tragic endeavor to gain what we have already been given.

Yet the Holy Spirit is shared by Christ with us so that, according to the Torrances, we might be turned out of ourselves (*homo excurvatus ex se*) to share in the life of Christ. When we are re-oriented by the Spirit to find our lives in Christ, this is the basis of a holy life. Scripture exhorts us to fix our eyes upon Jesus, which is the true meaning of repentance. This presents a challenge in particular to the introspective understanding of repentance found within the current movement to reclaim Puritan teaching. Furthermore, for the Torrances, God's purposes for humanity are primarily filial over federal; we are reconciled for relationship, not to have a second chance at adhering to the law. As we share by the Spirit in the Son's communion with the Father, we grow to reflect the reality of who we are in Christ.

Incurvatus In Se

The eschatological reserve created by Jesus's ascension means the abiding presence of sin in the world. Although God has chosen to unite humanity to himself in Christ by the Spirit, T. F. believes that there is a mysterious absurdity that some nevertheless reject God:[1]

> Sin is utter separation from God, alienation from God—but the distance between God and man is not constituted by any metaphysical magnitude such as the infinite distance between the creator and the creature. The distance between God and man is due precisely to the nearness of God to man, to the antagonism between God's holy will of love and our sin. The nearer God comes, the more intense the conflict and we are forced to cry, 'Depart from me, for I am a sinful man, O Lord' and 'I am not worthy to have you come under my roof.' Those were words spoken to God incarnate as he came near in Jesus Christ, spoken in the very presence of God, and they bring out into sharp relief the difference, the conflict between humanity and God which is minimised when God is thought of at a distance. Sin presupposes the nearness of God.[2]

A person's rejection of God is only possible in his presence.[3] For T. F., sin is intrinsically relational: "sin is a personal act against the very person of God."[4]

---

1. A discussion of the irrational nature of sin can be found in chapter 1. Cf. David Kelsey conceives of sin according to Wisdom Literature's presentation of sin as folly and argues that to attempt to explain it is a conceptual mistake. See Kelsey, *Eccentric Existence*, 408–11. He writes, "Sin is a type of negative mystery. It is not mystery in the sense of something in principle explicable but about which we presently have insufficient information for an explanation. Nor is it mystery in the sense of something too richly complex for our finite minds to be able to grasp its rationale. Rather it is a mystery in the sense of something undeniably real but a-rational, without cause or reason. Hence, to pose the question, "How do you explain the presence of sin and evil in the created realm?" is to fall prey to a conceptual mistake." (411)

2. T. F. T., *Incarnation*, 247.

3. Ibid., 252. He writes, "Sin is only possible in the presence of God, in the relation of the creature to the creator."

4. Ibid. Cf. Jüngel: "We must *locate* sin, we must give it its true place. This place is the *relationship to God*." Jüngel, *Justification*, 93. Cf. Kelsey describes sin as "a distortion of proper human response to God," which is a relational understanding of sin

> Sin is repudiated fellowship with God within mankind's existential relation to God. It is the act which seizes upon that very relation which they have in fellowship with God, the relation which constitutes the very being of humanity, and perverts it into its opposite, into separation from God, rebellion against him, in the will to be independent and autonomous.[5]

In rejecting God, a person is seeking the place of God for himself or herself: "When men and women assert themselves against the Godness of God they are actually asserting themselves to be God, and so placing themselves in direct contradiction to the Godness of God."[6] As Barth considers, although God intended mankind to participate in his lordship, man seeks to exalt himself autonomously.[7] Man seeks to take the role of judge from Christ and to be his own judge.[8] Man seeks to be self-governing, as Adam did in the Garden of Eden.[9] In so doing, man self-destructively alienates himself from God.[10] Barth conceives of man's exaltation of himself to the place of God as the essence of sin.[11]

Barth's understanding of sin complements the Torrances' theology. For Barth, sin is driven by two errors: a misunderstanding of humanity as self-determining and, even more decisively, a misunderstanding of God either as remote or as a despotic ruler.[12] Here we come back again to the importance of the self-revelation of God in Christ that, in the words of J. B., "God is a covenant God not a contract God," and T. F.'s assertion that "there

---

rather than a failure to fulfill, or the breaking of, rules. Kelsey, *Eccentric Existence*, 402.

5. T. F. T., *Incarnation*, 254.
6. Ibid., 249.
7. Barth, *Church Dogmatics* IV/1, 435–36.
8. Ibid., 445.
9. Ibid., 420–21.

10. Ibid., 432, 35–36. T. F. also saw this as self-destructive: "Sin is to be understood as the contradiction introduced into this life-relation or life-unity of man with the creator, for in sin the human creature who depends on the creator for existence and life rebels against the creator. Sin is therefore destructive of the creature—a form of suicide. By rebelling against the creator and by asserting his or her independence, the creature is rebelling against the innermost relation which constitutes their very being as a creature, as human being. Sin is therefore an 'impossible possibility,' as the medieval schoolmen sometimes called it." T. F. T., *Incarnation*, 247–48.

11. Barth, *Church Dogmatics* IV/1, 418–19. Jesus acts in obverse to man's self-exaltation by humbling himself in his assumption of humanity (432). Essentially, man "wants to be his own god and lord and judge." (459)

12. Ibid., 463, 465–67. In seeking to be his own judge, man is delusional. For Barth, sin is driven by falsehood (459).

is no God behind the back of Jesus."[13] Furthermore, Christ not only shows us the nature of God, but the nature of humanity. We are determined by the eschatological orientation of the risen humanity of Christ. This may mean that we are not self-determined individuals, but it does radically liberate us to be "personalized persons" and "humanized humans" who are given to share by the Spirit in Christ's intimate relationship with the Father.[14]

This ultimately means that sin is driven by not knowing what has been objectively achieved for us in Christ. In a sermon on Colossians 3:3, T. F. preaches that we behave as though we are not dead to sin because we do not believe that we are dead to sin: "That is one of the strange things about men and women. Although Christ has died for them, and they are dead to their old selves, they refuse to believe it; and act as though they were not dead!"[15] As 2 Peter 1:9 suggests, those who are not practicing godliness have forgotten that they have been cleansed from sin.[16] Similarly, Murray believes that we continue to sin when we do not realize that it has been conquered.[17] He proposes that this problem is linked to an external understanding of the atonement: some Christians know that Christ died *for* sin, but they do not realize that he died *to* sin.[18]

Sin is driven by the fear of a perceived lack and expresses itself in the attempt to gain what we believe that we do not have. Barth considers that sin is motivated by the attempt to get that which we do not realize we have already been given:

> Why is all that we can do, our effective progress, only an ascent or descent from one Titanism to another? Why are we so strikingly the same in spite of all the changes in costume and scenery throughout the centuries? Obviously because the fault lies much deeper. Because the goal of all these strivings is the thing which is an illusion. Because the compelling force behind all these strivings is the false idea that—if only we can acquire this or

---

13. J. B. T., "Introduction," 1; T. F. T., *Scottish Theology*, 294.
14. T. F. T., *Mediation*, 78–79.
15. T. F. T., "Colossians 3:3," 3.
16. Cf. Paul's words, "Do you not know that you are God's temple and that God's Spirit dwells in you?" (1 Cor 3:16) and, "Do you not know that your body is a temple of the Holy Spirit within you . . . ?" (6:19), which suggest that we experience sin because we do not know the truth of God.
17. Murray, *Abide*, 128.
18. Murray, *Like Christ*, 155–58.

that—we will succeed in being our own helper and redeemer and saviour.[19]

T. F. saw this striving to acquire salvation as the most terrible expression of sin: "The more they strive in their self-will to save themselves, the more they sin—in fact that is the very movement of sin at its subtlest and in its very worst form, self-justification."[20] Eberhard Jüngel also perceives how the falsehood associated with sin leads to legalistic striving: "The untruth of sin places the unconditional nature of the gospel under the condition of the law and thus makes the good news into a new morality."[21]

Essentially, sin is *homo incurvatus in se* (man turned in upon himself).[22] Although we have been reconciled for relationship, to share by the Spirit in the Son's communion with the Father, there is an irrational mystery that people choose to make themselves their own center. T. F. writes, "The central point in every human being is their relation to God, and sin means that this central point has been violated. Sin means that men and women have fallen out of the central thing in their life and existence, that they have thus become ec-centric."[23] Barth describes this as "man rotating about himself."[24] Jenson suggests that the varieties of sin, such as pride, sloth and falsehood, essentially fall under the one conceptual umbrella of *homo incurvatus in se*.[25]

Excurvatus Ex Se

Although we live in the eschatological reserve, with the continuing presence of sin, we also live in the power of Pentecost. At Pentecost, Jesus shared the Holy Spirit with humanity so that humanity might share by the Holy Spirit in Christ.[26] The role of the Holy Spirit is to turn us out of ourselves to

19. Barth, *Church Dogmatics* IV/1, 461.

20. T. F. T., *Incarnation*, 253.

21. Jüngel, *Justification*, 110. He writes, "The epitome of evil is sin in its basic form of the lie . . . Instead of 'take and eat' it says 'first perform, then you eat.'"

22. Jenson traces the notion of *incurvatus in se* from Augustine to Luther to contemporary theologians. See Jenson, *Gravity of Sin*.

23. T. F. T., *Incarnation*, 248.

24. Barth, *Church Dogmatics* IV/1, 422. Cf. Noble defines sin as the mind set on the flesh. Noble, *Holy Trinity*, 35. Cf. Athanasius, *Contra Gentes*, I–III.

25. Jenson, *Gravity of Sin*, 5. Noble agrees with Jenson that self-centeredness is a unifying category for sin. Noble, *Holy Trinity*, 123.

26. T. F. T., *Reconstruction* 241. This is what T. F. believes is expressed by the concept of *theosis*. *Theosis* is not the deification of the believer but the inclusion of the

participate in the life of Christ.²⁷ T. F. writes that the church finds its true center of existence in Christ:

> The church is the community of the reconciled, redeemed through the blood of Christ, for in him God has abolished the enmity and sin that estranged us from him and has given us the Spirit of true love. Through union with Jesus Christ the church shares in his life and in all that he has done for mankind. Through his birth its members have a new birth and are made members of the new humanity. Through his obedient life and death their sins are forgiven and they are clothed with a new righteousness. Through his resurrection and triumph over the powers of darkness they are freed from the dominion of evil and are made one body with him. Through his ascension the kingdom of heaven is opened to all believers and the church waits for his coming again to fulfil in all humanity the new creation which he has already begun in it. Thus the church finds its life and being not in itself but in Jesus Christ alone, for not only is he the head of the church but he includes the church within his own fullness.²⁸

T. F. perceives this truth to be reflected in Paul's language of the church as the "body of Christ" (Rom 12:4–5; 1 Cor 12:12–27; Eph 1:22–23; 5:29–32; Col 1:18):

> The term body of Christ directs us at once to Christ himself, laying the emphasis not on the body but on Christ. Thus it does not focus attention on the church as an entity in itself or as something that exists for its own sake, but upon the church as the immediate property of Christ which he has made his very own and gathered into the most intimate relation with himself.²⁹

T. F. considers the church to be "constantly directed away from itself to find in Christ alone its justification and its sanctification."³⁰ The essential theme of Paul's letters to the Corinthians, and in the Epistle to the Hebrews, J. B. argues, is that Christ is our living center, upon whom we must keep our eyes fixed:

---

believer in the divine life, whereby he finds his true center of existence not in himself but in God (243).

27. Ibid., 238.
28. T. F. T., *Atonement*, 361.
29. Ibid., 363.
30. Ibid., 371.

> We need to remind ourselves constantly that the centre of the church is not ourselves, but Jesus Christ our living Lord. Under the pressures of our culture, and of theological controversy, are we not in danger of losing that living centre—of forgetting that the real agent in the life of the Church is not ourselves, but Jesus Christ?[31]

This danger of losing Christ as the living center can arguably be seen, inadvertently, in the teaching of those who piously seek to reclaim Puritan theology. As Beeke and Jones consider, an integral aspect of Puritanism is self-examination.[32] Following this Puritan concern, Packer encourages Christians to introspectively examine themselves until they have discovered and repented of all their sins.[33] In contrast, J. B. asserts, "In faith we look primarily away from ourselves to Jesus Christ, desiring to be found 'in him,' clothed with his righteousness (Phil. 3:7–11)."[34]

Transformed by the Renewing of the Mind

When we turn away from ourselves (*homo incurvatus in se*) to Christ (*homo excurvatus ex se*), this is the essence of repentance. The Greek word *metanoia*, translated in English as "repentance," essentially means "a change of mind."[35] This challenges an introspective, anthropocentric notion of repentance whereby we are turned in on ourselves to examine our sinfulness and endeavor to offer satisfactory grief. This is exemplified by Packer's understanding of repentance as "binding one's conscience to God's moral law, confessing and forsaking one's sins, making restitution for past wrongs, grieving before God at the dishonour one's sins have done him, and forming a game plan for holy living."[36] Packer's articulation of repentance tends towards dependence upon our own endeavors: "Repentance means altering one's habits of thought, one's attitudes, outlook, policy, direction, and behaviour, just as fully as it is needed to get one's life out of the wrong shape and into the right one."[37] Yet for the Torrances, we do not have to rely upon the adequacy of our efforts because our repentance is a sharing in Christ's

---

31. J. B. T., *Worship*, 107. Cf. J. B. T., "Prayer and the Priesthood of Christ," 64.
32. Beeke and Jones, *A Puritan Theology*, 906.
33. Packer, *Rediscovering Holiness*, 139.
34. J. B. T., *Worship*, 23.
35. T. F. T., *Atonement*, 3.
36. Packer, *Rediscovering Holiness*, 33.
37. Ibid., 123.

perfect vicarious repentance on our behalf.[38] According to Packer, "Repenting is never a pleasure. Always, in more sense than one, it is a pain, and will continue as long as life lasts."[39] J. B., in contrast, describes repentance as a "joyful" activity.[40] This is because J. B. conceives of repentance as a turning away from ourselves to Christ, in whose intimate communion with the Father we may freely participate.[41]

As we live in the eschatological reserve, the Church is directed away from itself to turn to Christ and to hold to what is true of our lives in Christ: "So if you have been raised with Christ, seek the things that are above, where Christ is, seated at the right hand of God. Set your minds on things that are above, not on things that are on earth, for you have died, and your life is hidden with Christ in God" (Col 3:1–3).[42] Thus T. F. asserts, "While in the new time we are complete in Christ Jesus, yet in the conflicts and abstractions of fallen time we are unable to realise that wholeness, but must nevertheless reckon that we are dead to the old life and created again in the new."[43] Not only are we directed *to* Christ, but we are directed to share *in* Christ, and in his very mind and truth (1 Cor 2:16). T. F. urges the church to "let the mind that was in Christ be its mind, in order that the whole understanding of the church may be transformed and renewed in him, and in order that the whole structure of its thought may be determined by his truth."[44]

This means that our beliefs should be shaped by the truth of God rather than our own human experience. In the context of sanctification, this means that what we believe should be formed by the truth of our identity as saints in Christ, as opposed to our earthly experiences of sinfulness. Paul often exhorts the early Christians to turn from their experience of sin to God and his truth. He writes to the Galatians, "Formerly, when you did

---

38. T. F. T., *Mediation*, 94–95; T. F. T., *Atonement*, 71.

39. Packer, *Rediscovering Holiness*, 122.

40. J. B. T., "Christ in Our Place," 50.

41. Ibid., 48.

42. Although there is a tension between the Spirit and the flesh, we are directed by the Spirit away from ourselves to "set [our] minds on the things of the Spirit" (Rom 8:5). See also: "So we fix our eyes not on what is seen, but on what is unseen. For what is seen is temporary, but what is unseen is eternal." (2 Cor 4:18); "fixing our eyes on Jesus, the author and perfecter of faith" (Heb. 12:2).

43. T. F. T., "Eschatology," 420.

44. T. F. T., *Atonement*, 376. For more on reconciliation of the mind see 437–47. See Søren Kierkegaard's discussion of the transformation that comes from God's revelation of the truth. Johannes Climacus, *Philosophical Fragments*. See also Murray Rae's study of Kierkegaard in relation to the New Testament concept of *metanoia*: Rae, *Kierkegaard's Vision of the Incarnation*.

not know God, you were enslaved to beings that by nature are not gods. Now, however, that you have come to know God, or rather to be known by God, how can you turn back again to the weak and beggarly elemental spirits? How can you want to be enslaved to them again?" (Gal 4:8–9). In the context of the Corinthians's jealousy and quarrelling, Paul writes, "Do you not know that you are God's temple and that God's Spirit dwells in you? If anyone destroys God's temple, God will destroy that person. For God's temple is holy, and you are that temple" (1 Cor 3:16–17). Shortly afterwards, in the context of their fighting and sexual immorality, Paul writes similarly, "Do you not know that your body is a temple of the Holy Spirit within you, which you have from God, and that you are not your own?" (1 Cor 6:19).

Barth considers that Paul's method of moral instruction is to remind the early Christians of what has already been accomplished in Christ: "To oppose the raging flood of human vice a barrier by which it is set effectively in the past all that is needed is the ἀλλά of recollection of what has taken place in Jesus Christ, and in Him for them and to them."[45] Since sin is driven by a misunderstanding of God and of humanity, it is necessary to have correct knowledge in order to lead holy lives.[46] As Hays argues,

> Insofar as we perceive the truth about God's redemptive work in the world, we will participate gladly in the outworking of God's purpose; conversely, if we fail to act in a way consonant with God's will, we are living in a state of contradiction: we are failing to understand what is going on about us. Consequently, much of Paul's moral exhortation takes the form of reminding his readers to view their obligations and actions in the cosmic context of what God has done in Christ.[47]

---

45. Barth, *Church Dogmatics* IV/2, 517. Here Barth is commenting on 1 Cor 6:11.

46. "The preparation (καταρτισμός) of the saints consists in the recollection, first of what Christ already is, that as the Head of all things He is their Head, and second of what they already are in Him, that as the community they are His body, summoned to hasten towards this being of His and theirs, and therefore to that ἑνότης. This is the truth by which they are determined, and it is absolutely superior to every sleight of men 'method of error' (v. 15). The preparation of the saints consists in their equipment for ἀληθεύειν, i.e., for a life which here and now is lived by and for this truth; in a love for their Head which will not fail to give inner unity to the Church.' Ἀληθεύοντες ἐν ἀγάπῃ in virtue of this preparation, the saints will do the ἔργον τῆς ιακονίας (v. 12) and therefore fulfil the meaning of their existence as saints. They will "grow" . . . i.e., grow εἰς αὐτόν, into Christ who is their Head, in the direction which He thus gives, and towards the goal which He thus appoints." Barth, *Church Dogmatics* IV/2, 626. Here Barth is exegeting Eph 4:12–15.

47. Hays, *Moral Vision*, 39.

Murray asserts, "The whole Christian life depends on the clear consciousness of our position in Christ."[48] He writes,

> Get hold of your union to Christ; believe in the new nature within you, that spiritual life which you have from Christ, a life that has died and been raised again. A man's acts are always in accordance with his idea of his state. A king acts like a king, otherwise we say, "That man has forgotten his kingship," but if a man is conscious of being a king, he behaves like a king. And so I cannot live the life of a true believer unless I am filled with a consciousness of this every day . . . As long as I do not know it, I cannot act according to it, though it be in me . . . know yourselves as dead indeed unto sin.[49]

It may not always necessarily follow that we lead holy lives when we are given to know our identity in Christ; the irrational nature of sin prevents a definite logico-causal connection. Nevertheless, the idea that our perceived identity is significant for how we behave is supported by Paul's frequent affirmation of our identity in Christ, followed by an exhortation to live according to this new identity. For example, in Romans 6, Paul explains that we have been crucified with Christ and have risen with him to new life. He goes on to encourage the Romans to focus on their new identity in Christ: "So you also must consider yourselves dead to sin and alive to God in Christ Jesus" (Rom 6:11). Then he exhorts them to live righteously (6:12–13). In the same way, Paul tells the Colossians that they have died with Christ (Col 3:2), and this is followed by the exhortation to put to death their sinful behavior (3:5–9). Paul reminds the Colossians of their identity as "God's chosen ones, holy and beloved" and exhorts them to holy living (3:12ff.). In his letter to the Ephesians, Paul encourages them to live no longer according to the old nature as the Gentiles do but to grow up into Christ (Eph 4:1, 15, 17), reminding them that they are "created according to the likeness of God in true righteousness and holiness" (4:24). He instructs the Ephesians to live in the likeness of Christ (5:1–2) and to avoid impurity "as is proper among saints" (5:3). Paul's pattern of affirmation of our identity followed by exhortation to live accordingly is also echoed in the first letter of Peter which affirms, "You are a chosen people, a royal priesthood, a holy nation" (1 Pet 2:9) and then goes on in exhortation to abstain from sin and live holy lives (2:11–12ff.). Scriptural exhortations to godly behavior are

---

48. Murray, *Abide*, 51.
49. Murray, *The Master's Indwelling*, 71.

often preceded by directing the early Christians to the truth of their identity in Christ.[50]

T. F.'s preaching reflects this biblical pattern. In a sermon on Romans 6, T. F. preached that the new life we have as a result of our inclusion in Christ's vicarious humanity leads to a change in moral behavior. He encouraged his congregation to live knowing that they are dead to sin and alive to God, believing this to be the basis of living free from sin.[51] Similarly, in a sermon on Philippians 2:12, T. F. affirmed his congregation's identity as saints in Christ and spoke of this as the basis of a holy life:

> Don't you see, in God's sight, you are already secluded in the heart of Jesus Christ, you are already a new creature though to all outward appearances you may be far from it, you are already a saint though you know yourself to be a sinner. That is the glorious paradox of the Gospel. Christ has been tempted in all points as we are, He has tasted death for every man, and now presents us with a perfect redemption—and it is only because He has done that, that we may pluck up our courage and work, for it is God that worketh in us.[52]

Hauerwas regrets that modern Christian ethics has forgotten this orientation towards God and his truth, instead becoming self-centered and focused upon what we do.[53] He suggests, "Because contemporary Christian ethicists have assumed that "the ethical" primarily concerns action and decision, they have found little moral significance in basic affirmations about God, Christ, grace, and sanctification."[54] Yet as Paul's teaching appears to

---

50. Horton also understands sanctification in terms of the believer's behavior being brought into line with our identity. Horton, *Pilgrim Theology,* Kindle ed., Loc 6356. However, he understands this within a wider forensic framework, which fails to offer an account of the transformation of humanity in our ontological depths. Since Horton understands the believer's righteousness as "*alien,* that is, belonging properly to someone else" (5899), it is difficult to see how the behavior of the believer, who is "actually unrighteous in himself/herself" (5640), could begin to attain to the standards of someone else, that is, Christ.

51. T. F. T., "Romans 6," 5.

52. T. F. T., "Philippians 2:12," 3–4.

53. Hauerwas, *Vision and Virtue,* 30.

54. Ibid., 45. For Hauerwas, the Christian life is about growing into the reality of these affirmations of God's action in Christ (46). He writes, "The Christian is one so formed as he assumes the particular description offered him through the Church. This formation is the determination of our character through God's sanctifying work. Sanctification is thus the formation of the Christian's character that is the result of his intention to see the world as redeemed in Jesus Christ" (67). Hauerwas proposes a form of virtue ethics that he calls an "ethics of character." He argues that the traditional

suggest, the truth of God's accomplishment in Christ and who humanity is in him is of utmost significance for how we lead our lives. When we are turned out of ourselves by the Spirit to find our lives in Christ, this is the basis of holy living.

Sharing by the Spirit in the Son's Communion with the Father

The outworking of sanctification comes not only from this noetic process but, more fundamentally, participatory relationship. We were reconciled not only so that we may look to Christ as an example but so that we may participate *in* Christ and share by the Spirit in his intimate communion with the Father. Our sanctification is, according to T. F., a "sharing in his holy relation to the Father through the Holy Spirit."[55] It is union not atonement that is the goal of God's reconciling purposes; we are not only saved but given to share in the life of God.[56] J. B. often asserts, "In love God created us for 'sonship,' to find our true being-in-communion, and in Jesus Christ

---

Protestant understanding of morality as obedience to the law and will of God, which defies our own moral efforts or attempts to determine the good, does not appreciate the influence of our inner nature on our acts and how the self is determined through its acts (*Character and the Christian Life*, 3–5). He writes, "To be sanctified is to have our character determined by our basic commitments and beliefs about God. It is a willingness to see and understand ourselves as having significance only as our agency is qualified under the form of Christ and the task he entrusts us. Christian character is the formation of our affections and actions according to the fundamental beliefs of the Christian faith and life" (203). Hauerwas is concerned that without an ethics of character, either we turn to following external laws or to an automatic, mechanical process of grace producing holy living (194). His ethics of character highlights the importance of a change in our being if our beliefs are to have significance for our behavior (227). Yet although Hauerwas's ethics of character recognizes the importance of placing our focus upon Christ, he does not employ a concept of participation *in* Christ. It is not sufficient to have an external relationship with God or to know basic affirmations about Christ; we must share in his very life by the Spirit. Hauerwas describes a person's self-determination of character as "dependent upon his ability to fix attention on descriptions and act accordingly" (*Vision and Virtue*, 55; see also *Character and the Christian Life*, 188, 215). This is in danger of throwing us back upon our own efforts; rather, it is the work of the Spirit to turn us out of ourselves to Christ and to lead fruitful lives.

55. T. F. T., *Atonement*, 386. T. F. writes, "In its ultimate sense, the holiness of the church is its relation to God, its participation in the fellowship of the divine being and life and truth" (385).

56. T. F. T., *Mediation*, 77.

gives us that gift of communion, through the Spirit, of being daughters and sons of the Father."[57]

J. B. distinguishes between three theological models: (1) the Harnack (Hick) model; (2) the existential, present-day experience model; and (3) the incarnational trinitarian model.[58] The first is exemplified by nineteenth-century modern liberalism and J. B. perceives it to be in part responsible for moralistic Christianity. It offers an external account of Jesus as a teacher of moral principles and leads to the Christian's onerous task of following his exceptional example.[59] The second model recognizes the God-humanward movement in Christ and the work of atonement on the cross; yet it has no concept of his life-long vicarious humanity and the human-Godward movement in Christ, thereby making our response burdensome because it is detached from participation in Christ.[60] The third model, which J. B. commends, appreciates both the God-humanward movement, the human-Godward movement and the trinitarian dynamics of these movements.[61] It conceives of the Christian life as "the gift of participating through the Spirit in the incarnate Son's communion with the Father."[62]

Noble suggests that, if we are to take Christ as an example, it should be of his intimate relationship with the Father in which we are also given to share by the Holy Spirit. Jesus lives a holy life because of his relationship with the Father in the Spirit and, as we share in that relationship, the outworking of sanctification follows.[63] Noble considers that Christ's victory over evil is not the key to living a holy life but the consequence; "The inner secret is his relationship *with the Father*, and that relationship is a relationship *in the Spirit*."[64] In order to attempt to express this marvelous, mysterious transforming relationship, Noble offers the analogy of the experience of a man falling in love with a woman. The man finds that he is turned out

---

57. J. B. T., "Introduction," 1. See also J. B. T., "Prayer and the Priesthood of Christ," 60; J. B. T., *Worship*, 26–7. J. B. upholds McLeod Campbell as an example of one who appreciates God's filial purposes. See McLeod Campbell, *Nature of the Atonement*.

58. J. B. writes this in the context of worship but it can be applied to Christian activity more broadly.

59. J. B. T., *Worship*, 12–13.

60. Ibid., 13–18. J. B. suggests that it is this model that is most widespread (22). This model is exemplified in some modern evangelical Protestantism, as explored in chapter 2.

61. J. B. T., *Worship*, 18–25, 8–11.

62. Ibid., 18.

63. Noble, *Holy Trinity*, 200.

64. Ibid., 186.

of himself and she brings out the best in him.[65] The man does not seek of itself this change for the better; the end is her, to be with the woman, and his transformation is a byproduct.[66] Noble argues, "It is objective experience of the real and living God that results in the subjective inner and outward change we call 'sanctification.'"[67]

Conceived in terms of participatory relationship, this challenges an external, legal understanding of the outworking of sanctification. J. B. regrets the way in which the Puritans sought to inspire people to holiness through the law and fear of the consequences of disobedience, thereby subordinating God's filial purposes to an overarching legal framework.[68] William Perkins's preaching method was to preach law first, in order to terrify and provoke repentance, and then to preach the gospel as the offer of solace to those who choose to embrace Christ.[69] As Beeke and Jones write, "Not only did the Puritans seek to stir up a longing for heaven, they also sought to instill a terror of hell."[70] Packer believes that Christians today have the "most to learn from their stern side."[71] For Packer, it is law, rather than God's grace, that leads to repentance: "The self-knowledge in which a Christian's repentance is rooted comes from the law. It is a result of being made to face God's prescribed moral standards for us his creation."[72] Likewise, with regard to the outworking of sanctification, Packer seems to direct the Christian primarily to a relationship with the law rather than to Christ: "Holiness sets its sights on absolute moral standards and unchanging moral ideals, established by God himself."[73] Packer's understanding of sanctification prioritizes a legal framework over God's filial purposes:

---

65. Ibid., 15–16. Noble's analogy could be taken further because when a man falls in love with a woman, he can find that he cannot take his eyes off her. This resonates with the biblical call to fix our eyes on Jesus and, as we look to him, be transformed in his image.

66. Ibid., 16. Cf. Augustine: *"dilige et quod vis fac"* ("Love, and do what you will"). Augustine, *In epistulam Ioannis ad Parthos*, VII/8. See also Jesus's words: "If you love me, you will keep my commandments" (John 14:15).

67. Noble, *Holy Trinity*, 17.

68. J. B. T., "Strengths and Weaknesses," 49.

69. Beeke and Jones, *A Puritan Theology*, 694, 701.

70. Ibid., 830.

71. Packer, *Rediscovering Holiness*, 109.

72. Ibid., 150. Packer refers to Rom 7:7–28 for support and yet here Paul seems to be confirming that the law serves to fuel disobedience.

73. Ibid., 175–76.

> The purity and uprightness of God's own character, and his judgments of value (what is good and worthwhile, and what is neither) are fixed and immutable. He cannot be other than hostile to individuals and communities that flout his law. He cannot do other than visit them some of late in displays of retributive judgment, so that all his rational creatures may see the glory of his moral inflexibility.[74]

This legal understanding is accompanied by a tendency towards reliance upon our own anthropocentric endeavors:

> Those who neglect the discipline of thorough repentance for their shortcomings, along with regular self-examination so as to discern those shortcomings, are behaving as if God just turns a blind eye to our moral flaws—which is actually to insult him, since such indifference would be a moral flaw itself. But God is not morally indifferent, and we must not act towards him as if he were. The truth is that the only way to show real respect for God's real purity is by realistically setting oneself against sin. That means not only a wholehearted purpose of pleasing God by consecrated zeal in keeping his law, it also means repentance. And repentance means not more routine words of regret as one asks for pardon without one's heart being involved, but a deliberate confessing, an explicit self-humbling, and a sensing of shame in the presence of God as one contemplates one's failures.[75]

Smail regrets the tendency in modern evangelicalism towards the legalistic following of rules:

> Evangelicals have tended to major on initiation into the Christian life, to concentrate on its beginnings and to run out of steam when it comes to its growth and maturing by talking of the saved life in legal and moralistic terms, almost as if it were a matter of conformity to rather external standards of ethical conduct, religious practice and evangelistic duty.[76]

We have not simply been forgiven and given a second chance to adhere to the law. T. F. is emphatic that the church is not a group of individuals who seek to follow common moral principles; the church is a community of persons ontologically transformed in Christ who share by the Spirit in

---

74. Ibid., 135.

75. Ibid., 145–46.

76. Smail, *Reflected Glory*, 44. Noble links this to the tendency towards an exclusively penal understanding of the atonement. Sanctification is not rooted in the atonement and therefore demands our own moral endeavors. Noble, *Holy Trinity*, 30–31.

his relationship with the Father.[77] Canlis writes of Calvin's conception of the "identity-forming ministry" of the Spirit, who reveals who we are as adopted sons of the Father. The Spirit directs us out of ourselves, away from our own attempts at perfect performance, to God and our relationship with him, which is the basis of living the Christian life.[78] She writes, "The Holy Spirit ushers us into adoption, not workaholism; the Spirit tells us not so much what to do, but *who we are*."[79] For T. F., any external conception of holy living by adhering to laws is excluded by Paul's language of the church as the "body of Christ." The church inheres in Christ; it does not follow abstract rules.[80]

J. B. argues that Scripture is not a book of law but a revelation of grace.[81] Looking to the New Testament witness, Hays believes that it is not meant to be taken as a static book of rules: "Paul nowhere sets forth a systematic presentation of "Christian ethics." Nor does he offer his communities a "manual of discipline," a comprehensive summary of community organization and duties."[82] Breaking with the norm of the ancient world, Paul responds dynamically to issues that arise, in all things pointing to the person of Christ.[83] 1 Timothy is testament to the problem of a second-generation reception of Paul whereby his teaching is taken for granted and morality becomes static.[84] Hays writes,

> 1 Timothy articulates the moral vision of a Christian community that has achieved a measure of institutional and symbolic stability; the writer is no longer thinking through ethical issues from their theological foundations. All that needs to be done is to guard the tradition entrusted by the apostle. The result?

---

77. T. F. T., *Mediation*, 82. Cf. Noble, *Holy Trinity*, 147.
78. Canlis, "Living as God's Children," 343–45.
79. Ibid., 345.
80. T. F. T., *Reconstruction*, 201.
81. J. B. T., "The Doctrine of the Trinity," 36. Bavinck maintains that scriptural exhortations to holiness are derived not from the law but from the gospel. They are rooted in Christ, "in the Lord" (cf. Eph 4:21ff; 5:2, 5–6, 8). See Bavinck, *Our Reasonable Faith*, 482. Berkouwer points to the people of Israel as indication that following the law is not sufficient: "For too often men have talked about the command to be holy in such as way as to mutilate the biblical message. It is certainly not enough for a man to say that he honors the law of God and for that reason strives towards holiness. The people of Israel offer proof that one may live in the climate of absolute imperatives and still perish." Berkouwer, *Faith and Sanctification*, 19.
82. Hays, *Moral Vision*, 17.
83. Ibid., 17, 43.
84. Ibid., 71.

> A gain in stability, but a loss in profundity and freedom. In the authentic Pauline letters, the churches are repeatedly exhorted to discern the will of God anew under the guidance of the Holy Spirit; in 2 Timothy, there is no call for discernment because the will of God has already been sufficiently made known in the "sound teaching" of the tradition.[85]

As Hauerwas argues, "The specification of the Christian life, even in its most appealing and cogent form, always runs the risk of being made an end in itself—a program to be achieved rather than a mode of being to be lived out."[86] He regrets that law can be used as a substitute for relationship with Christ:

> The proposal of the shape of the Christian life tends to be used as a substitute for him alone who can give substance to the proposal. The Christian life cannot be specified by a set of virtues to be achieved apart from their arising as a response to Jesus Christ; nor can it be interpreted solely as a pattern of rules to follow or good acts to do.[87]

We fulfill the law not by adhering to static rules, argues J. B., but dynamically through the presence of the Spirit in us and our participation in Christ.[88] For T. F., fulfillment of the law is actually a dark, not a virtuous, endeavor when it is detached from participation in the person of Christ:

> The human heart is so desperately wicked that it cunningly takes advantage of the hiatus between what we are and what we ought to be in order to latch on to the patterns and structures of moral behaviour required of us, so that under the image of what is good and right it masks or even fortifies its evil intentions. Such is the self-deception of our human heart and the depravity of our self-will that we seek to justify ourselves before God and our neighbours by a formal, impersonal fulfilment of the divine law in which we remain untouched in ourselves and uncommitted in our own persons. Yet all the time we are fostering the very

---

85. Ibid.

86. Hauerwas, *Character and the Christian Life*, 182. In advancing a dynamic, relational account of ethics, this is not to be confused with systems such as Joseph Fletcher's situation ethics. See Fletcher, *Situation Ethics*. Dynamism from an anthropocentric starting point is as erroneous as adhering to static rules. The dynamism must not be abstracted from its center in Christ; it comes from participating by the Spirit in his relationship with the Father.

87. Hauerwas, *Character and the Christian Life*, 182.

88. J. B. T., "Prayer and the Priesthood of Christ," 61

processes of dehumanisation at work in the depths of our beings and trapping ourselves inescapably in insincere and hypocritical personalities.[89]

Similarly, Barth believes that ethical behavior is a matter of following God's will by the Spirit through participating in Christ.[90] It is futile and sinful for humanity to attempt to be its own judge and distinguish between good and evil, which is how the serpent tempted Adam and Eve.[91] Godly living is dynamic, not static, flowing from relationship with God rather than from our own beliefs about what is right and wrong.[92] Bonhoeffer likewise argues that the moral Christian life comes not by being turned in upon ourselves, judging what is good and evil, but rather by being turned out of ourselves in relationship with God.[93] What distinguishes Christian ethics from other ethical systems is that it is not concerned with the knowledge of good and evil. Only God has this knowledge and to try and attain it is to attempt to assume the role of God. When Adam and Eve ate the forbidden fruit in the Garden of Eden, they were turning away from God and in upon themselves.[94]

Bonhoeffer suggests that Jesus comes into opposition with the Pharisees on account of their being wholly centered upon the knowledge of good and evil.[95] When they ask Jesus questions which concern the conflict between the knowledge of good and evil, his answer seems to elude them, for his concern is not with the knowledge of good and evil but centered upon God.[96] Bonhoeffer writes, "He seems to be answering quite a different question from that which has been put to Him . . . He speaks with a complete freedom which is not bound by the law of logical alternatives."[97] Jesus's actions are not influenced by moral dilemmas, but by a sure trust in the will of God: "He lives and acts not by the knowledge of good and evil but by the will of God."[98] When we seek to know Christ and our reconciliation with

---

89. T. F. T., *Mediation*, 81. Focusing not on Christ but on the law arguably hinders the outworking of our sanctification. As Paul asserts, sin abounds under the law (Rom 5:20).

90. Barth, *Church Dogmatics* II/2 451; IV/2, 372–74.

91. Barth, *Church Dogmatics* IV/1, 446.

92. Barth, *Church Dogmatics* II/2, 646–47.

93. Bonhoeffer, *Ethics*, 3–37.

94. Ibid., 3–6.

95. Ibid., 12–13.

96. Ibid., 13.

97. Ibid., 14.

98. Ibid., 15.

God instead of good and evil, we discover true knowledge and are set free for whole-hearted devotion to the will of God.[99] He writes,

> The knowledge of Jesus is entirely transformed into action, without any reflection upon a man's self . . . His deed has become entirely unquestioning; he is entirely devoted to his deed and filled with it; his deed is no longer one possibility among many, but the one thing, the important thing, the will of God.[100]

Bonhoeffer argues that we should be turned out of ourselves, not judging our own actions or those of others, and live faithfully through relationship with God. The New Testament is not so much concerned with ethical problems as with our reconciliation in Christ.[101] The outworking of sanctification comes not from knowledge of good and evil but from our union with God.[102]

David W. Torrance laments the sermons preached today which emphasize cumbersome exhortations concerning what is the right thing to do.[103] This tendency can be seen in John Piper's recent book of sermons, *Sanctification in the Everyday*.[104] The strategy that Piper presents as to how to fight against sin, which he articulates using the pneumonic, "ANTHEM," begins with our willpower ("AVOID. Say NO! Within five seconds."), only secondly points to Christ ("TURN to something magnificent, like Christ crucified."), and continues with exhortations that rely upon our willpower ("HOLD the pure thing in the mind until the dirty thing is gone. ENJOY the greater pleasure of the blood-bought promises of God. MOVE on to meaningful Christ-exalting activity.").[105] This obscures Christ as the ground of our definitive sanctification in whose intimate communion with the Father we may participate freely by the Spirit. D. W. calls for preaching that is centered upon the person of Christ so that we might come into relationship with the Father:

> If you look at ministry today, probably ninety percent of all our preaching is telling people what to do. We lay tremendous

---

99. Ibid., 18–20.
100. Ibid., 19–20.
101. Ibid., 11.
102. Regrettably Bonhoeffer's thoughts are cut short because his work is unfinished.
103. David W. Torrance, "The Grace of the Finished Work of Christ."
104. Piper, *Sanctification in the Everyday*.
105. Piper, *Sanctification in the Everyday*, 10. See also Packer's "behavioural strategy." Packer, *Rediscovering Holiness*, 174. See also J. I. Packer, "Sanctification and the Fight."

burdens on the congregation. Our congregations get weary and tired, and many slip away. And the ministers themselves, they get frustrated and they leave. They're trying to go ahead in ministry, but under their own steam, using their own efforts, their own resources. I believe quite strongly that in the ministry we are called here to proclaim Christ, the person of Christ . . . If we keep our eye on Christ and seek to present Christ to the world, this is something very exciting, something very living and alive. We see people coming face-to-face with God in Jesus Christ.[106]

J. B. extends this to all pastoral situations, believing that instead of directing people with which is the right or wrong action to take, the first and foremost mission is to direct people to Christ so that we might share by the Spirit in his intimate relationship with the Father:

> It seems to me that in a pastoral situation, our first task is not to throw people back on themselves with exhortations and instructions as to what to do and how to do it, but to direct people to the gospel of grace to Jesus Christ, that they might look to him to lead them, open their hearts in faith and in prayer, and draw them by the Spirit into his eternal life of communion with the Father.[107]

When J. B. speaks of God's filial purpose in the context of atonement, this might also be applied to the outworking of sanctification in the Christian life: "God's primary purpose for humanity is 'filial,' not just 'judicial,' where we have been created in the image of God to find our true being-in-communion, in 'sonship,' in the mutual personal relations of love."[108] In the outworking of sanctification, God's primary purpose for humanity is not to adhere to external rules and regulations (judicial) but to participate by the Spirit in the Son's communion with the Father (filial).

Conclusion

The outworking of our sanctification comes as we are turned out of ourselves by the Spirit to Christ and the truth of our identity in him so that we might share in his communion with the Father and grow into who we are in Christ.

106. D. W. T., "The Grace of the Finished Work of Christ."

107. J. B. T., *Worship*, 34.

108. J. B. T., "Doctrine of the Trinity," 15; See also J. B. T., *Worship*, 26–27; J. B. T, "Prayer and the Priesthood of Christ," 60.

As we live in the eschatological reserve, the Torrances recognize that sin is an abiding presence. It is the irrational rejection of God whereby a person seeks to usurp the place of God. This arises from a misunderstanding of God as cruel or distant and from a misunderstanding of humanity as self-determining. Essentially sin is fed by a lack of knowing what has been objectively achieved for humanity in Christ. Through fear of a perceived lack, a person wretchedly attempts to acquire what we already have in Christ. He does not enjoy what he already has in Christ; he is turned in upon himself. Sin may thus be characterized as *homo incurvatus in se*.

The Torrances believe that the Holy Spirit turns a person out of himself (*homo excurvatus ex se*) to find his life satisfied in Christ. Our true center of existence is Christ, which is expressed in the language of the church as the body of Christ. When we turn to Christ, this is the meaning of repentance. It is not a miserable, burdensome endeavor, a perspective unfortunately perpetuated by the movement to reclaim Puritan teaching on sanctification. We are directed away from ourselves to Christ and to hold to what is true of our lives in him. We are to share in his mind and be determined by his truth. This means that our beliefs should be shaped by the truth of who we are in Christ, rather than our earthly experiences of sinfulness. Knowing what we have already been given in Christ is significant for acting accordingly, evident by Paul's repeated affirmation of the early Christians' identity in Christ followed by exhortations to live accordingly. Yet the outworking of sanctification comes not only from knowing *about* God but, more fundamentally, knowing God.

This means that the outworking of sanctification is not an external, legal process and Scripture is not a static book of rules. God does not intend for us to be turned back in upon ourselves, judging what is good and what is evil, and directing others to burdensome activities in detachment from Christ. God's purposes are primarily filial, not federal: the outworking of sanctification is the free gift of sharing by the Spirit in Christ's intimate communion with the Father.

Conclusion

THIS BOOK HAS SOUGHT TO PRESENT THE SIGNIFICANCE OF THE TORRANCES' filial, ontological, and objective soteriology in the face of current fervent criticism by Federal theologians, and to constructively extend the implications more fully to sanctification, particularly in light of the current movement to reclaim Puritan theology, but also with the broader practices of the church in mind. In so doing, it seeks to offer a vital, liberating message: salvation and sanctification are not burdensome endeavors but the free gift of enjoying communion with the triune God of grace. Although humanity lives in the eschatological reserve, in a world of continuing sin and evil, we are neither defined nor ruled by it; we are determined by the risen humanity of Christ. The Holy Spirit turns us out of ourselves to participate in the life of Christ and, as we do so, we grow to reflect the reality of who we are in him.

This line of argument seeks to be faithful to what God has revealed to us in Christ. The Torrances believe that it is impossible to understand God's ways within our own rational frameworks of thought. Salvation and sanctification defy logico-causal reasoning and the eschatological reserve means that God's purposes are fully accomplished and yet not fully manifest. If we attempt to make God's mysteries black and white, we will only glimpse a part of the truth. There can be truth in opposing arguments. It is a tricky task to express faithfully the eschatological tension and the seeming paradox of participation. Different contexts will necessarily need to address different issues, thereby shifting emphases.[1] This book has sought to redress an imbalance that leans towards a poor view of humanity and the outworking of our sanctification. The argument for confidence in the nature of our humanity and the outworking of our sanctification may be the most

---

1. The Torrances seek to emphasize Christ's priestly office over against his prophetic and kingly offices in order to counteract attitudes that bypass his vicarious and mediatorial role and therefore throw people back upon themselves.

challenging premise.[2] Yet it is not to deny the eschatological tension and the continuing presence of sin in the world, nor is it a boast in our own efforts. It seeks to reflect the confidence of the biblical witness and appreciate what has been accomplished for us in Christ.

A comprehensive summary of this book's line of argument can be found in the chapter conclusions. The purpose of this final conclusion is to highlight some key issues concerning the Torrances' claim that the whole of humanity has its being in Christ and to suggest that which might benefit from further discussion.

The Prospective Life

The Torrances' soteriology helpfully draws attention to the prospective aspect of the atonement: we are not only retrospectively forgiven of our sins but also adopted as sons and daughters of God to share by the Spirit in the Son's communion with the Father. Yet some who are appreciative of the Torrances regret that they do not adequately elaborate on the nature of the prospective life.[3] It is true that, although the Torrances have a profound understanding of what Christ by the Spirit has done for us vicariously in human flesh, there is much less exposition on what a person's life in Christ by the Spirit might look like.[4]

Although the Torrances do not spell out the shape of the Christian life, their lives are a dynamic testament to the radical ethical and sociopolitical imperatives of their theology. T. F. sought to preserve the life of the unborn child in the face of the abortion debate and J. B. felt compelled to challenge boldly apartheid in South Africa.[5] The Torrances saw that God's claiming of humanity in Christ had far-reaching implications for how we

---

2. For those not of a Pentecostal-Charismatic or Wesleyan tradition, this may be particularly difficult to agree with.

3. Habets, *Theosis*, 186–9; Eugenio, "Communion with God," 185.

4. For T. F., there is an inherent difficulty in describing the prospective aspect of the atonement: "We are permitted to speak here of the new age only with a prayer of forgiveness, for the very language we use is improper and must pass away with the nomistic forms of this world . . . We can speak about it only in stammering ways, in the fragmented figures of apocalyptic imagery." T. F. T., *Space, Time and Resurrection*, 100. Hauerwas reflects on the difficulty of making statements about the prospective nature of our mystical union with Christ since it will not be fully consummated until the end. Hauerwas, *Character and the Christian Life*, 184.

5. T. F. T., *The Being and Nature of the Unborn Child*; J. B. T., "Calvin and Puritanism in England and Scotland"; J. B. T., "Southern Africa Today," 42–45. J. B. also engaged with the Northern Irish conflict.

engage with every facet of human existence. Students of the Torrances and others continue to explore the implications of their theology for the nature of the Christian life.[6] Yet the benefit of not statically spelling out the shape of the Christian life is that they evade the danger of moralistic interpretation. Moreover, whilst the Torrances' theology might leave us with various questions regarding the Christian life, they direct us to where we can find the ultimate answer: through participating by the Spirit in the Son's intimate communion with the Father.

Our Human Response

The Torrances' objective account of salvation attracts the recurrent criticism that our human freedom and activity is negated or diminished. Yet this is to misunderstand the nature of human freedom and the way in which our activity relates to God in Christ. Our sinful self-will is mistaken for freedom, yet it only serves to usurp our freedom. It is true that our sinful self-will is set aside by God's objective activity but this is for the sake of our liberation, that we might gain real freedom.

Likewise, the only human activity that is negated is that which keeps us captive, and it is for the sake of humanizing us and enabling activity in its proper place. When our human activity is conceived of as an independent, logico-causal response, or in any way contributing to our salvation or sanctification, it becomes a heavy burden for us. Our faith and works are intended as a free response to God's grace, rather than as a means to earn it. Moreover, this is not an independent, logico-causal response; our response is a participation by the Spirit in a response already made by Christ. This means that we do not have to depend upon the adequacy of our own response; we are upheld by the faithfulness of Christ. Human activity that is independent, merit-based, and burdensome is diminished, for the sake of affirming human activity in its proper place, that is, as a free and joyful participation by the Spirit in what God has already accomplished in Christ.

---

6. E.g., Alan Torrance, "Forgiveness," 47–59; Kruger, *The Great Dance*; Redding, *Prayer and the Priesthood of Christ*; Dawson, *Jesus Ascended*; Purves, *Reconstructing Pastoral Theology*; Parry, *Worshipping Trinity*; Anderson, "The Practical Theology of Thomas F. Torrance," 65–78. See also *Participatio: The Journal of the Thomas F. Torrance Theological Fellowship: A Tribute to James B. Torrance*, Supp. Vol. 3. 2014. Habets suggests, "Perhaps this is the greatest legacy [T. F.] Torrance has left to those of us working within the Reformed tradition—to meditate upon his work (along with the rest of the tradition) and to add our own critical insights in service of the church." Habets, "T. F. Torrance: Mystical Theologian," 92.

Universalism

Despite the Torrances asserting otherwise, their theology is often misunderstood for universalism. This is because universal atonement seems to lead logically to universalism. T. F. argues against universalism for the reason that we cannot understand God's ways according to logico-causal categories. He points to the irrational reality of sin whereby some choose to reject God. Yet T. F.'s argument is perhaps also subject to logico-causal categories. Whilst sin is irrational, it is logical to maintain that, from our earthly experience of people rejecting God, these people must not ultimately be saved.

However, extending the implications of the Torrances' soteriology more fully to sanctification, we see that our lives are determined by the eschatological orientation of the risen humanity of Christ. This is our ultimate reality, although it will not be fully manifest until the Parousia. Until then, we are directed away from ourselves to Christ, to shape our beliefs by the truth of who we are in him, rather than by our earthly experiences of sinfulness. With this in mind, it might be argued that we should not assume that those who reject God now will not ultimately be saved. Despite contrary earthly experience, we should hold to the truth of our eschatological orientation revealed in Christ and have hope in the possibility of the ultimate reconciliation of all humanity.

Robin Parry draws upon T. F.'s repeated phrase that "there is no God behind the back of Jesus," pointing out that, if we do not come to a universalist conclusion regarding people whom we see reject God, "then *something other than the gospel of Christ is determining their end.*"[7] He argues, "Far more theologically satisfying, to my mind, is the proposal that the resurrection-ascension of Christ is the revelation of the destiny of humanity and the promise that it will come to pass."[8]

T. F. argues that the reality of hell and the necessity of evangelism defy a universalist position. Yet the reality of hell can be upheld alongside universalism as only a temporary fate. The irrational rejection of God accounts for the reality of hell but not for an eternal hell. Nor does universalism exclude the necessity of evangelism. First, hell is very much a reality, albeit temporary. Second, if all of humanity is to be possibly ultimately reconciled, evangelism is made universal in scope. Third, evangelism means that people's

---

7. MacDonald, *The Evangelical Universalist*, xx.

8. Ibid. In his book, Parry argues for universalism from philosophical reasoning, the biblical metanarrative and biblical-theological context, and addresses the hell passages in Revelation. Although T. F. denied universalism, he once made a suggestive comment to an enquiring student that hell itself would eventually be destroyed (Rev 20:14).

lives are transformed in the present as they discover the gift of sharing by the Spirit in the Son's communion with the Father.

T. F. also believes that universalism destroys the free decision of faith. Yet this does not necessarily follow. Parry argues that true freedom actually liberates us to accept God's salvation. God's self-revelation is liberating, not oppressive: "By so revealing himself, God is not forcing an agent to act against free will but simply clarifying the situation in such a way that the will changes . . . The only way for God to keep the damned continually choosing to resist him forever is by shielding them from the real consequences of their actions, thus denying them the possibility of making a *fully informed* decision."[9] This resonates with the Torrances' belief that God's objective claiming of humanity is ultimately liberating, and grace leads to the free response of godly living.

It is not within the scope of this book to debate universalism but, from the implications regarding sanctification that arise from the Torrances' soteriology, it does seek to show that it is an issue which requires further consideration. Whilst the possible universalist implications of the Torrances' theology is a cause of contention for critics, perhaps it might be found to be a positive aspect. Robin Parry felt compelled to publish his work on universalism under a pseudonym on account of the unorthodoxy of his position. Yet perhaps if the Church were guided more by confidence in Christ, we might be more hopeful about the eschatological orientation of our humanity.

Conclusion

This book presents the Torrances' claim that the whole of humanity has its being in Christ. Whilst it has sought to defend this claim, it does not argue for uncritical adoption of the Torrances' theology. Since our lives are determined by the eschatological orientation of the risen humanity of Christ, and scripture exhorts us to focus on heavenly truth rather than earthly experience, this seems to make it difficult for the Torrances not to openly hope in the possibility of the ultimate reconciliation of all humanity. Furthermore, the Torrances' profoundly personal, relational, and participatory scheme of salvation indicates a God whom humanity can not only know but experience intimately. A greater openness to and consideration of the mystical and experiential aspects of the Christian life would therefore complement this scheme of salvation. In relation to this, a more detailed exposition of the Spirit's action upon Jesus's humanity would aid a better understanding

---

9. Ibid., 30.

of the Spirit's action upon us today. Whilst it is imperative to make a proper distinction between God and humanity to avoid the "danger of vertigo," it is also important to take proper account of the likeness which God calls us to through participating in Christ by the Holy Spirit. The Torrances' theology would be complemented by a greater appreciation of what humanity has received and is called to in Christ.

A fuller appreciation of this present reality challenges the tendency to conceive of humanity primarily in terms of sinfulness and, in relation to this, of sanctification as a life-long struggle. Whilst T. F. displays an intense confidence on account of our new eschatological orientation in Christ, there is little positive discussion of what this means for humanity in the outworking of sanctification. This is perhaps due to the Torrances' concern to emphasize Christ's priestly office in order to counteract attitudes that throw people back upon themselves. Yet a deeper exploration of Christ's kingly office would further this concern for it declares that we are seated in a place of victory and rest. The Torrances appear to be somewhat characteristic of their Reformed tradition in their emphasis upon the objective work of God and lack of exploration of the subjective nature of sanctification. Although this may have been due to a concern to avoid moralism, it is regrettable because the Torrances' soteriology actually offers the crucial foundation for challenging moralism whilst also appreciating the obligations of grace.

The Torrances' claim that the whole of humanity has its being in Christ liberates us from our own efforts to earn our relationship with God and, extending the implications to sanctification, become the kind of person that we ought to be. God has objectively claimed humanity for salvation in Christ prior to anything that we could contribute and the radical claim that this places upon humanity is to grow to reflect the ontological reality of who we are in him as we freely share by the Spirit in the Son's filial communion with the Father.

Bibliography

Alexander, Donald L., ed. *Christian Spirituality: Five Views of Sanctification*. Downers Grove, IL: InterVarsity, 1988.
———. "The Riddle of Sanctification." In *Christian Spirituality: Five Views of Sanctification*, edited by Donald L. Alexander, 7–12. Downers Grove, IL: InterVarsity, 1988.
Allen, R. Michael. *Justification and the Gospel: Understanding the Contexts and Controversies*. Grand Rapids: Baker Academic, 2013.
———. *Reformed Theology*. New York: T&T Clark, 2010.
Alston, Wallace Jr. and Michael Welker, eds. *Reformed Theology: Identity and Ecumenicity*. Grand Rapids: Eerdmans, 2003.
Anderson, Ray. "The Practical Theology of Thomas F. Torrance." *Princeton Theological Review* 14.2 (2008) 65–78.
Armstrong, Brian G. *Calvinism and the Amyraut Heresy: Protestant Scholasticism and Humanism in Seventeenth Century France*. Madison: University of Wisconsin Press, 1969.
Barth, Karl. *Church Dogmatics* II/2. Edited by G. W. Bromiley and T. F. Torrance. Translated by G. W. Bromiley et al. Edinburgh: T&T Clark, 1957.
———. *Church Dogmatics* IV/1. Edited by G. W. Bromiley and T. F. Torrance. Translated by G. W. Bromiley. Edinburgh: T&T Clark, 1956.
———. *Church Dogmatics* IV/2. Edited by G. W Bromiley and T. F. Torrance. Translated by G. W. Bromiley. Edinburgh: T&T Clark, 1958.
———. *A Shorter Commentary on Romans*. London: SCM, 1959.
———. "Simultaneous Saints and Sinners." *Concordia Journal* 9 (1983) 213–16.
———. *The Theology of Schleiermacher*. Grand Rapids: Eerdmans, 1982.
Bavinck, Herman. *Our Reasonable Faith*. Grand Rapids: Eerdmans, 1956.
Bebbington, David. "Holiness in the Evangelical Tradition." In *Holiness: Past and Present*, edited by Stephen Barton, 298–315. Edinburgh: T&T Clark, 2003.
Beeke, Joel R., and Mark Jones. *A Puritan Theology: Doctrine for Life*. Grand Rapids: Reformation Heritage, 2012.
Behr, John, trans. *Saint Athanasius the Great: On the Incarnation: (Greek/English) PPS44a*, translated and edited by John Behr, 19–49. Crestwood: St Vladimir's Seminary Press, 2012.
Bell, M. C. *Calvin and Scottish Theology: The Doctrine of Assurance*. Edinburgh: Handsel, 1985.
Berkhof, Louis. *Systematic Theology*. London: Banner of Truth Trust, 1988.
Berkouwer, G. C. *Faith and Sanctification*. Grand Rapids: Eerdmans, 1952.

Bevan, Andrew Maurice. "The Person of Christ and the Nature of Human Participation in the Theology of T. F. Torrance: A Post-Modern Realist Approach to Personhood." PhD thesis, University of London, 2002.

Bird, Michael, and Preston Sprinkle, eds. *The Faith of Jesus Christ: Exegetical, Biblical, and Theological Studies*. Carlisle, UK: Paternoster, 2009.

Bird, Michael. *The Saving Righteousness of God: Studies on Paul, Justification and the New Perspective*. Paternoster Biblical Monographs. Milton Keynes, UK: Paternoster, 2007.

Bonhoeffer, Dietrich. *Christology*. Translated by John Bowden. London: Collins, 1971.

———. *Ethics*. Edited by Eberhard Bethge. Translated by Neville Horton Smith. London: SCM, 1983.

Braatan, Carl E., and Robert W. Jenson, eds. *Union with Christ: The New Finnish Interpretation of Luther*. Grand Rapids, Eerdmans, 1998.

Brondos, David. *Paul on the Cross: Reconstructing the Apostle's Story of Redemption*. Minneapolis: Fortress, 2006.

Brother Lawrence. *The Practice of the Presence of God*. Boston: Oneworld, Reprint, 1999.

Bozeman, Theodore Dwight. *The Precisianist Strain: Disciplinary Religion and Antinomian Backlash in Puritanism to 1638*. Chapel Hill: University of North Carolina Press, 2004.

Burgess, Stanley, ed. *Encyclopedia of Pentecostal and Charismatic Christianity*. New York: Routledge, 2006.

Calvin, John. *Institutes of the Christian Religion*. Translated by John Thomas McNeill and Ford Lewis Battles. Philadelphia: Westminster, 1960.

Campbell, Douglas. *The Deliverance of God: An Apocalyptic Rereading of Justification in Paul*. Grand Rapids: Eerdmans, 2009.

———. *The Quest for Paul's Gospel*. London: T&T Clark, 2005.

Canlis, Julie. *Calvin's Ladder: A Spiritual Theology of Ascent and Ascension*. Grand Rapids: Eerdmans, 2010.

———. "Living as God's Children: Calvin's Institutes as Primer for Spiritual Formation." In *Evangelical Calvinism: Essays Resourcing the Continuing Reformation of the Church*, edited by Myk Habets and Bobby Grow, 331–52. Eugene, OR: Pickwick Publications, 2012.

Carson, D. A. "The Vindication of Imputation." In *Justification: What's at Stake in the Current Debates*, edited by Mark Husbands and Daniel Treier, 46–78. Downers Grove, IL: InterVarsity, 2004.

Cassidy, James. "T. F. Torrance's Realistic Soteriological Objectivism and the Elimination of Dualisms: Union with Christ in Current Perspective." *Mid-America Journal of Theology* 19 (2008) 165–94.

Chalke, Steve, and Alan Mann. *The Lost Message of Jesus*. Grand Rapids: Zondervan, 2003.

Chester, Stephen. "It is No Longer I Who Live: Justification by Faith and Participation in Christ in Martin Luther's Exegesis of Galatians." *New Testament Studies* 55 (2009) 315–37.

Climacus, Johannes. *Philosophical Fragments*. Translated and edited by Howard and Edna Hong. Princeton: Princeton University Press, 1985.

Coffey, John. *Politics, Religion and the British Revolutions: The Mind of Samuel Rutherford*. Cambridge Studies in Early Modern British History. Cambridge: Cambridge University Press, 1997.

Colyer, Elmer. *How to Read T. F. Torrance: Understanding His Trinitarian & Scientific Theology*. 2001. Reprinted, Eugene, OR: Wipf & Stock, 2007.

———. "The Incarnate Saviour: T. F. Torrance on the Atonement." In *An Introduction to Torrance Theology: Discovering the Incarnate Saviour*, edited by Gerrit Scott Dawson, 33–44. London: T&T Clark, 2007.

———, ed. *The Promise of Trinitarian Theology: Theologians in Dialogue with T. F. Torrance*. Lanham, MD: Rowman & Littlefield, 2001.

———. "Thomas F. Torrance on the Holy Spirit." *Word & World* 23 (2003) 160–67.

Dabney, D. Lyle. "Why Should the Last be First? The Priority of Pneumatology in Recent Theological Discussion." In *Advents of the Spirit: An Introduction to the Current Study of Pneumatology*, edited by Bradford Hinze and Lyle Dabney, 240–61. Milwaukee: Marquette University Press, 2001.

Davidson, Ivor. "Theologizing the Human Jesus: An Ancient (and Modern) Approach to Christology Reassessed." *International Journal of Systematic Theology* 3 (2001) 129–53.

Dawson, Gerrit Scott, ed. *An Introduction to Torrance Theology: Discovering the Incarnate Saviour*. London: T&T Clark, 2007.

Dawson, Gerritt Scott. "Far as the Curse is Found: The Significance of Christ's Assuming a Fallen Human Nature in the Torrance Theology." In *An Introduction to Torrance Theology: Discovering the Incarnate Saviour*, edited by Gerrit Scott Dawson, 55–74. London: T&T Clark, 2007.

———. *Jesus Ascended: The Meaning of Christ's Continuing Incarnation*. Phillipsburg, NJ: P&R, 2004.

Dawson, Gerrit Scott and Jock Stein, eds. *A Passion for Christ: The Vision that Ignites Ministry*. Edinburgh: Handsel, 1999.

Dearborn, Timothy. "God, Grace and Salvation." In *Christ in Our Place: The Humanity of God in Christ for the Reconciliation of the World: Essays Presented to James Torrance*, edited by Trevor Hart and Daniel Thimell, 265–93. Exeter, UK: Paternoster, 1989.

Deddo, Gary. "The Holy Spirit in T. F. Torrance's Theology." In *The Promise of Trinitarian Theology: Theologians in Dialogue with T. F. Torrance*, edited by Elmer Colyer, 81–114. Lanham, MD: Rowman & Littlefield, 2001.

Dodd, C. H. *The Epistle of Paul to the Romans*. New York: Harper & Brothers, 1932.

Dulles, Avery. "The Trinity and Christian Unity." In *God the Holy Trinity: Reflections on Christian Faith and Practice*, edited by Timothy George, 69–83. Grand Rapids: Baker, 2006.

Dunn, James D. G. "Once More, *Pistou Christou*." In *Pauline Theology Volume IV: Looking Back, Pressing On*, edited by Elizabeth Johnson and David Hay, 61–81. Atlanta, Scholars, 1997.

———. "*Pisteos*: A Key to the Meaning of *Pistis Christou*." In *The Word Leaps the Gap: Essays on Scripture and Theology in Honour of Richard B. Hays*, edited by. J. R. Wagner, C. Kavin Rowe, and A. Katherine Grieb, 351–67. Grand Rapids: Eerdmans, 2008.

———. *The Theology of Paul the Apostle*. Grand Rapids: Eerdmans, 1998.

Edwards, Jonathan. "Sinners in the Hands of an Angry God." Sermon at Enfield, Connecticut, 8 July 1741. Christian Classics Ethereal Library. http://www.ccel.org/ccel/edwards/sermons.sinners.html.

Eugenio, Dick. "Communion with God: The Trinitarian Soteriology of Thomas F. Torrance." PhD Thesis, University of Manchester, 2011.

Farrow, Douglas. *Ascension Theology*. London: T&T Clark, 2011.

———. *Ascension and Ecclesia: On the Significance of the Doctrine of the Ascension for Ecclesiology and Christian Cosmology*. Grand Rapids: Eerdmans, 1999.

Feazell, J. Michael. *The Liberation of the Worldwide Church of God*. Grand Rapids: Zondervan, 2001.

Ferguson, Sinclair B. "The Puritans: Can They Teach Us Anything Today?" Lecture Delivered at the Dedication of the Puritan Resource Centre, Grand Rapids, USA, 20/10/2005. Part 1: http://banneroftruth.org/us/resources/articles/2005/the-puritans-can-they-teach-us-anything-today-1/. Part 2: http://banneroftruth.org/us/resources/articles/2005/the-puritans-can-they-teach-us-anything-today-2/.

———. "The Reformed View." In *Christian Spirituality: Five Views of Sanctification*, edited by Donald L. Alexander, 47–76. Downers Grove, IL: InterVarsity, 1988.

Fergusson, David A. S. "Predestination: A Scottish Perspective." *Scottish Journal of Theology* 46 (1993) 457–78.

Fletcher, Joseph. *Situation Ethics: The New Morality*. Philadelphia: Westminster, 1966.

Florovsky, Georges. *Bible, Church, Tradition: An Eastern Orthodox View*. Collected Works of Georges Florovsky 1. Belmont, MA: Nordland, 1972.

Frost, R. N. *Richard Sibbes: God's Spreading Goodness*. Portland, OR: Cor Deo, 2012.

Garcia, Mark. "Attribution: Union with Christ, Reification and Justification as Declarative Word." *International Journal of Systematic Theology* 11 (2009) 415–27.

Gatewood, Tee. "Alive to God in Christ: The Spirit and the Church in the Torrance Tradition." *Crux* 44.2 (2008) 9–19.

Gibson, David, and Jonathan Gibson, eds. *From Heaven He Came and Sought Her: Definite Atonement in Historical, Biblical, Theological, and Pastoral Perspective*. Kindle Edition. Wheaton, IL: Crossway, 2013.

Gorman, Michael. *Inhabiting the Cruciform God: Kenosis, Justification, and Theosis in Paul's Narrative Soteriology*. Grand Rapids: Eerdmans, 2009.

Grudem, Wayne. *Systematic Theology*. Leicester, UK: InterVarsity, 1994.

Gundry, Stanley N., ed. *Five Views on Sanctification*. Grand Rapids: Zondervan, 1987.

———. "The Nonimputation of Christ's Righteousness." In *Justification: What's at Stake in the Current Debates*, edited by Mark Husbands and Daniel Treier, 17–45. Downers Grove, IL: InterVarsity, 2004.

Gunton, Colin. "Being and Person: T. F. Torrance's Doctrine of God." In *The Promise of Trinitarian Theology: Theologians in Dialogue with T. F. Torrance*, edited by Elmer Colyer, 115–38. Lanham, MD: Rowman & Littlefield, 2001.

———. *Father, Son & Holy Spirit: Toward a Fully Trinitarian Theology*. London: T&T Clark, 2003.

Habets, Myk, and Bobby Grow, eds. *Evangelical Calvinism: Essays Resourcing the Continuing Reformation of the Church*. Eugene, OR: Pickwick Publications, 2012.

———. "Introduction: *Theologia Reformata et Semper Reformanda*: Towards an Evangelical Calvinism." In *Evangelical Calvinism: Essays Resourcing the Continuing Reformation of the Church*, Myk Habets and Bobby Grow, 1–22. Eugene, OR: Pickwick Publications, 2012.

Habets, Myk. "The Doctrine of Election in Evangelical Calvinism: T. F. Torrance as a Case Study." *Irish Theological Quarterly* 73 (2008) 334–54.

———. "Reforming Theosis." In *Theosis: Deification in Christian Theology*, edited by Stephen Finlan and Vladimir Kharlamov, 146–67. Eugene, OR: Pickwick Publications, 2006.

———. "Spirit Christology: Seeing in Stereo." *Journal of Pentecostal Theology* 11 (2003) 199–234.

———. "T. F. Torrance: Mystical Theologian Sui Generis." *Princeton Theological Review* 39:2 (2008) 91–104.

———. *Theosis in the Theology of Thomas Torrance*. Farnham, UK: Ashgate, 2009.

———. "There is no God behind the back of Jesus Christ: Christologically Conditioned Election." In *Evangelical Calvinism: Essays Resourcing the Continuing Reformation of the Church*, edited by Myk Habets and Bobby Grow, 173–99. Eugene, OR: Pickwick Publications, 2012.

Hall, Basil. "Calvin against the Calvinists." In *John Calvin: A Collection of Distinguished Essays*, edited by Gervase Duffield, 19–37. Grand Rapids: Eerdmans, 1966.

Hardy, Daniel. "T. F. Torrance." In *The Modern Theologians: An Introduction to Christian Theology Since 1918*, edited by David Ford with Rachel Muers, 163–77. 3rd ed. Oxford: Blackwell, 2005.

Hart, Trevor. "Atonement, the Incarnation, and Deification: Transformation and Convergence in the Soteriology of T. F. Torrance." *Princeton Theological Review* 39 (2008) 79–90.

Hart, Trevor, and Daniel Thimell, eds. *Christ in Our Place: The Humanity of God in Christ for the Reconciliation of the World: Essays Presented to James Torrance*. Exeter, UK: Paternoster, 1989.

Hauerwas, Stanley. *Character and the Christian Life*. San Antonio, TX: Trinity University Press, 1985.

———. *A Community of Character: Toward a Constructive Christian Social Ethic*. Notre Dame: University of Notre Dame Press, 1981.

———. *Sanctify Them in the Truth: Holiness Exemplified*. Edinburgh: T&T Clark, 1998.

———. *Vision and Virtue*. Notre Dame: University of Notre Dame Press, 1981.

Hays, Richard B. *The Faith of Jesus Christ: An Investigation of the Narrative Substructure of Galatians 3:1—4:11*. SBL Dissertation Series 56. Chico, CA: Scholars, 1983.

———. *The Moral Vision of the New Testament: A Contemporary Introduction to New Testament Ethics*. London: T&T Clark, 1996.

Helm, Paul. *Calvin and the Calvinists*. Edinburgh: Banner of Truth Trust, 1982.

———. "The Logic of Limited Atonement." *Scottish Bulletin of Evangelical Theology* 3.2 (1985) 47–54.

Heron, Alasdair. "Foreword." In *Evangelical Calvinism: Essays Resourcing the Continuing Reformation of the Church*, xii–xvi. Eugene, OR: Pickwick Publications, 2012.

———. "James Torrance: An Appreciation." In *Christ in Our Place: The Humanity of God in Christ for the Reconciliation of the World: Essays Presented to James Torrance*, edited by Trevor Hart and Daniel Thimell, 1–8. Exeter, UK: Paternoster, 1989.

———. "T. F. Torrance in Relation to Reformed Theology." In *The Promise of Trinitarian Theology: Theologians in Dialogue with T. F. Torrance*, edited by Elmer Colyer, 31–50. Lanham, MD: Rowman & Littlefield, 2001.

Hesselink, I. John. "The Charismatic Movement and the Reformed Tradition." In *Major Themes in the Reformed Tradition,* edited by Donald McKim, 377–84. Grand Rapids: Eerdmans, 1992.

Hinze, Bradford, and Lyle Dabney, eds. *Advents of the Spirit: An Introduction to the Current Study of Pneumatology.* Milwaukee: Marquette University Press, 2001.

Hoekema, Anthony A. "The Reformed Perspective." In *Five Views on Sanctification,* edited by Stanley N. Gundry, 59–90. Grand Rapids: Zondervan, 1987.

Hooker, Morna. "Πίστις Χριστοῦ." *New Testament Studies* 35 (1989) 165–84.

Horton, Michael. *Pilgrim Theology: Core Doctrines for Christian Disciples.* Kindle ed. Grand Rapids: Zondervan, 2013.

———. *Covenant and Salvation.* Louisville: Westminster John Knox, 2007.

Hudson, D. Neil. "Worship: Singing a New Song in a Strange Land." In *Pentecostal Perspectives,* edited by Keith Warrington, 177–203. Carlisle, UK: Paternoster, 1998.

Hunsinger, George. "The Dimension of Depth: Thomas F. Torrance on the Sacraments." In *The Promise of Trinitarian Theology: Theologians in Dialogue with T. F. Torrance,* edited by Elmer Colyer, 139–60. Lanham, MD: Rowman & Littlefield, 2001.

Husbands, Mark, and Daniel Treier, eds. *Justification: What's at Stake in the Current Debates.* Downers Grove, IL: InterVarsity, 2004.

Jenson, Matt. *The Gravity of Sin: Augustine, Luther and Barth on homo incurvatus in se.* London: T&T Clark, 2007.

Johnson, Marcus. "The Highest Degree of Importance: Union with Christ and Soteriology." In *Evangelical Calvinism: Essays Resourcing the Continuing Reformation of the Church,* edited by Myk Habets and Bobby Grow, 222–52. Eugene, OR: Pickwick Publications, 2012.

Jüngel, Eberhard. *Justification: The Heart of the Christian Faith.* Edinburgh: T&T Clark, 2001.

Kapic, Kelly, and Randall Gleason, eds. *The Devoted Life: An Invitation to the Puritan Classics.* Downers Grove, IL: InterVarsity, 2004.

Kagarise, Robby J. "Theology of Experience." In *Encyclopedia of Pentecostal and Charismatic Christianity,* edited Stanley M. Burgess. New York: Routledge, 2006.

Kärkkäinen, Veli-Matti. "Introduction to Pneumatology." In *Holy Spirit and Salvation: The Sources of Christian Theology,* edited by Veli-Matti Kärkkäinen, xi–xxiv. Louisville: Westminster John Knox, 2010.

———. *One with God: Salvation as Deification and Justification.* Collegeville, MN: Liturgical, 2004.

Keating, Daniel A. "Trinity and Salvation: Christian Life as an Existence in the Trinity." In *The Oxford Handbook of the Trinity,* edited by Gilles Emery O.P. and Matthew Levering, 442–56. Oxford: Oxford University Press, 2011.

Kelsey, David. *Eccentric Existence: A Theological Anthropology: Volume 1.* Louisville: Westminster John Knox, 2009.

Kendall, R. T. *Calvin and English Calvinism to 1649.* Oxford: Oxford University Press, 1981.

Kettler, Christian D. *The Vicarious Humanity of Christ and the Reality of Salvation.* Lanham, MD: University Press of America, 1991.

Kolb, Robert. *Martin Luther: Confessor of the Faith.* New York: Oxford University Press, 2009.

Kruger, C. Baxter. *God Is for Us.* Jackson: Perichoresis, 1995.

———. *The Great Dance: The Christian Vision Revisited.* Jackson: Perichoresis, 2000.

Kümmel, W. G. *Romer 7 und die Bekenhrung des Paulus*. Leipzig: Hinrichs, 1929.
Lee, Kye Won. *Living in Union with Christ: The Practical Theology of Thomas F. Torrance*. New York: Lang, 2003.
Letham, Robert. *The Holy Trinity: In Scripture, History, Theology And Worship*. Phillipsburg, NJ: P&R, 2004.
———. "The Triune God, Incarnation, and Definite Atonement." In *From Heaven He Came and Sought Her: Definite Atonement in Historical, Biblical, Theological, and Pastoral Perspective*, edited by David Gibson and Jonathan Gibson. Wheaton, IL: Crossway, 2013. Kindle ed.
Lloyd-Jones, David Martyn. *The Puritans: Their Origins and Successors*. Edinburgh: Banner of Truth Trust, 1987.
Macchia, Frank. "Justification and the Spirit: A Pentecostal Reflection on the Doctrine by which the Church Stands or Falls." *Pneuma: The Journal of the Society for Pentecostal Studies* 22 (2000) 3–21.
———. *Justified in the Spirit: Creation, Redemption and the Triune God*. Grand Rapids: Eerdmans, 2010.
MacDonald, Gregory. *The Evangelical Universalist: The Biblical Hope that God's Love Will Save Us All*. 2nd ed. London: SPCK, 2012.
Macfarlane, Graham. "The Role of the Holy Spirit in Revival." In *On Revival: A Critical Examination*, edited by Andrew Walker and Kristin Aune, 43–55. Carlisle, UK: Paternoster, 2003.
Mackintosh, H. R. *The Divine Initiative*. London: SCM, 1936.
MacLean, Stanley. *Resurrection, Apocalypse and the Kingdom of Christ: The Eschatology of Thomas F. Torrance*. Eugene, OR: Pickwick Publications, 2012.
Macleod, Donald. "Dr T. F. Torrance and Scottish Theology: A Review Article." *Evangelical Quarterly* 72 (2000) 57–72.
Mannermaa, Tuomo. *Christ Present in Faith: Luther's View of Justification*. Minneapolis: Fortress, 2005.
Matlock, Barry. "The Rhetoric of *pistis* in Paul: Galatians 2.16, 3.22, Romans 3.22, and Philippians 3.9." *Journal for the Study of the New Testament* 30 (2007) 173–203.
Matlock, Barry. "Detheologizing the *pistis Christou* Debate: Cautionary Remarks from a Lexical Semantic Perspective." *Novum Testamentum* 42 (2000) 1–23.
McGrath, Alister. *Historical Theology*. Oxford: Blackwell, 1998.
———. *Justification by Faith*. Grand Rapids: Zondervan, 1991.
———. *T. F. Torrance: An Intellectual Biography*. London: T&T Clark, 1999.
McCormack, Bruce. "The End of Reformed Theology? The Voice of Karl Barth in the Doctrinal Chaos of the Present." In *Reformed Theology: Identity and Ecumenicity*, edited by Alston Jr., Wallace M., and Michael Welker, 46–64. Grand Rapids: Eerdmans, 2003.
———. "What's at Stake in Current Debates over Justification? The Crisis of Protestantism in the West." In *Justification: What's at Stake in the Current Debates*, edited by Mark Husbands and Daniel Treier, 81–117. Downers Grove, IL: InterVarsity, 2004.
McGowan, A. T. B. "The Atonement as Penal Substitution." In *Always Reforming: Explorations in Systematic Theology*, edited by A. T. B. McGowan, 183–210. Leicester, UK: Apollos, 2006.
———. "Federal Theology as a Theology of Grace." *Scottish Bulletin of Evangelical Theology* 2 (1984) 41–50.
———. *The Federal Theology of Thomas Boston*. Edinburgh: Rutherford House, 1997.

———. "Justification and the Ordo Salutis." *Foundations* 51 (2004) 6–19.
McLeod Campbell, John. *The Nature of the Atonement*. Cambridge: Macmillan, 1856.
McWilliams, D. "The Covenant Theology of the Westminster Confession of Faith and Recent Criticism." *Westminster Theological Journal* 53 (1991) 109–24.
Migne, J. P. *Patrologia Cursus Completus Series Graeca*. 165 vols. Paris: 1857–1886.
———. *Patrologia Cursus Completus Series Latina*. 217 vols. Paris: 1844–1864.
Molnar, Paul. *Incarnation and Resurrection: Toward a Contemporary Understanding*. Grand Rapids: Eerdmans, 2007.
———. *Thomas F. Torrance: Theologian of the Trinity*. Farnham, UK: Ashgate, 2009.
Moltmann, Jürgen. *Jesus Christ for Today's World*. Translated by Margaret Kohl. London: SCM, 1994.
———. *The Spirit of Life: A Universal Affirmation*. Translated by Margaret Kohl. Minneapolis: Fortress, 1992.
———. "The Trinitarian Personhood of the Holy Spirit." In *Advents of the Spirit: An Introduction to the Current Study of Pneumatology*, edited by Bradford Hinze and Lyle Dabney, 302–14. Milwaukee: Marquette University Press, 2001.
Moule, C. F. D. "The Biblical Conception of 'Faith.'" *The Expository Times* 68 (1957).
Muller, Richard. *After Calvin: Studies in the Development of a Theological Tradition*. Oxford: Oxford University Press, 2003.
———. "The Barth Legacy: New Athanasius or Origen Redivivus? A Response to T. F. Torrance." *The Thomist* 54 (1990) 673–704.
———. *Calvin and the Reformed Tradition: On the Work of Christ and the Order of Salvation*. Grand Rapids: Baker Academic, 2012.
———. *The Unaccommodated Calvin: Studies in the Foundation of a Theological Tradition*. New York: Oxford University Press, 2000.
Murray, Andrew. *Abide in Christ*. New Kensington: Whitaker, Reprint, 2002.
———. *Absolute Surrender: And Other Addresses*. Chicago: Moody, Reprint, 1980.
———. *Experiencing the Holy Spirit*. New Kensington: Whitaker House, Reprint, 1985.
———. *The Holiest of All*. Springdale: Whitaker House, Reprint, 1996.
———. *Like Christ*. New Kensington: Whitaker House, Reprint, 1983.
———. *The Master's Indwelling*. USA: Merchant, Reprint, 2009.
———. *The Secret of God's Presence*. New Kensington: Whitaker House, Reprint, 1982.
Nettles, Thomas J. "A Better Way: Reformation and Revival." *Reformation & Revival* 1.2 (1992) 23–64.
Noble, T. A. *Holy Trinity: Holy People: The Theology of Christian Perfecting*. Eugene, OR: Cascade Books, 2013.
Oberman, Heiko. *The Reformation: Roots and Ramifications*. Translated by Andrew Colin Gow. Grand Rapids: Eerdmans, 1994.
Olsen, Roger E. *Arminian Theology: Myths and Realities*. Downers Grove, IL: InterVarsity, 2006.
Ortlund, Dane. "Justified by Faith, Judged According to Works." *Journal of the Evangelical Theology Society* 52 (2009) 323–39.
Overy, Michael, and Andrew Sach. *Pierced for Our Transgressions: Rediscovering the Glory of Penal Substitution*. Nottingham, UK: Inter Varsity, 2007.
Packer, J. I., and Mark Dever, *In My Place Condemned He Stood: Celebrating the Glory of Atonement*. Wheaton, IL: Crossway, 2008.

Packer, J. I. "Foreword." In *From Heaven He Came and Sought Her: Definite Atonement in Historical, Biblical, Theological, and Pastoral Perspective*, edited by David Gibson and Jonathan Gibson. Kindle ed. Wheaton, IL: Crossway, 2013.

———. *Puritan Portraits: J. I. Packer on Selected Classic Pastors and Pastoral Classics*. Fearn, UK: Christian Focus, 2012.

———. *A Quest for Godliness: The Puritan Vision of the Christian Life*. Wheaton, IL: Crossway, 1990.

———. *Rediscovering Holiness: Know the Fullness of Life with God*. Ann Arbor: Servant, 1992.

———. "Sanctification and the Fight." Talk delivered to Greenville Presbyterian Theological Seminary and Mt. Olive, North Carolina, USA, 19/02/2004. http://www.sermonaudio.com/sermoninfo.asp?SID=219048305.

———. "What Is Sanctification?" Talk delivered to Greenville Presbyterian Theological Seminary and Mt. Olive, North Carolina, USA, 19/02/2004. http://www.sermonaudio.com/playpopup.asp?SID=2190482917.

Parry, Robin. *Worshipping Trinity: Coming Back to the Heart of Worship*. Eugene, OR: Cascade Books, 2012.

Partee, Charles. "The Phylogeny of Calvin's Progeny: A Prolusion." In *Evangelical Calvinism: Essays Resourcing the Continuing Reformation of the Church*, edited by Myk Habets and Bobby Grow, 23–66. Eugene, OR: Pickwick Publications, 2012.

Peterson, David. *Possessed by God: A New Testament Theology of Sanctification and Holiness*. Leicester, UK: Apollos, 1995.

Pinnock, Clark. *Flame of Love: A Theology of the Holy Spirit*. Downers Grove, IL: InterVarsity, 1996.

Piper, John. *Counted Righteous in Christ: Should We Abandon the Imputation of Christ's Righteousness?* Wheaton, IL: Crossway, 2002.

———. *The Future of Justification: A Response to N. T. Wright*. Nottingham, UK: Inter Varsity, 2008.

———. *Sanctification in the Everyday*. Minneapolis: Desiring God, 2012.

Popkes, Wiard. "Two Interpretations of 'Justification' in the New Testament: Reflections on Galatians 2:15–21 and James 2:21–25." *Studia Theologica* 59 (2005) 129–46.

Pratz, Gunther. "The Relationship between Incarnation and Atonement in the Theology of Thomas F. Torrance." *Journal for Christian Theological Research* 3.2 (1998).

Purves, Andrew. "The Christology of Thomas F. Torrance." In *The Promise of Trinitarian Theology: Theologians in Dialogue with T. F. Torrance*, edited by Elmer Colyer, 51–80. Lanham, MD: Rowman & Littlefield, 2001.

———. *Reconstructing Pastoral Theology: A Christological Foundation*. Louisville: Westminster John Knox, 2004.

Purves, Jim. *The Triune God and the Charismatic Movement: A Critical Appraisal from a Scottish Perspective*. Carlisle, UK: Paternoster, 2004.

Radcliff, Jason. *Thomas F. Torrance and the Church Fathers: A Reformed, Evangelical, and Ecumenical Reconstruction of the Church Fathers*. Eugene, OR: Pickwick Publications, 2014.

Rae, Murray. *Kierkegaard's Vision of the Incarnation: By Faith Transformed*. Oxford: Clarendon, 1997.

Rainbow, Paul A. *The Way of Salvation: The Role of Christian Obedience in Justification*. Milton Keynes, UK: Paternoster, 2005.

Rankin, W. D. "Carnal Union with Christ in the Theology of T. F. Torrance." PhD thesis, University of Edinburgh, 1997.
Redding, Graham. "Calvin and the Cafe Church: Reflections at the Interface between Reformed Theology and Current Trends in Worship." In *An Introduction to Torrance Theology: Discovering the Incarnate Saviour*, edited by Gerrit Scott Dawson, 121–34. London: T&T Clark, 2007.
———. *Prayer and the Priesthood of Christ: In the Reformed Tradition*. London: T&T Clark, 2003.
Robeck, Cecil M., Jr. "Foreword." In Edmund Rybarczyk, *Beyond Salvation: Eastern Orthodoxy and Classical Pentecostalism on Becoming Like* Christ, xiii–xx. Carlisle, UK: Paternoster, 2004.
Roberts, Alexander, James Donaldson, and Philip Schaff, and Henry Wace, eds. *The Ante Nicene Fathers*. Peabody, MA: Hendrickson, 1994.
———. *Nicene and Post-Nicene Fathers*. Series I. 14 vols. Peabody, MA: Hendrick-son, 1994.
———. *Nicene and Post-Nicene Fathers*. Series II. 14 vols. Peabody, MA: Hendrick-son, 1994.
Robinson, J. A. T. "Universalism—Is It Heretical?" *Scottish Journal of Theology* 2 (1949) 139–45.
Rolston, Holmes, III. "Responsible Man in Reformed Theology: Calvin vs. The Westminster Confession." *Scottish Journal of Theology* 23 (1970) 129–56.
Romanides, John. *The Ancestral Sin*. Ridgewood: Zephyr, 2002.
Rybarczyk, Edmund. *Beyond Salvation: Eastern Orthodoxy and Classical Pentecostalism on Becoming Like Christ*. Carlisle, UK: Paternoster, 2004.
Ryken, Leland. *Wordly Saints: The Puritans as They Really Were*. Grand Rapids: Zondervan, 1986.
Saucy, Robert L. "'Sinners' Who Are Forgiven or 'Saints' Who Sin?" *Bibliotheca Sacra* 152 (1995) 400–412.
Seifrid, Mark. *Christ, Our Righteousness: Paul's Theology of Justification*. Downers Grove, IL: InterVarsity, 2000.
Smail, Thomas, Andrew Walker and Nigel Wright, eds. *Charismatic Renewal: The Search for a Theology*. London: SPCK, 1995.
Smail, Thomas. *The Forgotten Father*. London: Hodder & Stoughton, 1981.
———. *The Giving Gift: The Holy Spirit in Person*. London: Hodder & Stoughton, 1988.
———. *Reflected Glory: The Spirit in Christ and Christians*. London: Hodder & Stoughton, 1975.
———. "Third Person Singular—The Trinitarian Spirit." Presidential Address to the annual meeting of the Scottish Church Theology Society, Crieff, 10–14 January 2011.
Speidell, Todd, ed. *Participatio: The Journal of the Thomas F. Torrance Theological Fellowship: A Tribute to James B. Torrance*. Supplement to Volume 3 (2014).
———. *Participatio: The Journal of the Thomas F. Torrance Theological Fellowship*. Supplement to Volume 1 (2011).
———. *Participatio: The Journal of the Thomas F. Torrance Theological Fellowship*. Volume 1 (2009).
Stackhouse, Ian. *The Gospel-Driven Church: Retrieving Classical Ministries for Contemporary Revivalism*. Milton Keynes, UK: Paternoster, 2004.

Stanglin, Keith D., and Thomas H. McCall, *Jacob Arminius: Theologian of Grace*. Oxford: Oxford University Press, 2013.
Stein, Jock, ed. *Gospel, Church, and Ministry: Thomas F. Torrance Collected Studies I*. Eugene, OR: Pickwick Publications, 2012.
———. "The Legacy of the Gospel." In *A Passion for Christ: The Vision that Ignites Ministry*, edited by Gerrit Scott Dawson and Jock Stein, 131–50. Edinburgh: Handsel, 1999.
Stott, John. *The Cross of Christ*. Leicester, UK: Inter Varsity, 1989.
Synan, Vinson. "Sanctification." In *Encyclopedia of Pentecostal and Charismatic Christianity*, edited Stanley M. Burgess. New York: Routledge, 2006.
Torrance, Alan. "The Bible as Testimony to Our Belonging: The Theological Vision of James B. Torrance. In *An Introduction to Torrance Theology: Discovering the Incarnate Saviour*, edited by Gerrit Scott Dawson, 103–20. London: T&T Clark, 2007.
———. "Forgiveness: The Essential Socio-political Structure of Personal Being." *Journal of Theology for Southern Africa* 56 (1986) 47–59.
Torrance, David W. "The Grace of the Finished Work of Christ." Interview with Mike Morrison, You're Included, Grace Communion International. http://www.gci.org/yi/dtorrance104GCI.
———. "Interview." *Participatio: The Journal of the Thomas F. Torrance Theological Fellowship*, Supplement to Volume 1 (2011) 22–38.
———. "Introduction: Discovering the Incarnate Saviour of the World." In *An Introduction to Torrance Theology: Discovering the Incarnate Saviour*, edited by Gerrit Scott Dawson, 1–22. London: T&T Clark, 2007.
———. "Thomas Forsyth Torrance: Minister of the Gospel, Pastor, and Evangelical Theology." In *The Promise of Trinitarian Theology: Theologians in Dialogue with T. F. Torrance*, edited by Elmer Colyer, 1–30. Lanham, MD: Rowman & Littlefield, 2001.
Torrance, James B. "Calvin and Puritanism in England and Scotland." Address to the Congress for the Advancement of Calvin Research, Pretoria, South Africa, 12–14 August 1980. 264–86.
———. "The Concept of Federal Theology—Was Calvin a Federal Theologian?" In *Calvinus Sacrae Scripturae Professor: Calvin as Confessor of Holy Scripture*, edited by Wilhelm Neuser, 15–40. Grand Rapids: Eerdmans, 1994.
———. "The Covenant Concept in Scottish Theology and Politics and Its Legacy." *Scottish Journal of Theology* 34 (1981) 143–62.
———. "Covenant or Contract? A Study of the Theological Background of Worship in Seventeenth-century Scotland." *Scottish Journal of Theology* 23 (1970) 51–76.
———. "The Doctrine of the Trinity in Our Contemporary Situation." In *The Forgotten Trinity: A Selection of Papers Presented to the BCC Study Commission on Trinitarian Doctrine Today*, edited by Alasdair I. C. Heron, 3–17. London: British Council of Churches, 1991.
———. "The Incarnation and 'Limited Atonement.'" *Evangelical Quarterly* 55 (1983) 83–94.
———. "Introduction." In *The Nature of the Atonement* by J. McLeod Campbell, 1–16. Edinburgh: Hansel, 1996.

———. "Prayer and the Priesthood of Christ." In *A Passion for Christ: The Vision that Ignites Ministry*, edited by Gerrit Scott Dawson and Jock Stein, 55–67. Edinburgh: Handsel, 1999.

———. "The Priesthood of Jesus: A Study in the Doctrine of Atonement." In *Essays in Christology for Karl Barth*, edited by T. H. L. Parker, 153–73. Plymouth: Latimer, Trend, 1956.

———. "Southern Africa Today: The Kairos Debate: Listening to its Challenge." *Journal of Theology for Southern Africa* 55 (1986) 42–45.

———. "Strengths and Weaknesses of the Westminster Theology." In *The Westminster Confession in the Church Today: Papers Prepared for the Church of Scotland Panel on Doctrine*, edited by Alasdair C. Heron, 40–53. Edinburgh: Saint Andrews Press, 1982.

———. *Worship, Community and the Triune God of Grace*. Carlisle, UK: Paternoster, 1994.

Torrance, Thomas F. *Atonement: The Person and Work of Christ*, edited by Robert T. Walker. Downers Grove, IL: IVP Academic, 2009.

———. "The Atonement, the Singularity of Christ and the Finality of the Cross: The Atonement and the Moral Order." In *Universalism and the Doctrine of Hell*, edited by Nigel M. De S. Cameron, 225–56. Carlisle, UK: Paternoster, 1992.

———. *The Being and Nature of the Unborn Child*. Edinburgh: Handsel, 2000.

———. *Calvin's Doctrine of Man*. London: Lutterworth, 1949.

———. *The Christian Doctrine of God: One Being Three Persons*. London: T&T Clark, 1996.

———. "The Christ Who Loves Us." In *A Passion for Christ: The Vision that Ignites Ministry*, edited by Gerrit Scott Dawson and Jock Stein, 9–20. Edinburgh: Handsel, 1999.

———. "Colossians 3:3." Sermon to Alyth Parish in 1940 and Beechgrove Parish in 1948. The Thomas F. Torrance Manuscript Collection, Princeton Theological Seminary, Box 47.

———. "The Death of Christ in St Paul." The Thomas F. Torrance Manuscript Collection, Princeton Theological Seminary, Box 21.

———. "Eschatology" (1950–2). The Thomas F. Torrance Manuscript Collection, Princeton Theological Seminary, Box 21.

———. *God and Rationality*. New York: Oxford University Press, 1971.

———. *The Ground and Grammar of Theology: Consonance Between Theology and Science*. Edinburgh: T&T Clark, 1980.

———. *Incarnation: The Person and Life of Christ*, edited by Robert T. Walker. Downers Grove, IL: IVP Academic, 2008.

———. "Introduction." In *The Incarnation: Ecumenical Studies in the Nicene Constantinopolitan Creed A.D. 381*, edited by Thomas F. Torrance, xi–xxii. Edinburgh: Handsel, 1981.

———. "*Itinerarium Mentis In Deum*: My Theological Development." The Thomas F. Torrance Manuscript Collection, Princeton Theological Seminary, Box 10.

———. "Karl Barth and the Latin Heresy." *Scottish Journal of Theology* 39 (1986) 461–82.

———. *Kingdom and Church: A Study in the Theology of the Reformation*. 1956. Reprinted, Eugene, OR: Wipf & Stock, 1996.

———. *The Mediation of Christ*. Exeter, UK: Paternoster, 1983.

―――. *The Mediation of Christ: Revised Edition*. Colorado Springs: Helmers & Howard, 1992.
―――. "My Parish Ministry: Alyth, 1940–43." In *Gospel, Church, and Ministry: Thomas F. Torrance Collected Studies I*, edited by Jock Stein, 25–73. Eugene, OR: Pickwick Publications, 2012.
―――. "One Aspect of the Biblical Conception of Faith." *The Expository Times* 68 (1957) 11–14; 221–22.
―――. "Philippians 2:12." Sermon to Alyth Parish in 1940 and Beechgrove Parish in 1949. The Thomas F. Torrance Manuscript Collection, Princeton Theological Seminary, Box 46.
―――. "Preaching Christ Today." In *Gospel, Church, and Ministry: Thomas F. Torrance Collected Studies I*, edited by Jock Stein, 220–256. Eugene, OR: Pickwick Publications, 2012.
―――. "Preaching Jesus Christ." In *A Passion for Christ: The Vision that Ignites Ministry*, edited by Gerrit Scott Dawson and Jock Stein, 23–32. Edinburgh: Handsel, 1999.
―――. "Predestination in Christ." *Evangelical Quarterly* 13 (1941) 108–41.
―――. *Reality and Evangelical Theology: The Realism of Christian Revelation*. Philadelphia: Westminster, 1981.
―――. "Romans 6." Sermon to Alyth Parish in 1943. The Thomas F. Torrance Manuscript Collection, Princeton Theological Seminary, Box 45.
―――. *Royal Priesthood*. Edinburgh: Oliver & Boyd, 1955.
―――, trans. and ed. *The School of Faith: The Catechisms of the Reformed Church*. London: James Clarke, 1959.
―――. *Scottish Theology: From John Knox to John McLeod Campbell*. Edinburgh: T&T Clark, 1996.
―――. *Space, Time and Resurrection*. Edinburgh: Handsel, 1976.
―――, ed. *Theological Dialogue Between Orthodox and Reformed Churches: Volume 1*. Edinburgh: Scottish Academic, 1985.
―――, ed. *Theological Dialogue Between Orthodox and Reformed Churches: Volume 2*. Edinburgh: Scottish Academic, 1993.
―――. *Theological Science*. London: Oxford University Press, 1969.
―――. *Theology in Reconciliation: Essays towards Evangelical and Catholic Unity in East and West*. 1975. Reprinted, The Torrance Collection, Eugene, OR: Wipf & Stock, 1996.
―――. *Theology in Reconstruction*. 1965. Reprinted, The Torrance Collection, Eugene, OR: Wipf & Stock, 1996.
―――. "Thomas Torrance Responds." In *The Promise of Trinitarian Theology: Theologians in Dialogue with T. F. Torrance*, edited by Elmer Colyer, 303–40. Lanham, MD: Rowman & Littlefield, 2001.
―――. *The Trinitarian Faith: The Evangelical Theology of the Ancient Catholic Church*. Edinburgh: T&T Clark, 1988.
―――. "Universalism or election?" *Scottish Journal of Theology* 2 (1949) 310–18.
Tugwell, Simon. *Did You Receive the Spirit?* London: Darton, Longman & Todd, 1972.
Walker, Robert T. "Recollections and Reflections," *Participatio* 1 (2009) 39–48.
Waters, Guy Prentiss. *Justification and the New Perspectives on Paul: A Review and a Response*. Phillipsburg, NJ: P&R, 2004.

Watson, Francis. "Did Christ Die as Our Substitute? Reconstructing the Logic of Atonement." Paper presented in a seminar of the Research Institute in Systematic Theology, Kings College London (1993).

———. *Paul, Judaism, and the Gentiles: Beyond the New Perspective*. Grand Rapids: Eerdmans, 2007.

Webber, Robert. *Ancient-Future Faith*. Grand Rapids: Baker, 1999.

Webster, John. *Holiness*. London: SCM, 2003.

———. "Introduction." In *Justification: The Heart of the Christian Faith*, edited by Eberhard Jüngel, vii–xvi. Edinburgh: T&T Clark, 2001.

———. "Perfection and Participation." In *The Analogy of Being: Invention of the Antichrist or the Wisdom of God?* Edited by Thomas Joseph White, 379–94. Grand Rapids: Eerdmans, 2010.

———. "*Rector et iudex super omnia genera doctrinarum*? The Place of the Doctrine of Justification." In *What Is Justification About?*, edited by Michael Weinrich and John Burgess, 35–56. Grand Rapids: Eerdmans, 2009.

———. "T. F. Torrance 1913-2007." *International Journal of Systematic Theology* 10.4 (2008).

Welker, Michael, ed. *The Work of the Spirit: Pneumatology and Pentecostalism*. Grand Rapids: Eerdmans, 2006.

Wright, N. T. *Justification: God's Plan and Paul's Vision*. London: SPCK, 2009.

www.ingramcontent.com/pod-product-compliance
Lightning Source LLC
Chambersburg PA
CBHW070256230426
43664CB00014B/2547